PHOTOSHOP 7

SCOTT KELBY

The Adobe® Photoshop® 7
Down & Dirty Tricks
Team

CREATIVE DIRECTOR
Felix Nelson

TECHNICAL EDITOR
Chris Main

COPY EDITOR
Barbara Thompson

PROOFREADER
Richard Theriault

PRODUCTION LAYOUT
Dave Damstra

PRODUCTION ART
Ted LoCascio

COVER DESIGNED BY
Felix Nelson

The New Riders Team

PUBLISHER
David Dwyer

ASSOCIATE PUBLISHER
Stephanie Wall

EXECUTIVE EDITOR
Steve Weiss

MANAGING EDITOR
Sarah Kearns

PRODUCTION
Wil Cruz

PROOFREADER
Linda Seifert

STOCK IMAGES
The stock images used
in this book are courtesy of

digitalvision
www.digitalvisiononline.com

PUBLISHED BY
New Riders Publishing

International Standard Book Number: 0-7357-1237-9

Library of Congress Catalog Card Number: 2001096934

06 05 04 03 02   7 6 5 4 3 2

Interpretation of the printing code: the rightmost double-digit number is the year of the book's printing; the rightmost single-digit number is the number of the book's printing. For example, the printing code 02-1 shows that the first printing of the book occurred in 2002.

Composed in Myriad and Minion by New Riders Publishing.

Trademarks

Warning and Disclaimer

www.downanddirtytricks.com

For my brother Jeff,
the craziest, most fun, most
honorable, and most admirable
big brother a guy could ever have.
I love you man.

ACKNOWLEDGMENTS

I'm very blessed to be surrounded with such wonderful people, and I have so many of them to thank for their help with this book that I'm either going to have to add pages or shrink the type to fit them all in.

First, I want to thank my amazing wife Kalebra. She's the greatest gift life could bring me and her spirit, hilarious sense of humor, beauty, patience, and understanding continue to prove what everybody always says—I'm the luckiest guy in the world.

I owe a deep debt of gratitude to my creative team, who worked harder on this book than almost any project we've undertaken. They turned it around in record time, and right on time, while juggling a dozen other projects, and I've never been prouder of them than I am today.

Felix Nelson: Your input, ideas, techniques, and artwork have made this a better book and your tireless dedication to raising the bar is what makes you the amazing talent and wonderful person that you are. My humble thanks for everything you did to make this, and all our projects, something to be proud of. I feel very lucky to have you on our team.

Chris Main: This is the fifth book you've worked on with me, and you just keep getting better and better at it. After testing every tip and every technique in all my books, you're getting pretty darn scary in Photoshop too. You've done an awful lot in the short number of years you've been on the team—you have a lot to be proud of, and a lot of people are proud of you—especially me.

Dave Damstra: You've proved once again why I tell everyone you're the absolute best layout guy in the business, and your attitude in work, and in life, continues to be an inspiration to us all.

Barbara Thompson: You really rose to the occasion on this book and did an outstanding job, with your as-usual, first-rate attitude, and I can't thank you enough.

Richard Theriault: Thanks for once again lending us your special talents. You're absolutely a pleasure to work with and I'll continue to try to force you out of retirement every chance I can.

Ted (T-Lo) LoCascio: Thanks for keeping all our other projects moving ahead at full speed while we were deeply immersed in "bookland."

Jim Workman and *Jean A. Kendra:* It's great having business partners who understand what it takes to do what we do. I can't thank you enough for your constant support, understanding, freedom, and help in accomplishing my goals. You guys rock.

Dave Moser: You truly are our "secret weapon." We're constantly amazed at your enthusiasm and absolute dedication to making everything we do better than what we've ever done before. You're a great friend, an amazing individual, and I'm honored to have you on our team.

Gina Profitt: Thanks for keeping me on track, organized, and for making sure I had the time I needed to get the job done.

Jerry Kelby: Thank you for being the father everybody wishes they had.

Jordan Kelby: I have good news, little buddy—Daddy's done writing the book—let's go to Disney World.

Thanks to all my friends at Adobe Systems, especially Barbara Rice, Julieanne Kost, Jill Nakashima, Karen Gauthier, Kevin Connor, Rye Livingston, and Terry White.

Thanks also to my Photoshop buddies from whom I've learned so much, and continue to learn from, including Jack Davis, Ben Willmore, Deke McClelland, Robb Kerr, and Felix Nelson.

A heartfelt thanks to my mentors whose wisdom and whip-cracking have had an immeasurable effect on my life: John Graden, Jeff Kelby, Dave Gales, and Jim Lemminn.

Kudos and continued thanks to my home team: Julie Stephenson, Stacy Behan, Ronni O'Neil, Melinda Gotelli, Scott "Dude" Stahley, Kleber Stephenson, Tommy Maloney, and Jon Gales.

Most importantly, I want to thank God for leading me to the woman of my dreams, for giving me a family I adore, for allowing me to make a living doing what I love, for always being there when I need Him, and for blessing me with such a wonderful, fulfilling, and happy life.

Scott Kelby

Scott is Editor-in-Chief of *Photoshop User* magazine and President of the National Association of Photoshop Professionals (NAPP), the trade association for Adobe Photoshop users worldwide. Scott is also President of KW Media Group, Inc., a Florida-based software training and publishing company.

He is author of *Photoshop Photo-Retouching Secrets, Photoshop 6 Down & Dirty Tricks,* and *Macintosh... The Naked Truth,* all from New Riders Publishing. He is also co-author of *Photoshop 6 Killer Tips,* also from New Riders Publishing. In addition, Scott is a contributing author to the following books: *Photoshop 6 Effects Magic* from New Riders; *Maclopedia (the Ultimate Reference on Everything Macintosh)* from Hayden Books; and *Adobe Web Design and Publishing Unleashed* from Sams Publishing.

Scott is Training Director for the Adobe Photoshop Seminar Tour, Technical Chair for PhotoshopWorld (the annual convention for the National Association of Photoshop Professionals), and is a frequent speaker at graphics trade shows and events. He's also featured in a series of Photoshop, Adobe Illustrator, and Web design training videos and has been training Photoshop users around the world since 1993.

Scott lives in the Tampa Bay area of Florida with his wife Kalebra and his 5-year-old son Jordan. For more background info, visit www.scottkelby.com.

TABLE OF CONTENTS

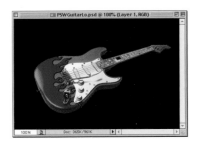

T A B L E   O F   C O N T E N T S   www.downanddirtytricks.com

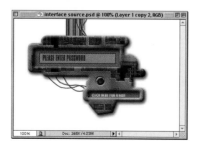

INTRODUCTION

Before we get into how this book works, what it's all about, and the boring stuff that usually winds up in introductions, I want to say right up front that you're going to have so much fun with this book, you're going to absolutely lose your mind.

I know it sounds crazy, but this book is going to change your life. Because after reading and applying the techniques learned here, you'll be able to walk in the door of virtually *any* secret underground religious cult, and they'll take you as a member—no questions asked, right on the spot. Not only that, you'll put up little or no resistance whatsoever when asked to sign over all your personal belongings, and you'll willingly agree to cut off all contact with your family and friends because after all, they no longer share your glorious dream of becoming "one with the pixel." They're "outsiders," "nonbelievers," and therefore can't be trusted.

What's more amazing is that I was able to find both professional editors and a respected publisher to let me start the introduction of my book with this whole "cult" thing. You know what that says to me? Even *they* don't read book introductions. But you, you're different, you're a rebel—someone who looks convention in the face and then quickly looks away, so as not to be rude. You're ready for a different kind of Photoshop book. An edgy Photoshop book: A Photoshop book that takes risks—just like you.

You don't want chapter after chapter waxing philosophical about resolution, color management, file formats (and the women who love them). You don't want lengthy technical explanations of how each tool mathematically interacts before you're allowed to touch any of them. No, that's not you. You're alive. You're unbound. You want to do the cool stuff now! You want to sit down in front of your computer and the next time you look up, it's 4:15 in the morning—you've been up all night, and you don't even care. Why? Because you've been having a blast (and because you're going to bill your client for every minute). When your client gets the invoice, there's a reasonable chance they'll black out, perhaps more than once, but it'll all be worth it when they see your work. That's what this book is all about—teaching you the coolest special effects that will blow your clients away, make you truckloads of money, and give you the most fun you've ever had using Photoshop—*without* all the boring technical stuff.

If this is who you are. If this is who you want to be. This, my friend, is the book for you. Embrace it. Feel it. Feed it (feed it?). But what if this isn't who you are, and not who you want to be? Buy this book anyway. It's good for the economy.

How this book works

Think of this as a "Photoshop special effects cookbook." Need to create a studio backdrop for a product shot? Turn to page 177. Need a cool chrome effect for an ad? Turn to page 104. Need to do cool stuff right now, for a project due tomorrow? Just turn to the page that has the effect you need, and follow the step-by-step instructions.

You'll be able to re-create *every* technique in this book, regardless of your level of Photoshop experience, and you'll unlock the secrets for creating today's hottest Photoshop effects—the same ones you see in national magazines, on TV, and on the Web that would otherwise have taken years to learn, but are simple—once you know the secrets. You'll be absolutely amazed at how easy these tricks really are, and they're all here, including those closely guarded "insider tips" and down and dirty tricks of the trade. There are no years of study, no complex mathematical concepts to master, no baloney. It's (as we say) "Just the funk and not the junk!"

...you'll unlock the secrets for creating today's hottest Photoshop effects —the same ones you see in magazines, on TV, and on the Web.

Okay, so now you know what the book is all about—special effects and cool tricks—but you probably have other questions. Probing, lingering personal questions whose answers may be too uncomfortable for our studio audience, so instead I thought we'd do something safer—a simple Q&A section where I make up the questions I'd like to have answered if I was the person buying this book, and then I answer them, as if I'd written the book (which coincidentally, I did). If this sounds at all confusing, it should. Here we go:

Q. Where should I start in the book?
A. Honestly, it doesn't matter. This book isn't designed to be read like a novel, starting with chapter 1, then chapter 2, etc.—this is a jump-in-anywhere book and start "effecting." To learn a little bit more about what's in each chapter, make sure you read the chapter intros. I say "a little" more, because I wrote those at about 2:00 a.m., and I was half in the bag (I mean, quite tired after many hours of work). Also, if you're a seasoned Photoshop user, don't be put off because I give full explanations of steps in the tutorials. For example, instead of just saying "Create a new layer" I generally say "Create a new layer by clicking on the New Layer icon at the bottom of the Layers palette." I do that because I want any user, at any level of Photoshop experience, to be able to jump in any place in the book and pull off the technique. There's no "intro to Photoshop" chapter—I figured if you bought this book, instead of one of those 1,000-page "learn everything about Photoshop" books, you want to do the cool stuff now, so I start on page 1 with the first special effect and I don't stop again until the back cover. (Okay, they made me put an index in the back, but wouldn't you really rather have had another special effect instead? Come on, admit it. See, I knew this book was for you!)

Q. How is this book different from your 6.0 book?
A. This book is better (you knew I was going to say that. Heck, even I knew that you knew that I was going to say that). In fact, not even taking into account all the new Photoshop 7 stuff, I think it's a much better book. It's yummier, cooler, rockin'-er—anything good you can think of ending with an "-er." That's what this book is. I've learned a lot of slick, new effects since I wrote the last version of this book, and I've been fortunate enough to have Photoshop users all over the world send me some of their favorite tips and techniques as well, so there's a lot of brand-new stuff in this book. But...I also updated some of the most popular effects from the 6.0 version of the book as well. In many cases, I've found easier ways to do them, interesting new ways to use them, some little shortcuts that make them more fun, and basically I just can't stop trying to find ways to make them even better. It's a sickness.

Q. Where do all these cool effects come from?
A. France.

Q. No, really, where do they come from?
A. Actually, the book is a combination of a lot of different things. The whole "Down & Dirty" concept started back in 1993 with a session I did called "Photoshop Down & Dirty Tricks" at a Photoshop seminar held in Ft. Lauderdale, Florida. It turned out to be the hit of the seminar, and I think the reason it resonated with the crowd was that I was teaching them the exact same things I'd been trying so hard to learn just a few months

...I figured if you bought this book, instead of one of those 1,000-page "learn everything about Photoshop" books, you want to do the cool stuff now.

earlier. At the time, I had my own "wish list" of Photoshop effects that I wanted to learn, and once I learned them, I couldn't wait to share them with other Photoshop users. We had fun that day. We laughed, we cried (okay, I cried), we learned, and at the end of the day, I don't know who was more excited, the attendees or me, but I knew then that this is what I wanted to do.

It's nine years later and I still do a constantly updated version of the "Photoshop Down & Dirty Tricks" session live at the Adobe Photoshop Seminar Tour as well as at PhotoshopWorld. Out of those sessions came my best-selling Photoshop "Down & Dirty Tricks" video series, and some of my favorite techniques from there are here too. I also included techniques from the "Down & Dirty Tricks" column that I write with Felix Nelson in *Photoshop User* magazine, and I included lots of new Down & Dirty Tricks that I've never done anywhere else. In short, this book takes some of my favorite Photoshop techniques and combines them all into one resource. It's the book that I wish I'd found when I was trying to learn these types of effects, and I'm thrilled to be able to bring this new updated version to you.

Actually, finding ideas for new Photoshop effects is easy because Photoshop is literally everywhere. Open a magazine, look at TV, or just drive down the street and look at the billboards—you're looking at Photoshop work. There are two things about that reality that I truly love: (1) figuring out how they did those effects, and (2) sharing *how* they did them with other people like yourself. It's how I get my kicks. That, and doing crack—kidding (you knew that, right?).

Q. This book has lots of cool images, do I get those too?
A. You're kinda greedy, aren't you? Okay, you can have the images. Here's the scoop: When I was preparing to write this new version of the book, as you might imagine, I wanted it to have great-looking images, and that's why I asked Digital Vision if I could use their royalty-free stock images in the book. I honestly feel that they have the hottest royalty-free images in the market today and that's why I contacted them, and only them, to arrange to use their images.

Luckily, besides having the hottest images, they're incredibly nice people and I was able to use that to guilt them into letting you download the images used in the book from the book's companion Web site at *www.downanddirtytricks.com.* How cool are Digital Visions images? Why don't you see for yourself at *www.digitalvisiononline.com?* In particular, make sure you check out their Infinity collection to see some of the hottest, cutting-edge work from Europe's smartest young designers. Yes, that's totally a plug, but they didn't ask me to do it. (If they had, I would have, but they didn't.)

Now, you may also notice that there are some photos in the book that are, well…not quite as good as others. For example, there's a head shot of Felix taken outside our offices. Believe it or not, that's *not* a royalty-free image from Digital Vision (although it certainly should be). In certain cases, we took some snapshots using our trusty (rusty? crusty?) digital camera, so any photo that doesn't look really slick is probably one of those—and not from Digital Vision. We let you download those photos as well. Please be kind to them (i.e., don't use Liquify on them)…especially the one of Felix.

I wanted any user, at any level of Photoshop experience, to be able to jump in at any place in the book and pull off the technique.

Q. Okay, who is Felix?

A. Felix Nelson is about the coolest, most creative, Photoshop guy in the world. He's the Creative Director for *Photoshop User*, and Art Director for *Mac Design Magazine*, and he has an amazing ability to do things in Photoshop that I can't even begin to understand. I'm fortunate to work with Felix every day and I have to honestly say that I learn more about Photoshop from Felix than from anyone else on the planet, and I'm delighted to pass on some of his ideas and techniques throughout the book.

Q. Is this for Mac, Windows, or both?

A. Both! It covers the Macintosh and PC versions of Photoshop. (Honestly, it was pretty easy because Photoshop is identical on both the Macintosh and PC platforms.) However, even though the software is the same, the Mac and PC keyboards are slightly different so every time I give a keyboard shortcut in the book, I give both Mac and PC keyboard shortcuts...see, I care.

Q. What are in those sidebars on every page?

A. In the previous version of this book, I put a Photoshop tip on every page. Some were little shortcuts, some were timesavers, some were just advice (stocks, mutual funds, relationships, etc.), and as best as I can tell—nobody really noticed. Everybody got sucked into all the cool special effects and figured the sidebars hid all the boring technical stuff, instead of cool tips. So when I started updating the book, my first thought was to pull out all the tips because, frankly, it's hard coming up with almost 300 tips. But when Felix heard I was taking out the tips, he started whining, "Ahhh man, you can't take those out—I thought that was the coolest part—it's a special effects book, but it also had hundreds of sidebar tips." So, I left 'em in, added some new ones for Photoshop 7, and replaced any lame ones. I'm counting on you to do your part and read at least some of them. I even added the header, "Quick Tip," to each one hoping they'd catch your attention. These are the acts of a desperate tips man.

Q. What if I'm still using Photoshop 6?

A. Well, then it's time to upgrade—big time—because honestly, Photoshop 7 blows Photoshop 6 out of the water, especially if you're a photographer. In the meantime, if you still have 6, you *can* use this book and get a lot out of it until you do upgrade (which, incidentally, you should do tonight).

So why is it that a Photoshop 6 user would use this Photoshop 7 book? It's because a lot of the things Adobe added to Photoshop 7 weren't special effects-related. For example, there aren't many cool effects you can do with the spell checker. I love the spell checker; I crave the spell checker. Apparently, I desperately need a spell checker, but I can't teach you really cool smoke effects, flames, or chrome effects with the spell checker—sad, but true. Photoshop 7 was a major productivity upgrade, with cool stuff like the File Browser (great for photographers, but again, makes for a lame special effect), the absolutely amazing Healing Brush (the best tool for photo retouching ever, but as a special effects tool, it's no drop shadow), Mac OS X and Windows XP Support (again, no glass, no metal, no flames) and the hundred or so other tweaks, fixes, new features, improvements, and enhancements that make it the best overall Photoshop ever. That's why I included lots of sidebar tips on cool new stuff in Photoshop 7 throughout the book, and of course, the

You're now ready to enter a world of special effects delights that dare not speak its name...

tutorials in the whole book were done using Photoshop 7 (hence the book's name). Now, what if you're using Photoshop 5.5 or 5.0? Don't tell anyone, just hide yourself away in a tower somewhere until you can upgrade to Photoshop 7.

Q. Blah, blah, blah. Enough already, eh?

A. You're right, I've said enough. You're now ready to enter a world of special effects delights that dare not speak its name. A world where drop shadows intermingle with bevels amidst a starry sky created entirely with the Noise filter and a tasteful hint of Gaussian Blur. This is your world. This is your time. Launch Photoshop, go forth, and make cool stuff that will generate client invoices so large it would make a government military contractor blush.

Q. What's the Web site again?

A. The book's companion Web site is at *www.downanddirtytricks.com*. It's where you can download the images used in the book, and if you go there, it will save me the trouble of publicly plugging my other books, including *Photoshop Photo-Retouching Secrets* and *Photoshop Killer Tips* (I couldn't help myself), now quick, turn the page before I plug again...

Have fun kids, and don't stay up too late.

I know what you're thinking. Are the techniques in this chapter really "cool effects," or is this just marketing hype?

Suspicious Characters
Cool Type Effects

First, I want to point out that there are strict guidelines set in place by a large, scary-sounding government agency to make sure that when a claim is made about a particular product, the claim is true. So, to substantiate the fact that these type effects are indeed worthy of the glitzy marketing term "cool," I formed a blue-ribbon panel that was charged with putting together a crack team of addicts to find Arthur Fonzarelli and get his full endorsement of these effects. Sadly, the panel was not able to locate Mr. Fonzarelli within the allotted time. However, a woman identified only as Pinky Tuscadero, with whom he was once romantically linked, did render her expert opinion in his stead. Her opinion proved beyond reasonable doubt that the effects in this chapter would be considered by Mr. Fonzarelli, or any of the Happy Days' cast (with the notable exception of Chachi), to be "cool effects." I think that pretty much settles it.

Instant 3D Type

In previous editions of this book, I included an effect similar to the one shown here, but this technique is so much easier and so much more versatile that I wanted to include it. Plus, the first four steps of this technique show you how to apply a perspective transformation to your type while it's still vector which, as you're probably aware, just isn't possible with a regular Type layer.

STEP ONE: Open a document in RGB mode, and use the Type tool to create your type.

STEP TWO: You're going to use Free Transform to add a perspective effect to your type, but you can't do that while you actually have a Type layer. But we don't want to Rasterize the type or our perspective effect will look blurry, so instead, go under the Layer menu, under Type, and choose Convert to Shape. This way, your type retains its smooth vector lines.

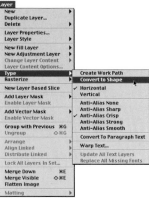

STEP THREE: Press Command-T (PC: Control-T) to bring up Free Transform. Hold Shift-Option-Command (PC: Shift-Alt-Control) and grab the top right Free Transform control point and drag upward to create a perspective effect. When it looks like the type shown at right, press Return (PC: Enter) to lock in your transformation.

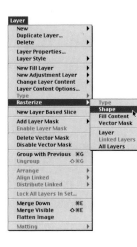

STEP FOUR: Now that we've added the perspective effect and our lines are still smooth, we can safely rasterize our type by going under the Layer menu, under Rasterize, and choosing Shape (as shown).

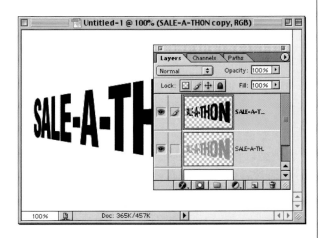

STEP FIVE: In the Layers palette, make a copy of your text layer by dragging it to the New Layer icon at the bottom of the Layers palette. Press "d" to set your Foreground color to black, then press Shift-Option-Delete (PC: Shift-Alt-Back-space) to fill your type with black (as shown). Next, in the Layers palette, drag this black text layer beneath your original text layer.

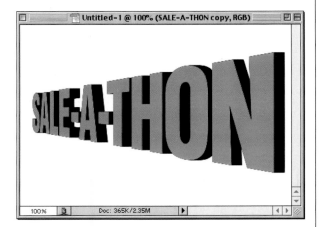

STEP SIX: Here's where you create the 3D effect. Hold Option-Command (PC: Alt-Control) and press-and-hold the Right Arrow key on your keyboard. As you do this, you'll see the 3D effect emerge. What's happening is that you're duplicating and simultaneously nudging to the right the black text layer over and over again very quickly. In the example shown here, it added 27 layers, yet it only took about 15 seconds. Don't worry about the extra layers, we'll deal with them in the next step.

continued

Quick Tip:
How to move your layers without touching them

Okay, the title up there is a little misleading: You can't move them without touching them, but you can move them around in the Layers palette without clicking on them by using the following keyboard shortcuts:

• To move your current layer down in the Layers palette, press Command-Left Bracket (PC: Control-Left Bracket).

• To move your current layer up in the Layers palette, press Command-Right Bracket (PC: Control-Right Bracket).

Now, if you really want to move a layer around within your image without using the mouse, just switch to the Move tool and use the Arrow keys on your keyboard.

Quick Tip:
Zoom shortcuts
To jump instantly to a 100% view of your image, double-click on the Zoom tool. To have your image instantly "Fit on Screen," double-click on the Hand tool.

STEP SEVEN: In the Layers palette, your original text layer should be on top of the layer stack (as shown). Hide this layer from view by clicking once on the Eye icon in the first column beside your text layer (as shown here). Then, scroll down to the bottom of the Layer stack and hide the Background layer from view as well, leaving only the 20+ black type layers still visible.

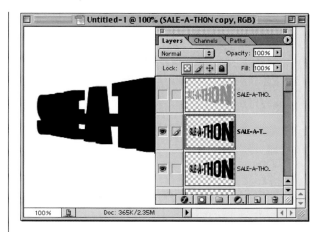

STEP EIGHT: Go to the Layers palette's pop-down menu and choose Merge Visible to combine the 20+ text layers into just one layer. Now you can make both your Background layer and the top type layer visible again by clicking in the first column beside them where the Eye icon used to appear.

STEP NINE: This last step is totally optional. Because your 3D effect is all one layer, click on that layer and then click on the Lock Transparency button at the top of the Layers palette. Now you can drag a gradient through your type to create the effect shown here (I used a gradient that starts with dark gray then goes to light gray. I also added a drop shadow...just because.

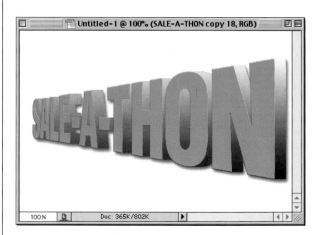

Gel Type Made Easy

Apple Computer made this effect famous with the giant "X" used in their Mac OS X ad campaign and product packaging. The technique shown here is about the fastest and easiest way to get the "Gel type" look without breaking a sweat. In fact, 90% of the work is done in the Layer Styles dialog box alone.

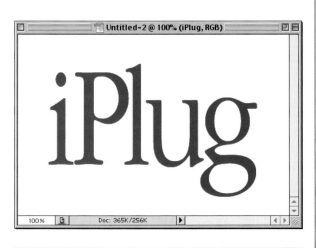

STEP ONE: Open a document, in RGB mode at 72 ppi. Choose a dark blue as your Foreground color, then use the Type tool to create your type (in this example, I used Garamond Condensed Light at about 200 points).

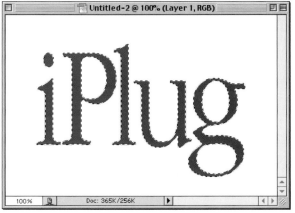

STEP TWO: Switch your Foreground color to a lighter shade of blue (kind of a powder blue). In the Layers palette, Command-click (PC: Control-click) on your Type layer to put a selection around your type. Next, create a new blank layer by clicking on the New Layer icon at the bottom of the Layers palette.

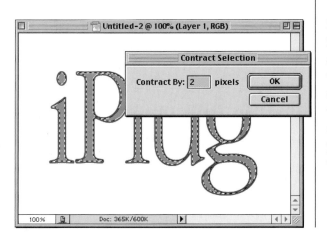

STEP THREE: Go under the Select menu, under Modify, and choose Contract. When the Contract dialog appears, enter 2 pixels, and click OK, then press Option-Delete (PC: Alt-Backspace) to fill your contracted selection with light blue.

continued

Quick Tip:
Putting a selection around your type

In this book, when I want you to put a selection around your type, I generally have you Command-click (PC: Control-click) on the Type layer in the Layers palette. There's another way to do this but because it's not just a keyboard shortcut, it takes longer to get to. I still thought you'd want to know it (especially if you're charging by the hour).

Just go under the Select menu and choose Load Selection. When the dialog pops up, click OK, and it'll put a selection around your type.

Quick Tip:
Sharpen that gel

Gel effects are another one of those effects that seem to really jump off the page if you apply the Unsharp Mask filter (under Sharpen in the Filter menu). In fact, try these settings and run the filter twice in a row: Amount: 150%, Radius: 1, and Threshold: 7.

STEP FOUR: Deselect by pressing Command-D (PC: Control-D). Duplicate this layer by dragging it to the New Layer icon at the bottom of the Layers palette. Go under the Filter menu, under Blur, and choose Gaussian Blur. When the dialog box appears, enter 3 pixels, and click OK to apply a slight blur that's primarily visible on the inside of your type.

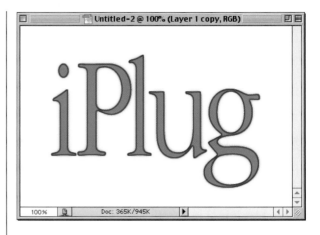

STEP FIVE: Choose Bevel and Emboss from the Layer Styles pop-up menu at the bottom of the Layers palette. When the dialog appears for Style, choose Emboss. Increase the Depth to 300 and Size to 12. Under Shading, increase the Highlight Opacity to 100% and decrease the Shadow Opacity to 40%. Change the Shadow Mode to Color Dodge, click on the black Color Swatch, change the shadow color to white, and then click OK.

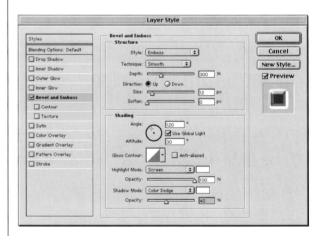

STEP SIX: In the Layers palette, click on the Eye icon beside the Background layer to hide it from view. Then, choose Merge Visible from the palette's drop-down menu. Choose Drop Shadow from the palette's pop-up Styles menu and click OK to apply a drop shadow and complete the effect.

Type on a Circle

In the last incarnation of this book, I included a tedious step-by-step technique for wrapping type around a globe. It was tedious because it didn't make use of the cool Text Warp feature, which makes the job much faster and easier. Here's the new improved version.

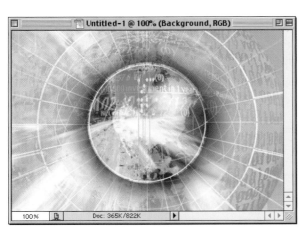

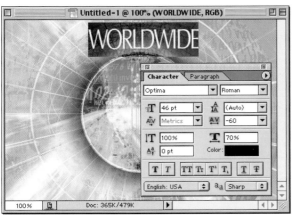

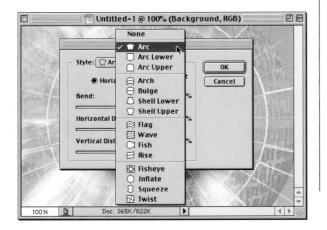

STEP ONE: Open the image you want to place circular type around. (Note: You can apply this technique to a blank document by drawing a circular selection and adding a 1-pixel black stroke to it as a guide for the rotation of your text.)

STEP TWO: Use the Type tool to set your type. Once set, go to the Layers palette and double-click on the "T" thumbnail to highlight your type (as shown). In the Options Bar, click the Character palette button (it's the last icon on the right before the Cancel and Commit buttons). When it appears, lower the Horizontal Scale (width) to 70% as shown. (We do this because the next step tends to stretch the type out, so we condense it first.)

STEP THREE: While your type is still highlighted, click the second to last icon in the Options Bar (it has the letter "T" on it with a bent line beneath it). This brings up the Warp Text dialog box. From the dialog's Style pop-up menu, choose Arc (as shown).

continued

Quick Tip:
Is there an another way than this?
Yes. Actually you to have Adobe Illustrator (or FreeHand, or CorelDRAW) so that you can put your type on a path in that application, save it as an EPS, and use Photoshop's Place command (under the File menu) to import the type on a path.

Quick Tip:
Formatting ®, ™, and other symbols in Photoshop

To visually adjust the baseline shift (great for adjusting trademark and registration mark symbols), highlight the character you want to affect and press Shift-Option-Up Arrow (PC: Shift-Alt-Up Arrow) to move the character above the baseline, and of course, use the same shortcut with the Down Arrow to move text below the baseline (for things such as H_2O, etc.).

STEP FOUR: While the dialog box is open, move your pointer outside the box, click on your type, and drag it into position in your image. Adjust the amount of Bend (dragging the slider to the right) until it looks about right. You can see how it will look (while it's still highlighted) by temporarily hiding the highlighting by pressing Command-H (PC: Control-H). Click OK to complete the top Arc.

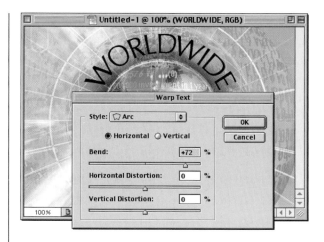

STEP FIVE: Make a duplicate of your arc's layer by dragging it to the New Layer icon at the bottom of the Layers palette. Next, go to the Layers palette and double-click on the "T" thumbnail to highlight your type. Once highlighted, type in the word you want for the bottom of the circle type (it will replace the copied text, as shown here).

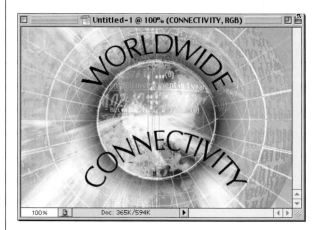

STEP SIX: Click on the Warp Text button again in the Options Bar. Move your pointer outside the box, click on your type, and drag it into position at the bottom of the circle. This time you'll move the Bend slider to the left to create the arc effect with your type.
TIP: You can use the highlight to help you align the type around the circle. Just leave the dialog and position it manually, and look at how the highlight matches the shape of your circle.

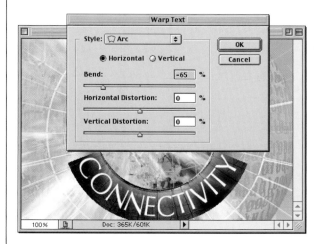

STEP SEVEN: Lastly, click OK to complete the bottom Arc. Two tips for using Warp Text: (1) longer words require more Bend amount than shorter words; and (2) make sure your type doesn't seem too stretched after using Warp Text. If it does, try the technique again but before you do, condense the type even further than the 70% we used here.

Quick Tip:
Accessing Free Transform functions

Although we're constantly accessing Free Transform functions, such as Skew, Scale, Flip Horizontal, etc., from either the contextual pop-up menu or by use of a keyboard shortcut, you can access these functions by going under the Edit menu, under Transform.

Quick Tip:
Don't confuse Clipping Groups with Clipping Paths

The layer term "clipping group" is often confused with the well-known path term "clipping path," but the two are entirely different. Okay, they're not entirely different in what they do: a clipping group puts your image inside type (or anything black) on the layer beneath it, so you could say it clips off everything outside the type. A clipping path is created with the Pen tool and you can choose to save this path with your document, so when you import your image into another application (such as QuarkXPress, Adobe InDesign, Adobe Illustrator, etc.), everything outside the path is clipped off. This is most often used for clipping off the white backgrounds that appear behind objects.

In short, it'll help if you remember that a clipping group is a layer technique, while a clipping path is a path created with the Pen tool that's used mostly in print for silhouetting images against their backgrounds.

Putting an Image into Type (Clipping Group)

This technique lets you take any image and place it inside type that you've set on the layer directly beneath it. This is a pretty flexible effect because you can reposition your image inside the type once you've created it and if for some reason you don't like the results, you can undo the effect.

STEP ONE: Open a new document in RGB mode. Press the letter "d" to set your Foreground color to black. Create some large display-sized type (tall thick typefaces work well for this effect).

STEP TWO: Open the image you want to put inside your type. Switch to the Move tool by pressing the letter "v," then click-and-hold on this image and drag-and-drop it into your original document. This should give you three layers: (1) your Background layer, (2) your Type layer, and (3) a layer with the image that you want clipped into your type.

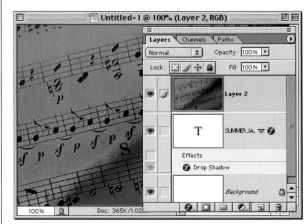

STEP THREE: Make sure your top layer (the image) is active (click on it in the Layers palette), and then press Command-G (PC: Control-G) and your image will now appear inside your type.

STEP FOUR: You can now reposition your image within your type by clicking-and-dragging with the Move tool. To undo this effect, press Shift-Command-G (PC: Shift-Control-G).

STEP FIVE: In most cases, it helps if you add a drop shadow to your Type layer to better define the edges of your letters (plus it looks cool). Click on the Type layer (in the Layers palette), then add the drop shadow by choosing Drop Shadow from the Layer Style pop-up menu at the bottom of the Layers palette (it's the little *f* icon).

STEP SIX: Here's an example of the effect in use. Because we knew we would be putting some type beside the logo, we backscreened the top quarter of the image. We did that by creating a new layer, then we made a rectangular selection that covered about the top quarter of the image. We set white as our foreground color, then pressed Option-Delete (PC: Alt-Backspace) to fill the selection with white. In the Layers palette, we lowered the opacity to 70% to let the trumpet show through, and of course, we added a drop shadow to the layer, just for good measure.

Quick Tip:
The letter-by-letter version
A popular version of this effect is to put a different image into each letter of your type. I've seen a lot of companies do this—they take their name and put a different image in each letter to represent one of their products or a facet of their company.

This is very easy to do, but it's a little more time-consuming (if you use a long word, it can be very time-consuming). Here are a couple of tips if you decide to go this route:

(1) Use large thick typefaces. The thicker the better.

(2) Use tall rectangular images. I usually crop all of my images to be tall and rectangular before I begin adding them to my main document.

(3) When you're trying to position your image over a letter, lower the Opacity of that layer so that you can see the letter's outline on the layer below it. This little tip will keep you from going postal.

(4) Then just press Command-G (PC: Control-G) to put your image within the letter. Then, on to the next letter.

Quick Tip:
The old "Bring up the last filter dialog box" trick

If you've applied a filter and you want to reapply the same filter with different settings, there's a keyboard shortcut for just that. You can bring up the dialog box for the last filter you ran, with the same settings you last used, by pressing Option-Command-F (PC: Alt-Control-F).

If you want to reapply the last filter using the exact same settings, just press Command-F (PC: Control-F).

Stroke Effects on Type

The inspiration for this effect came from my pantry, when one day I noticed that the logo on the large bag (yes, the large bag) of Oreo® cookies totally rocked. It had bevels, strokes, shadows, and a yummy filling sandwiched between two chocolate cookies. I'm not ashamed to admit that I gained six pounds while researching this technique (which required numerous large bags of Oreos).

STEP ONE: Open a new document at 150 ppi in RGB mode. Press "g" to get the Gradient tool, then up in the Options Bar, click on the Gradient thumbnail to bring up the Gradient Editor. Click on the third gradient under Presets (the Black to White gradient).

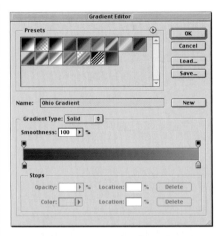

STEP TWO: Double-click on the left (black) Color Stop. When the Color Picker appears, click on the Custom button, choose PANTONE 654, and click OK. Next, double-click on the right (white) Color Stop. When the Color Picker appears, choose PANTONE 631. Give this gradient a name, and then press the New button to Save it. Drag this gradient within your Background layer as shown.

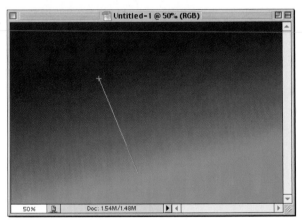

STEP THREE: Press "d" then "x" to set your Foreground color to white. Then press "t" to switch to the Type tool, and enter your type. (The font used here is Futura Extra Bold. I also set the Horizontal Scaling to 120% in the Character palette).

STEP FOUR: In the Layer's palette, double-click directly on the "T" thumbnail of your Type layer to have Photoshop automatically highlight your type. From the Options Bar, click on the Warp Text icon (it looks like a "T" with a half circle under it). When the dialog appears, choose Arc for Style. Lower the Bend to 8%, lower the Horizontal Distortion to –13% (as shown), and click OK.

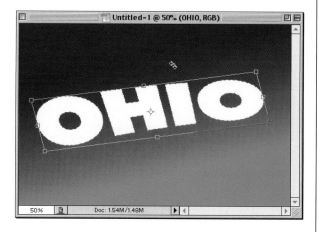

STEP FIVE: Press Command-T (PC: Control-T) to bring up Free Transform. Rotate the word a little counterclockwise, then hold the Command key (PC: Control key), grab the top center point, and drag to the left to Skew the entire word to the left. When it looks like the type shown here, press Return (PC: Enter) to complete the transformation.

STEP SIX: To apply a drop shadow, choose Drop Shadow from the Layer Styles pop-up menu at the bottom of the Layers palette. Enter 10 for both Distance and Size and click OK.

Quick Tip:
Understanding Layer Styles

Although most of the Layer Styles are often thought of as filter effects (e.g., glows, bevels, drop shadows, etc.), it's important to understand that you ARE NOT applying a filter. You are applying an effect to an entire layer. For example, let's say you have an image of a basketball on its own layer, and you apply the Drop Shadow Layer Style to that layer. Once you've done that, anything else you do to that layer will also have the exact same drop shadow as the basketball. Paint a brush stroke? Boom, it has a drop shadow. Drag a square selection and fill it with a blur? Boom—another drop shadow. Remember they're called *Layer* Styles because they affect the entire layer.

continued

Quick Tip:
Making the Glow Layer Style work

Have you ever applied the Outer Glow or Inner Glow Layer Style and didn't see the glow appear on screen—even after you increased the Size to 20 or 30 pixels? That's because by default the Blend Mode for the Glow Layer Style is set to Screen. In many cases, depending on what you have on the layers beneath your Glow layer, you won't be able to see the glow at all. The way around it? Just change the Blend Mode (in the Glow Layer Style dialog box) from Screen to Normal. Then, increasing the Size and Spread amount will make a visible difference.

STEP SEVEN: Choose Bevel and Emboss from the Layer Styles pop-up menu at the bottom of the Layers palette. Increase the Depth to 201%, the Size to 15, and Soften to 2. Lower the Opacity of the Shadow to 50% and click OK to apply a wide bevel to your Type layer.

STEP EIGHT: Hold the Command key (PC: Control key) and in the Layers palette, click once on your Type layer to put a selection around your type. Then, go under the Select menu, under Modify, and choose Expand. When the dialog box appears, Expand by 16 pixels and click OK to increase the size of your selection (as shown).

STEP NINE: Press "w" to switch to the Magic Wand. You'll notice (in the capture in Step Eight) that the centers of the letters are selected, but unfortunately we don't want that, so just hold the Shift key and click the Magic Wand tool once inside each of the two "O's" to remove those selections.

STEP TEN: Your selection should still be in place. Create a new blank layer by clicking on the New Layer icon at the bottom of the Layers palette. Then, go under the Edit menu and choose Stroke. When the Stroke dialog box appears, for Width enter 8, and for Location choose Inside, then click OK to apply an 8-pixel black stroke around your selection. Deselect by pressing Command-D (PC: Control-D).

STEP ELEVEN: Choose Bevel and Emboss from the Layer Styles pop-up menu at the bottom of the Layers palette. Increase the Depth to 400%, and the Size to 10. Click on the down-facing triangle next to the Gloss Contour sample to bring up the Contour Picker. Choose the same contour shown in the inset at left (called Rounded Steps), turn on Anti-aliased, and click OK to apply the bevel to your black stroke.

STEP TWELVE: Choose Color Overlay from the Layer Styles pop-up menu at the bottom of the Layers palette. When the dialog box appears, click on the Color Swatch, then click on the Custom button in the Color Picker, choose PANTONE 7461, and click OK to apply a bright blue color to cover your black beveled stroke (as shown here).

Quick Tip:
Get those palettes out of the way
If your palettes are cluttering your work area, here's a quick tip to tuck them safely off to the side. Just hold the Shift key and double-click on the palette's title bar. It will instantly snap to the nearest edge of your screen, opening up the work area in the center of your screen.

continued

Quick Tip:
Toggle through your Preferences windows

This is one of those little-known shortcuts that can be a great timesaver. When you open any of Photoshop's Preference dialogs (General Preferences, Plug-ins & Scratch Disks, Units & Rulers, etc.), just press Command-N (PC: Control-N) and the next set of Preferences will appear in the current dialog. To toggle back to the previous Preference, just press Command-P (PC: Control-P).

STEP THIRTEEN: Hold the Command key (PC: Control key) and in the Layers palette, click on your original Type layer to put a selection around your type (make sure to also select the centers of the "O's"). Go under the Select menu, under Modify, and choose Expand. Enter 18 pixels and click OK. Create a new blank layer. Press "d" to set your Foreground color to black, then press Option-Delete (PC: Alt-Backspace) to fill this layer with black. In the Layers palette, drag this black layer behind your original Type layer.

STEP FOURTEEN: Deselect by pressing Command-D (PC: Control-D). Choose Drop Shadow from the Layer Styles pop-up menu at the bottom of the Layers palette. Lower the Opacity to 65%, increase the Distance to 30 and the Size to 40, and click OK to apply a soft drop shadow to your black layer. Click OK.

STEP FIFTEEN: Choose Gradient Overlay from the Layer Styles pop-up menu at the bottom of the Layers palette. Click on the Gradient thumbnail and in the Gradient Picker, choose the original gradient you created in Step Two. For Style, choose Reflected and check the Reverse box. For Angle, choose 4°, and click OK to apply this gradient over your black fill.

STEP SIXTEEN: Choose Stroke from the Layer Styles pop-up menu at the bottom of the Layers palette. All you're going to do in this dialog box is to change the color from its default of red to white (by clicking on the Color Swatch and choosing white in the Color Picker), then click OK to apply a white stroke around your layer.

STEP SEVENTEEN: In the Layers palette, click in the second column beside Layers 1 and 2 (the top layer and the bottom layer below the original text) to link them together.

STEP EIGHTEEN: Press "v" to switch to the Move tool, then press the Left Arrow key twice, and the Down Arrow key twice, to offset the Bevel effect layers from the type to complete the effect.

Quick Tip:
Setting your tracking back to 0 (it's default)

The Tracking control (in the Character palette) controls the amount of space between your letters. A negative setting moves your letters closer together, a positive number moves them farther apart. If you're like me, you're constantly tweaking this spacing, and if you're like me, you'll be as happy as I was when I learned that you can reset the tracking back to zero for your selected type by simply pressing Shift-Command-Q (PC: Shift-Control-Q). The only catch is—your type has to be highlighted (which frankly is weird because you can increase or decrease the amount of tracking anytime the type layer is selected, but unless the type is highlighted that keyboard shortcut doesn't work. (See, it is weird isn't it?)

Mondo Cool Light Burst

A friend of mine showed me this effect a while back, and I was delighted—delighted because someone finally found a use for the Polar Coordinates filter. Besides that bonus, it's a pretty cool effect that simulates beams of light bursting, nah, exploding through your type.

STEP ONE: Open a new RGB document. Set your Foreground color to black by pressing the letter "d." Using the Type tool, set some very large type (72 points or higher). Rasterize your Type layer by going under the Layer menu, under Rasterize, and choosing Type. Hold the Command key (PC: Control key) and in the Layers palette click on your text layer to put a selection around it. Go under the Select menu and choose Save Selection. Click OK in the dialog box.

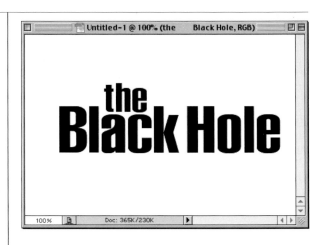

STEP TWO: Deselect your type by pressing Command-D (PC: Control-D). Switch your Foreground color to white by pressing the letter "x." Go under the Edit menu and choose Fill. In the Fill dialog box, change the Mode to Multiply and click OK. Go under the Filter menu, under Blur, and choose Gaussian Blur. Enter 2.5 pixels and click OK.

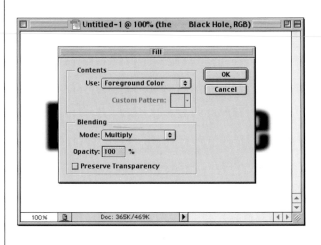

STEP THREE: Go under the Filter menu, under Stylize, and choose Solarize. Press Shift-Command-L (PC: Shift-Control-L) to run Auto Levels, brightening the image. Make a copy of your current layer by dragging it to the New Layer icon at the bottom of the Layers palette.

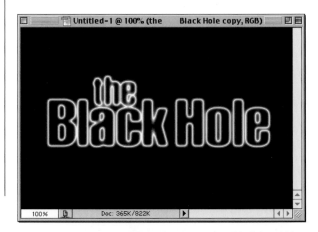

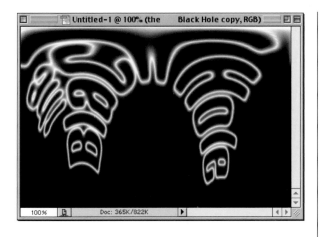

STEP FOUR: Next, go under the Filter menu, under Distort, and choose Polar Coordinates. In the Polar Coordinates dialog box, choose Polar to Rectangular and click OK. This makes your type look really, really bad, but don't let it dismay you—press on.

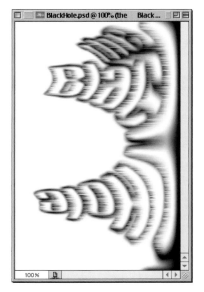

STEP FIVE: Go under the Image menu, under Rotate Canvas, and choose 90° CW. Invert your image by pressing Command-I (PC: Control-I). Go under the Filter menu, under Stylize, and choose Wind.

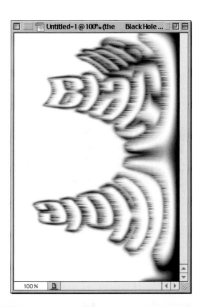

STEP SIX: When the Wind dialog box appears, choose Wind for Method and From the Right for Direction and click OK. Run this filter two more times by pressing Command-F (PC: Control-F) twice (for a total of three times).

Quick Tip:
Filters
• To change values in certain filter dialog boxes, use the Up/Down Arrow keys on your keyboard.

• To change the values in whole numbers or in increments of ten units at a time, hold the Shift key along with the Up/Down Arrow keys.

• Once you've made changes in the filter dialog, if you want to reset them to where you started, hold the Option key (PC: Alt key), and the Cancel button changes to a Reset button. Press it and you're back where you started.

• To return to a 100% preview, click on the Zoom percentage in the filter dialog box. (This works in most filter dialogs, but not all of them. Go figure.)

continued

Quick Tip:
Getting your last settings back

If you're working on a project in Photoshop, and you apply Levels or Curves, etc., and click OK, when you open the dialog box again, you start back at square one. For example, if you apply a custom curve, click OK, and go back to the Curves dialog box, all you'll find is the default straight curve. However, there's a trick for bringing back the last settings you used in a dialog—just add the Option key (PC: Alt key) when you press the keyboard shortcut. For example, to bring up Curves with the last curve setting you applied, press Option-Command-M (PC: Alt-Control-M) instead of just pressing Command-M (PC: Control-M), the regular keyboard shortcut.

STEP SEVEN: Press Command-I (PC: Control-I) to Invert the image again. Press Shift-Command-L (PC: Shift-Control-L) to run Auto Levels again to brighten. Press Command-F (PC: Control-F) three times to run the Wind filter three more times. Go under the Image menu, under Rotate Canvas, and choose 90° CCW. Go under the Filter menu, under Distort, and choose Polar Coordinates.

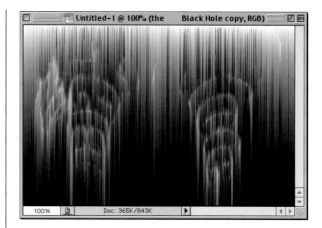

STEP EIGHT: In the Polar Coordinates dialog box, choose Rectangular to Polar and click OK to create your light burst. Change the Layer Blend Mode from Normal to Screen to bring in your original type (it will still look a bit blurry at this stage).

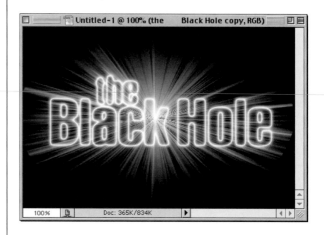

STEP NINE: To add color, create a new blank layer. Click on the Gradient tool, expand the Gradient Picker by clicking on the down-facing arrow next to the Gradient thumbnail in the Options Bar, choose the Violet Orange gradient, and drag the Gradient tool through this layer. Change the Blend Mode to Color and press Command-I (PC: Control-I) to invert the colors to red and orange.

STEP TEN: In the Layers palette, click on your text layer copy (should be the layer below the one you're currently on). Go under the Filter menu, under Blur, and choose Radial Blur. In the dialog box, choose Zoom for Blur Method. Increase the Amount to 66 and click OK. Now click on your original text layer, go under the Select menu, and choose Load Selection. In the Load dialog box, choose Alpha 1, and click OK. Press the letter "d" to set your Foreground color to black, then press Option-Delete (PC: Alt-Backspace). Deselect by pressing Command-D (PC: Control-D) to complete the effect.

Quick Tip:
Removing Layer Styles from layers

If you've applied a Layer Style to a layer and later decide you want to delete that Style, you can do it directly from the Layers palette. Just click on the named effect in the palette and drag it to the Trash icon at the bottom of the Layers palette.

If you just want to hide the effect from view (and not delete it entirely), click on the Eye icon next to the effect you want to hide. To reveal the effect again, click where the Eye icon used to be.

Quick Tip:
Kerning shortcuts
Increasing or decreasing the space between two letters is called "kerning," and Photoshop lets you kern your type either numerically or by using a keyboard shortcut (which is much better because kerning should be done by eye). To visually kern tighter (remove space between two letters) click your cursor between the two letters that you want to kern (just click, don't highlight), then press Option-Left Arrow (PC: Alt-Left Arrow) to tighten. Press Option-Right Arrow (PC: Alt-Right Arrow) to add space between the two letters.

Carved in Stone

This is a major update of the Carved in Stone effect I included in the previous version of this book. This technique is more realistic, has more depth, and is basically "more gooder" (as my five-year-old son would say) all around. Actually, I just think it's "bester."

STEP ONE: We're going to start by opening an appropriate image (this technique will work with almost any background image, but honestly, carving in stone looks best when the background image is, well…stone). Duplicate the Background layer by dragging it to the New Layer icon at the bottom of the Layers palette.

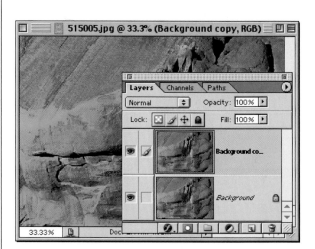

STEP TWO: Press "t" to choose the Type tool and type in your text at a large size. Then, click on the Eye icon next to your Type layer to hide the layer from view. Command-click (PC: Control-click) on your Type layer to put a selection around your type.

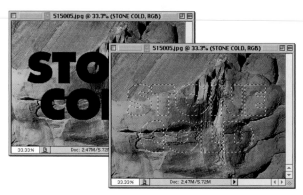

STEP THREE: Now, click on the Background copy layer in the Layers palette to make it the active layer. Press Shift-Command-I (PC: Shift-Control-I) to inverse the selection. Press Delete (PC: Backspace) to remove the excess background from the Background copy layer.

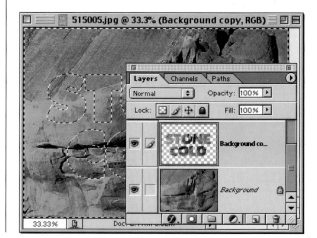

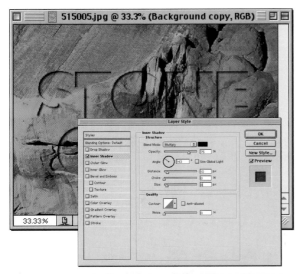

STEP FOUR: Press Command-D (PC: Control-D) to Deselect. Choose Inner Shadow from the Layer Styles pop-up menu at the bottom of the Layers palette. When the dialog box appears, uncheck the Use Global Light box, change the Angle to 143°, the Distance to 10, and the Size to 8. Don't click OK yet.

Quick Tip:
Using the Radial Blur in Best mode means "Coffee Break" time
When using Zoom set to Best as the Blur Method for a Radial Blur on a low-resolution image (for example, 72-ppi), it'll take a minute or two, maybe less. However, if you run a Radial Zoom Blur on a high-res, 300-ppi image, you have time to grab a cup of coffee. In fact, depending on your computer, you may have time to run out for lunch. This is one sloooooooow filter. It's doing a lot of that "Mr. Science"-type math, so it takes forever (in computer terms, forever is anything more than two minutes. A lifetime is 30 minutes). This filter sometimes takes a lifetime. Sorry 'bout that.

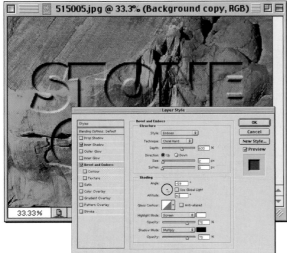

STEP FIVE: In the Styles list on the left side of the Layer Style dialog box, click on the name Bevel and Emboss. For Style, choose Emboss. For Technique, choose Chisel Hard. Change the Depth to 600 and the size to 2. In the Shading section, make sure the Use Global Light box is unchecked, and then change the Angle to –59° and the Altitude to 40. Don't click OK yet.

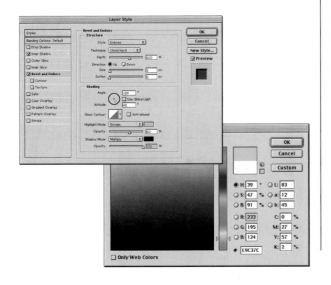

STEP SIX: Still in the Bevel and Emboss dialog—click on the Highlight Mode Color Swatch. When the Color Picker appears, move the dialog box so you can see the background image. Click on a light or highlight area directly on the image (a light yellow/beige color in our image), and click OK. Now, lower the Highlight Mode Opacity to 60% and raise the Shadow Mode Opacity to 100%.

continued

STEP SEVEN: Click on the name Color Overlay in the Styles list. Change the Blend Mode to Overlay and lower the Opacity to 23%. Click on the Color Swatch, choose black for the color and click OK. Now you can click OK to close the Layer Style dialog box.

STEP EIGHT: The final step is to darken the inside of the letters to help "sell" the effect that the type is carved into the background. To do this, press Command-L (PC: Control-L) to bring up the Levels dialog. Move the bottom-right Output Levels slider to the left until you reach approximately 210, then click OK to complete the effect.

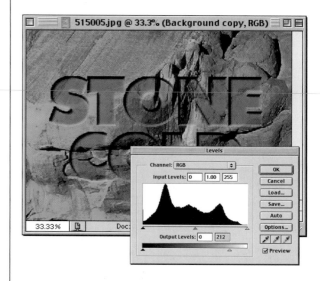

OPTIONAL STEP 1: This next trick I learned from my Creative Director, Felix Nelson, who learned it from Jack Davis, author of the fantastic *Photoshop WOW! Book* series. Command-click (PC: Control-click) on the Type layer once again to make a selection.

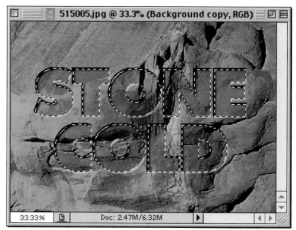

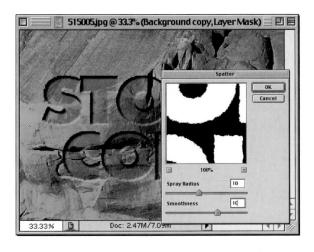

OPTIONAL STEP 2: Now, click on the Add a Layer Mask icon (the gray square with a little white circle in it) at the bottom of the Layers palette. Go under Filter, under Brush Strokes, and choose Spatter. Enter 10 for Spray Radius, 10 for Smoothness, and click OK. This will rough up the edges of the text.

OPTIONAL STEP 3: Duplicate the Background copy layer by dragging it to the New Layer icon at the bottom of the Layers palette. Chose Bevel and Emboss from the Layer Style pop-up menu at the bottom of the Layers palette. Change the Style from Emboss to Stroke Emboss, and set the Depth to 1000. Click on Color Overlay in the Styles list. Change the Blend Mode from Overlay to Multiply, set the Opacity to 30%, and click OK to complete the effect.

Quick Tip:
Faster duplicating

When you're duplicating an entire image in Photoshop, you go under the Image menu and choose Duplicate (seems easy enough). But if you want to bypass the annoying dialog box that asks you to name the duplicate of your document, just hold the Option key (PC: Alt key) when choosing Duplicate. This way, the duplicate will appear immediately rather than making you stop to dismiss the dialog.

Totally Distressed Type Effect

This is my version of a technique I first picked up from Kris Hunt at The Screaming Banana for giving type that beaten-up, weathered look that's all the rage, especially in Hollywood (HBO uses a similar effect for their excellent *Band of Brothers* series). The version shown here lets you do most of the set-up in layers, so you're hardly working in channels at all.

STEP ONE: Open a new document (RGB or Grayscale— your choice). Set your Foreground color to black by pressing the letter "d." Using the Type tool, set some very large type (in this example, I used the font Compacta Bold set at 120 points). This technique works equally well with a placed EPS logo, as long as the logo is black.

STEP TWO: Create a new blank layer by clicking on the New Layer icon at the bottom of the Layers palette. Now, hide your Type/logo layer by clicking on the Eye icon in the first column to the left of that layer. Don't actually change layers, just hide the type layer from view (as shown).

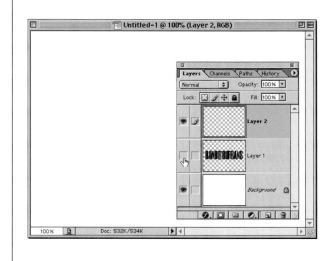

STEP THREE: Press Shift-U until the Line tool appears in the Toolbox. Up in the Options Bar, click on the third tiny icon from the left (as shown) to create lines with pixels, rather than a shape layer. Also, set your line Weight to 2 pixels (as shown).

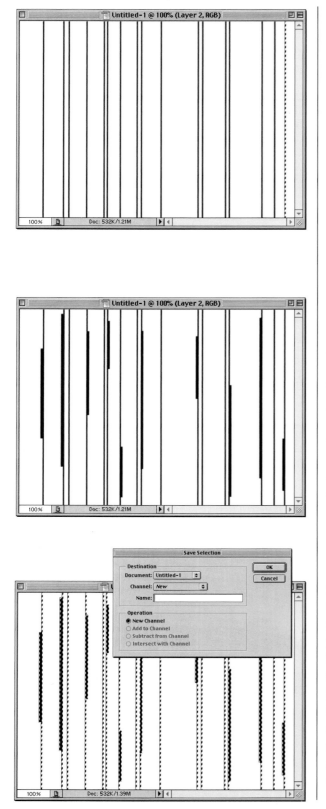

STEP FOUR: Draw a vertical line on the left side of your image area, from top to bottom. Command-click (PC: Control-click) on the layer's name (in the Layers palette) to put a selection around your line. Press "v" to get the Move tool, then hold Option-Command (PC: Alt-Control), click directly on your line, and drag to the right to make a duplicate of your line. Create a pattern of randomly spaced lines as shown here (all on that new blank layer you created).

STEP FIVE: Deselect by pressing Command-D (PC: Control-D), and then press "u" to switch back to the Line tool. In the Options Bar, increase the Weight to 4. Then draw another series of lines, only about half as many as the first time, and anywhere from one-half to three-quarters as long as the others. Also, draw these directly beside the existing lines (as shown).

STEP SIX: Command-click (PC: Control-click) on the Layer's name (in the Layers palette) to put a selection around all the lines on your Layer. Go under the Select menu and choose Save Selection. When the Save Selection dialog box appears, simply click OK and your selection will be saved as an Alpha Channel in your Channels palette.

Quick Tip:
A faster way to rasterize your Type layer
Tired of digging through the Layer menu to rasterize your type? Here's a shortcut: Go to the Layers palette, hold the Control key (PC: Right-click), and click-and-hold on your Type layer. A contextual pop-up menu will appear where you can choose Rasterize Layer. No more digging!

continued

Quick Tip:
Esoteric selection shortcut of the month

Okay, this one's pretty freaky: You probably already know that if you hold the Command-key (PC: Control-key) and click on a Layer's name (in the Layers palette, it puts a selection around the objects on that layer. So for example, if you had type on a layer, and Command-clicked (PC: Control-clicked) on the Type layer, it would put a selection around all your type. But here's the "esoteric selection shortcut" of the month: If after loading that selection, you then press Shift-Option-Command and click on another layer (in the Layers palette), it will load a selection that intersects with your original selection. Try it once and if you're like me, you'll wonder "When in the world would I use that?" Hey…I don't make these keyboard shortcuts, I just share them with my "peeps."

STEP SEVEN: Deselect by pressing Command-D (PC: Control-D) and drag your lines layer into the Trash at the bottom of the Layers palette to delete it. Go to the Channels palette and click on Alpha 1 (your saved lines channel). Your lines will appear white on black, so you'll have to press Command-I (PC: Control-I) to invert them so they're back to black lines on a white background.

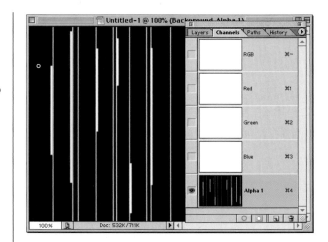

STEP EIGHT: Go under the Filter menu, under Pixelate, and choose Mezzotint. When the dialog box appears, from the Type pop-up menu choose Coarse Dots, then click OK to add some trauma to your lines. Then, to minimize the trauma (you want some, but not this much), go under the Edit menu and choose Fade Mezzotint. When the Fade dialog appears (shown right), change the Mode from Normal to Screen, and click OK.

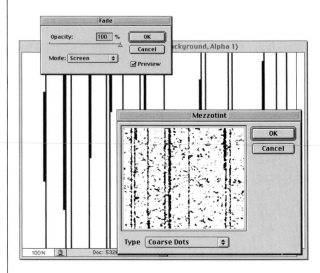

STEP NINE: Choose the Mezzotint filter again, but this time from the Type pop-up menu choose Medium Strokes, then click OK to add some horizontal trauma. Again, it's a bit too much, so go under the Edit menu and choose Fade Mezzotint. When the Fade dialog appears, lower the Opacity to 50%, and click OK.

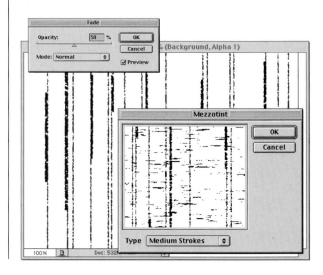

STEP TEN: Go to the Layers palette and click on your Type logo layer to make it active (as shown).

STEP ELEVEN: Go under the Select menu and choose Load Selection. When the dialog box appears, under Channel, choose Alpha 1 from the pop-up menu, and click OK to load your lines as a selection (as shown).

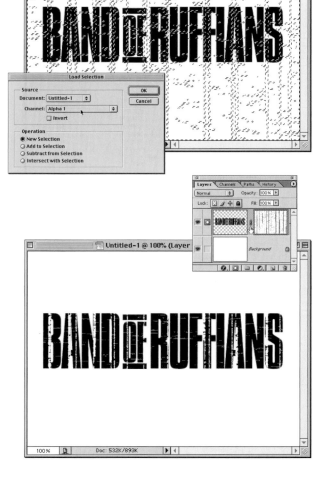

STEP TWELVE: Lastly, to get your lines to appear in white, solely within your black type, go under the Layer menu, under Add Layer Mask, and choose Reveal Selection. If you want to reposition your lines to better suit the text, in the Layers palette, click on the link icon between your layer thumbnail and the Layer Mask thumbnail, and then use the Move tool to move your Mask into position.

Quick Tip:
Canvas Size lies!
OK, this is really more of a half-truth. Here's the scoop: When you shrink the Canvas Size of your document (basically, you're cropping down the image without using the Crop tool), you get a warning dialog that reads "The new canvas size is smaller than the current canvas size. Some clipping will occur." If you go ahead and click the "Proceed" button, your new smaller, canvas size will appear. Here's the thing: Let's say you had a type layer with the word "Washington," on it, and when you took 3" off your Width in the Canvas Size dialog, all that was left on screen is "shingt" (it clipped off the left and the right side), you're really not as out-of-luck as Photoshop's warning dialog makes you think. That's because although you can't see it, the rest of the word was not deleted—it's just hidden from view. Grab the Move tool and drag your type left (or right) and you'll see the rest of your supposedly "clipped-off" word.

Quick Tip:
Controlling your tracking

Tracking is the space between a group of letters or words (kerning is the space between just two letters).

To visually (rather than numerically) set the tracking tighter (removing space between a group of letters), take the Type tool and highlight your text, then press Option-Left Arrow (PC: Alt-Left Arrow) to tighten. Press Option-Right Arrow (PC: Alt-Right Arrow) to add space between a selected group of letters or words.

Type R Us

This effect is similar to the one used by Toys R Us® in certain treatments of their logo. Thanks to Layers Styles it's really pretty easy—in fact most of the work takes place inside the Layer Styles dialog box.

STEP ONE: Open a new RGB document, then set your type at a large type size (I used the typeface Gill Sans Ultra).

STEP TWO: Highlight each letter individually, and recolor the letters as shown. Next, choose Drop Shadow from the Layer Styles pop-up menu at the bottom of the Layers palette. When the dialog box appears, increase the Size to 8, and then turn off the "Use Global Light" checkbox. Don't click OK yet.

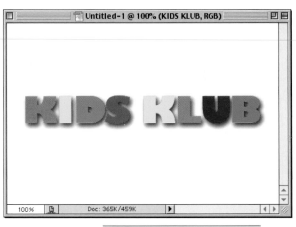

STEP THREE: In the list of Styles on the left side of the Drop Shadow dialog, click on the name Bevel and Emboss, then click on the checkbox (not the name) just below it for Contour. Increase the Depth to 160%, Size to 9, and Soften to 7. In the Shading section, set the Angle to 174° and the Altitude to 39°. Increase the Highlight Opacity to 87% and lower the Shadow Opacity to 37%. Don't click OK yet.

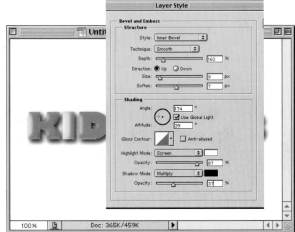

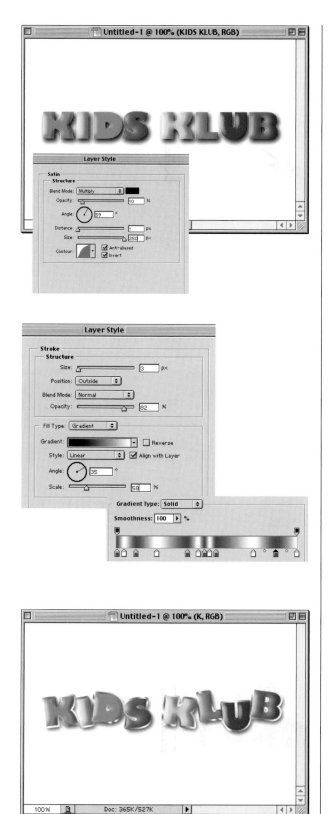

STEP FOUR: In the list of Styles, click on the name Satin to bring up its options. Lower the Opacity to 10% and change the Angle to 59%. Lower the Distance to 1 and increase the size to 250. Click on the down-facing triangle next to the Contour thumbnail, and in the Contour Picker choose the "Half Round" contour (shown at left).

STEP FIVE: In the list of Styles, click on the word Stroke. Set the Size to 3 and the Opacity to 82%. Under Fill Type, choose Gradient, and then click on the Gradient Thumbnail to open the Gradient Editor window. Using the example at left, create a new gradient (the gray Color Stops are 65% black, the lighter Color Stops are white. Double-click on the Stops to change their color and Option-[PC: Alt-] drag to duplicate them). For Style, choose Reflected and turn off "Align with Layer." Set the Angle to 35°, and lower the Scale to 58%.

STEP SIX: Now, you can finally click OK, and the resulting effect is shown here. As an optional step, you could Rasterize the type layer, select each letter individually, and choose "Layer via Cut" from the Layer menu (under New) to put each letter on its own separate layer. Then you could use Free Transform to slightly rotate each letter randomly for a more playful feel to the effect.

Quick Tip:
Importing artwork from Adobe Illustrator
There are at least five different ways to import artwork created in Adobe Illustrator but frankly, there's only one GOOD way to do it. In Adobe Illustrator, save the file as an EPS, switch to Photoshop, open the document you want to import your artwork into, and go under the File menu and choose Place. Choose your saved EPS Illustrator artwork and click OK. A bounding box will appear with a preview (if you saved it with a preview), and you can scale the image to any size you'd like (it's still EPS vector artwork at this point). When you get it to the exact size you like, press the Return or Enter key, and only then will it rasterize and become a pixel-based Photoshop image. When it rasterizes, it takes on the exact resolution and color mode of the document it was imported into. That's all there is to it.

Carved Wood Type

This technique (which my creative director Felix Nelson showed me) is similar to the one used by Disney® for their hit movie *Tarzan* (now available on video and DVD). What's neat is that you start by creating the texture from scratch using Photoshop's filters, then you wind up applying that custom-made texture to your type.

STEP ONE: Open a new document in RGB mode. Press "g" to get the Gradient tool. Up in the Options Bar, click on the Gradient thumbnail to bring up the Gradient Editor. When it appears, double-click on the left Color Stop. When the Color Picker appears, click on the Custom button, then choose PANTONE 722, and click OK. Double-click on the right Color Stop; this time choose PANTONE 732. Click OK. Name your gradient and click the New button to save it.

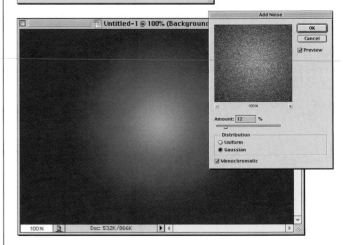

STEP TWO: In the Options Bar, click on the Radial Gradient icon (it's the second one from the left). Using this tool, click-and-drag from the center to the top of the Background layer. Go under the Filter menu, under Noise, and choose Add Noise. Enter 12% for Amount, choose Gaussian, check Monochromatic, and click OK.

STEP THREE: Then, go under the Filter menu, under Blur, and choose Motion Blur. Enter 33° for Angle and 10 for Distance. Click OK. Now, go under the Filter menu, under Sharpen, and choose Unsharp Mask. Enter 500% for Amount, 9.0 pixels for Radius, and 1 for Threshold, then click OK.

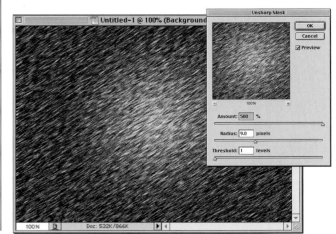

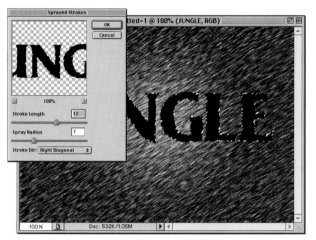

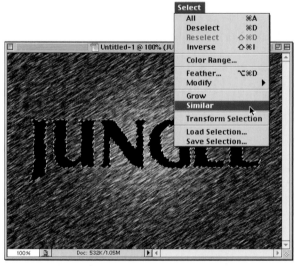

STEP FOUR: Press "t" to choose the Type tool, and enter your type (in a large point size). Go under the Layer menu, under Rasterize, and choose Type to convert your Type layer into a regular image layer. Now, under the Filter menu, under Brush Strokes, choose Sprayed Strokes. Type 12 for Stroke Length, 7 for Spray Radius, and Right Diagonal for Direction. Click OK.

STEP FIVE: Press "w" to switch to the Magic Wand. Click once in the first letter of your word. Then, go under the Select menu and choose Similar to select the rest of the letters. Under the Select menu, choose Inverse. Now, press Delete (PC: Backspace) to remove the little chunks of white space around the letters created by the Brush Strokes filter. Don't Deselect yet.

STEP SIX: Go under the Select menu and choose Inverse to reselect your text. Drag your text layer into the Trash to delete it, leaving just your selection on the Background layer. Press Command-J (PC: Control-J) to put the selected background area up on its own layer. In the Layers palette, click once on the Background layer to make it the active layer. Press Command-A (PC: Control-A) to Select All, then press Delete (PC: Backspace) to delete the background image. Press Command-D (PC: Control-D) to Deselect.

continued

Quick Tip:
Filter Before and Afters

One of the improvements to filters in Photoshop 7 is the new giant-sized filter preview windows that let you see what your image will look like with the filter applied to it. The tip is that you can make these previews even more usable by clicking in the Preview window to show what the image looks like before applying the filter; when you release the mouse button, you'll see what it looks like after. In essence, click to see a "before," release to see the "after."

Quick Tip:
Make multiple Lasso selections

In this tutorial, we have you make multiple selections with the Lasso tool by making one selection, then holding the Shift key while you make subsequent selections. There's another way to do this that you might find easier than holding down the Shift key the whole time. After you've made your first selection, go up to the Options Bar and click on the second icon from the left (called the "Add to Selection" button), and now you can add additional areas to your selection without holding the Shift key.

STEP SEVEN: Choose Bevel and Emboss from the Layer Styles pop-up menu at the bottom of the Layers palette. When the dialog box appears, increase the Depth to 400%, and decrease the Size to 4. Increase the Highlight Opacity to 90%. Don't click OK yet. From the list of Styles on the left side of the Layer Style dialog box, click on the word Drop Shadow to bring up its options. Increase the Size to 8, lower the Opacity to 50%, and then click OK to apply both the Bevel and the Drop Shadow.

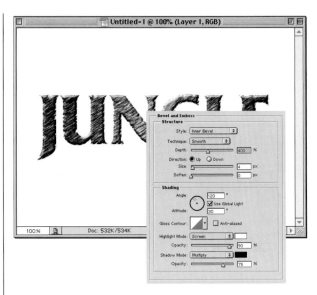

STEP EIGHT: Press "L" to choose the Lasso tool. Make a thin selection in the center of each letter (do one letter, hold down the Shift key, then add the other letters). These selections should be very random—the rougher, the better. Press Command-C (PC: Control-C) to copy the selected areas, create a new blank layer by clicking on the New Layer icon at the bottom of the Layers palette, and then press Command-V (PC: Control-V) to paste your selection onto this new layer. In the Layers palette, change the layer Mode from Normal to Color Burn.

STEP NINE: Duplicate your new layer by dragging it to the New Layer icon at the bottom of the Layers palette. Now drag the duplicated layer (Layer 2 copy) into the New Layer icon (this creates Layer 2 copy 2). Change the layer mode from Color Burn to Screen. Press "v" to choose the Move tool, then press the Right Arrow key twice and the Down Arrow key once to offset the layer.

Semi-transparent Type

This is a quick and easy way to give your type a glassy effect without jumping through all the hoops that are usually associated with glass type, like creating a Displacement Map and applying it to your image.

STEP ONE: Open the RGB image of your choice (we're using a mountain scene). Press "t" to get the Type tool and enter your text (we used Trajan in our example).

STEP TWO: Go to the Layers palette and Command-click (PC: Control-click) directly on your Type layer to make the type an active selection. Now, click on the Eye icon next to the Type layer to hide it from view. Finally, click on the original Background layer.

STEP THREE: Press Command-J to place the selection on its own layer (Layer 1). Click on the Add a Layer Style icon (the black circle with the "*f*" in it) at the bottom of the Layers palette, and choose Drop Shadow (don't click OK yet). Click directly on the words Inner Shadow in the Styles list on the left of the Layer Style dialog box (once again, don't click OK).

continued

Quick Tip:
Photoshop's Glass filter

If you've ever tried to use Photoshop's Glass filter (found under the Filter menu, under Distort), then you've already found that it doesn't work worth a darn (and that wording is overly kind). It just shouldn't be named "Glass." It should be named something like "Mess up your image" or "Junkiscizor"—something more indicative of the real effect it has on your image. There's one instance where you might consider using the Glass filter, and that's when creating a Glass effect on type. You start by creating an Alpha channel of your type, blurring it a pixel or two, and saving it as a Displacement Map. Then when you use the Glass filter, choose "Load Texture," and load the map you saved; it applies a glassy look to your type. It almost looks decent. It doesn't look like glass, mind you, but it looks decent.

Quick Tip:
Style Presets are actually in the Layers Styles dialog box

By now you probably know that if you create a series of Layer Styles (as we've done in this tutorial) you can save that combination of styles with all their options settings as a "Style," which then appears in the Styles palette. What you may not realize is that you can actually access these Styles right from the Layer Styles dialog box. You'll see at the top left of the dialog box the word "Styles" and below it a list of Styles you can apply. Well, I always thought that was just a text header telling you that the Styles were below it but actually if you click on that word, the Styles (saved in the Styles palette) will appear. It's freaky. It's odd. Try it once, and I guarantee you, you'll say "who cares" out loud.

STEP FOUR: Click on the words Inner Glow in the Styles list and click OK to apply all three styles to your text. Now you can click on your Type layer and drag it into the Trash at the bottom of the Layers palette to delete the layer.

STEP FIVE: This is really an optional step, but if you wanted the effect to stand out a bit more, you can either lighten or darken the background image (it depends on how dark/light your image is whether you'll lighten or darken the background). You do that by clicking on the Background layer in the Layers palette, pressing Command-L (PC: Control-L) to bring up the Levels dialog box, moving the left Output Levels slider toward the right to lighten, or drag the right slider to the left to darken.

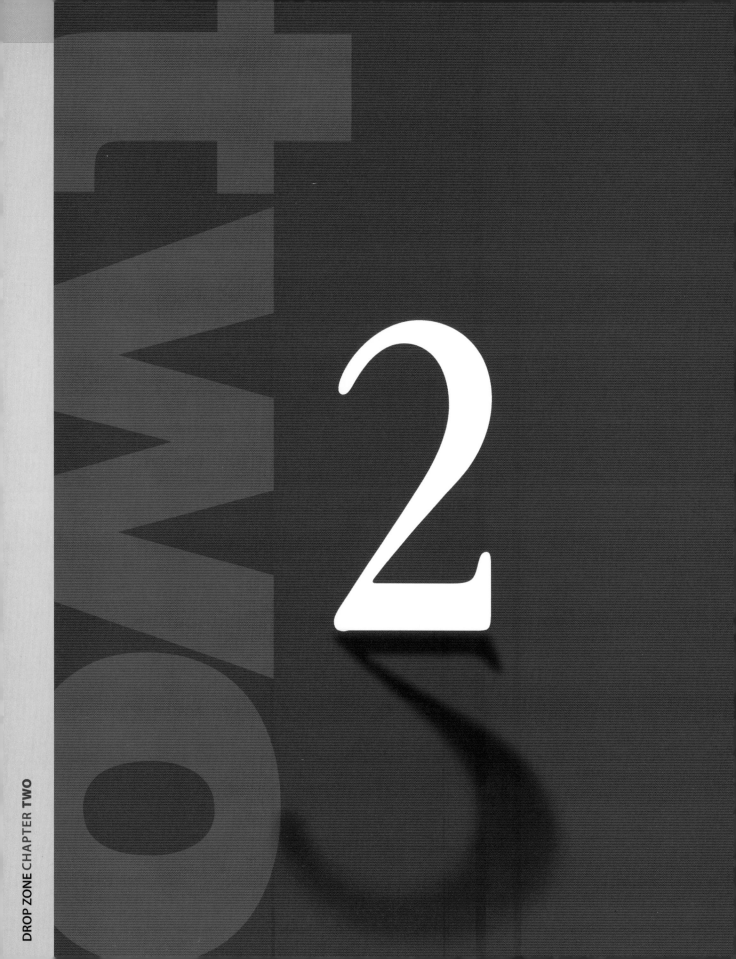

You know what I love about drop shadows? Everything. Seriously, I love 'em. But I'm not the only one—there are

Drop Zone
Drop Shadow Techniques

millions of us shadow freaks. It's not just guys, women love shadows as much, if not more than men. If what Carol Channing said is true—"Diamonds are a girl's best friend," then drop shadows are the bridesmaids at her wedding. Clients love 'em too. Spend 2½ hours color-correcting a photo they gave you and they'll smile politely, but add a drop shadow to it, and the next thing you know, you're an usher at their wedding. I guess the underlying message here is this—use lots of drop shadows and before you know it, you'll either be married, or at the very least, part of someone else's wedding party.

Quick Tip:
Ruler guide trick
Any time that you're
dragging out a guide
from your ruler, you can
change its orientation as
you drag it. (Just in case
you meant to grab a
horizontal guide and
instead you accidentally
grabbed a vertical guide.
Hey, it could happen.) To
change the guide from
vertical to horizontal (or
vice versa), press the
Option key (PC: Alt key)
while you're dragging,
and it'll switch to the
other orientation. Release
the key and it switches
back. That way you can
position it exactly how
you like before releasing
the mouse button.

Matrix Shadow Effect

This effect has really caught on in the past couple of years. The first time I remember seeing it was on the logo for the movie *The Matrix*, and since then, it has gotten more and more popular, and now it's very widely used in high-tech or Euro design projects.

STEP ONE: Press the letter "d" to set your Foreground color to black, and press Option-Delete (PC: Alt-Backspace) to fill the Background layer with black. Then press the letter "x" to swap your Foreground and Background colors, making your Foreground color white. Use the Type tool to create your type (as shown here).

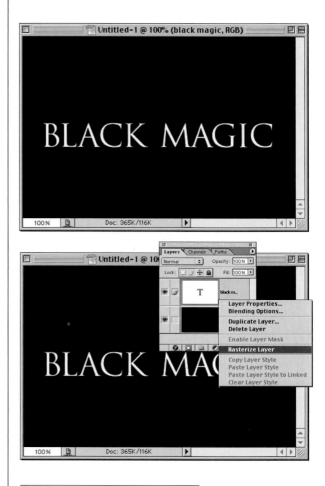

STEP TWO: Once your type is visible, you'll need to convert your Type layer into an image layer. You do that by Control-clicking (PC: Right-clicking) on the Layer's name in the Layers palette. A pop-up menu will appear. Choose Rasterize Layer Now that it's rasterized, you can run filters on the layer.

STEP THREE: Make a duplicate of your rasterized layer by dragging it to the New Layer icon at the bottom of the Layers palette. Go under the Filter menu, under Blur, and choose Motion Blur. When the Motion Blur dialog box appears, set the Angle to 0°, and increase the Distance of the Blur to 39 pixels. Click OK.

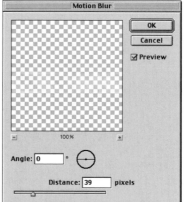

STEP FOUR: The capture at left shows the most common application of the effect, which just uses a horizontal motion blur, so you could end the technique right here. However, lately I've noticed some designers doing both a horizontal and vertical motion blur, so if you want to do that, continue on to Steps Five and Six, but that's totally optional.

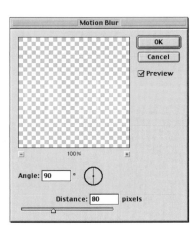

STEP FIVE: Make a duplicate of your original rasterized layer by dragging it to the New Layer icon at the bottom of the Layers palette. Go under the Filter menu, under Blur, and choose Motion Blur. When the Motion Blur dialog box appears, set the Angle to 90°, and increase the Distance of the Blur to 80 pixels. Click OK.

STEP SIX: The capture at left shows the final effect, if you decided to add both the horizontal and vertical motion blurs. This effect works equally well with black text on a white background, so don't think you're tied to the particular version we've shown here.

Quick Tip:
Want more tips?

If you like these sidebar tips, how'd you like a whole book of them? Check out *Photoshop 6 Killer Tips,* also published by New Riders Publishing (shameless plug?!). Well, I tried, didn't I?

Quick Tip:
Free Transform: the keyboard shortcut brain teaser

Most of the time when we use the Free Transform function, we Control-click (PC: Right-click) inside the Free Transform bounding box and choose our desired transformation from the handy pop-up menu. This way we only have to remember one keyboard shortcut—Control-click (PC: Right-click). But in actuality, there are keyboard shortcuts for almost every Free Transform function (except for rotate—just move your pointer outside the bounding box then move your mouse to rotate). Here's the list just in case you feel like learning them:
• Hold the Command key (PC: Control key) and drag a corner square handle to distort your object.
• Hold Shift and drag a square handle on any corner for proportional scaling of your object.
• Hold Shift-Option-Command (PC: Shift-Alt-Control) and grab a top or bottom corner square handle and drag outward to add a perspective effect.
• Hold Option-Command (PC: Alt-Control), grab the center handle, and drag right or left to skew.

Perspective Shadow

This shadow effect is widely used in print and on the Web to give the impression of a light source from behind the object, rather than in front or to the side, as Photoshop shadows are usually applied. I saw it recently on the logo for the movie *The Talented Mr. Ripley*.

STEP ONE: Open a new document, press "t" to get the Type tool and create your type. (Note: I put a Black to Medium gradient in the background for effect, but it's not necessary for this technique.) After you've created your type, press Command-J (PC: Control-J) to duplicate your Type layer (as shown in the inset).

STEP TWO: Press Command-T (PC: Control-T) to bring up the Free Transform function. Control-click (PC: Right-click) directly inside the Free Transform bounding box, and a pop-up list of possible transformations will appear. Choose Flip Vertical from this list. Don't press Return (PC: Enter) yet.

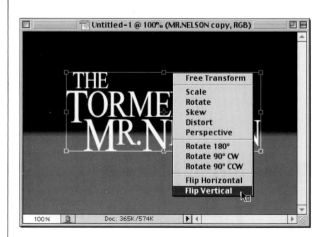

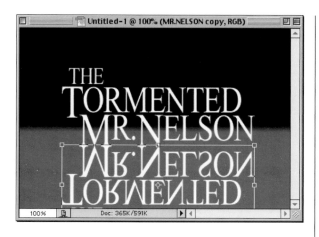

STEP THREE: Drag your flipped layer downward until the bottom of the letters of both sets of text nearly touch. Now, press Return (PC: Enter) to complete your transformation. Go under the Layer menu, under Rasterize, and choose Type to convert your flipped Type layer into an image layer.

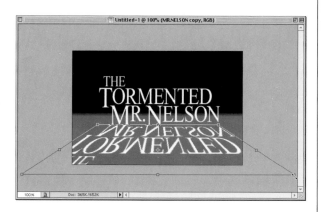

STEP FOUR: Press Command-T (PC: Control-T) to bring up the Free Transform function again. Control-click (PC: Right-click) directly inside the Free Transform bounding box and choose Perspective. Grab either the bottom left or right adjustment handle and drag outward to create the perspective effect.

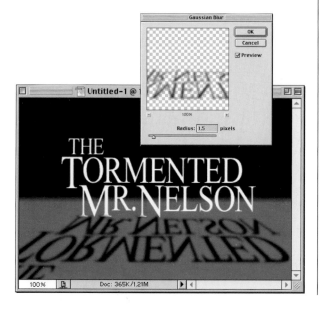

STEP FIVE: Next, grab either the top left or right adjustment handle and drag inward to accentuate the effect, and press Return (PC: Enter) to complete the transformation. Press "d" to make your Foreground color black, and press Shift-Option-Delete (PC: Shift-Alt-Backspace) to fill your text with black. Go under the Filter menu, under Blur, and choose Gaussian Blur. Add a slight 1.5-pixel blur to lightly soften the shadow.

continued

Quick Tip:
Getting out of a transformation
While you're using the Free Transform function, if you suddenly decide you don't want to transform your object after all, just press the Escape key on your keyboard to leave Free Transform. If you've made a transformation you don't like, you can undo your last step by pressing Command-Z (PC: Control-Z) while you're still in Free Transform.

Also, while you're in Free Transform, you can move your object by placing your pointer inside the bounding box (your pointer changes to an arrow) and dragging the box to a new location.

When you're transforming your object, you can lock in your transformation by either pressing Return (PC: Enter) or double-clicking within the bounding box.

COOL TIP: If you want to transform an object AND put a copy of it on its own layer at the same time, add the Option key (PC: Alt key) to the Free Transform keyboard shortcut, making it Option-Command-T (PC: Alt-Control-T).

Quick Tip:
Putting selections on their own layers

In this book, we often make a selection and put the selected area on its own layer by pressing Shift-Command-J (PC: Shift-Control-J). This performs the same function as going under the Layer menu, under New, and choosing Layer via Cut.

Layer via Cut cuts out your selection from the background image and moves it to its own layer (leaving a big white space in the layer below). If you want to move your selection to its own layer WITHOUT cutting (and leaving a knockout where you cut), leave out the Shift key and instead just press Command-J PC Control-J). This is the same as going under the Layer menu, under New, and choosing Layer via Copy (which leaves your original selected area intact on the layer below and places an exact duplicate of your selection on the layer above).

STEP SIX: Press "m" to switch to the Rectangular Marquee tool and drag a rectangular selection around the center of your shadow (as shown) Go under the Select menu and choose Feather. In the Feather Selection dialog box, choose 10 pixels as your Feather Radius. Click OK to soften the edges of your selected area.

STEP SEVEN: Go under the Filter menu, under Blur, and choose Gaussian Blur. Apply a 2-pixel blur. Deselect by pressing Command-D (PC: Control-D). Draw another, rectangular selection at the bottom of your image window (as shown).

STEP EIGHT: Apply one last 2-pixel Gaussian Blur. What this does is make your shadow appear more blurry as it moves away from the base of the type—just like a shadow would in real life. Deselect by pressing Command-D (PC: Control-D) to complete the effect.

Perspective Cast Shadow

This twist on the classic drop shadow effect adds realism in two ways: (1) It casts a shadow that's more like what an actual light source would cast; and (2) The shadow has a bit of a harder edge near the object but gets softer as it moves away.

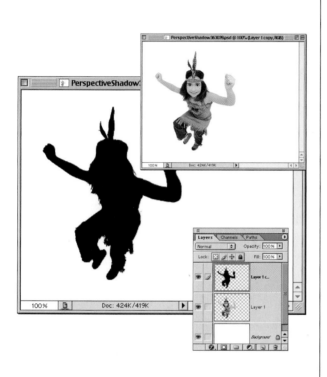

STEP ONE: Put an object on its own layer. Make a copy of that layer by dragging it to the New Layer icon at the bottom of the Layers palette. Press the letter "d" to change the Foreground color to black, then press Shift-Option-Delete (PC: Shift-Alt-Backspace) to fill your object copy with black.

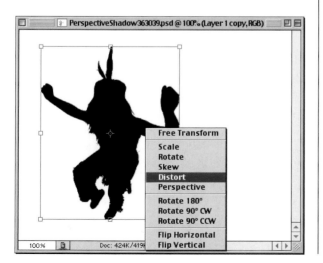

STEP TWO: Press Command-T (PC: Control-T) to bring up the Free Transform function. Control-click (PC: Right-click) directly inside the Free Transform bounding box and a pop-up list of possible transformations will appear. Choose Distort from this list.

continued

Quick Tip:
Making copies of layers

In this example, we make a copy of the layer by dragging the layer (in the Layers palette) to the New Layer icon at the bottom of the Layers palette. But there are other ways of creating copies of layers. The fastest is probably to press Command-J (PC: Control-J). This makes an instant duplicate of your current layer.

Another way is to take the Move tool, hold the Option key (PC: Alt key), click within your image on the layer you want to copy, and drag. As you drag, you'll see that a new layer copy has been created in the Layers palette.

Another method is to go under the Layer menu and choose Duplicate Layer. A dialog box will appear that enables you to name your newly copied layer and to choose whether you want this new layer to appear in your current document or in another open document, or you can choose to have it become a new document.

As a shortcut, you can Control-click (PC: Right-click) on your layer (in the Layers palette) and a pop-up menu will appear where you can choose Duplicate Layer.

STEP THREE: In this step, you need to make the copy filled with black lie almost flat on the ground, so grab the top center adjustment point and drag it downward (as shown). Press Return (PC: Enter) to complete your transformation.

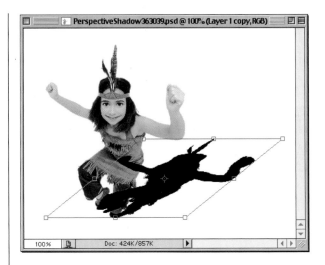

STEP FOUR: Make sure your Foreground color is still set to black and the Background color is set to white by pressing the letter "d." Then switch to the Gradient tool by pressing the letter "g." Look in the Options Bar to make sure your currently selected gradient is Foreground to Background. If it isn't, click on the down-facing arrow next to the Gradient thumbnail to bring up the Gradient Picker, and choose it from there.

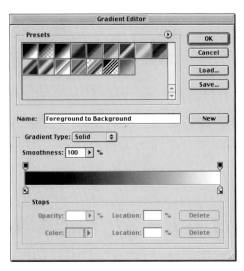

STEP FIVE: In the Layers palette, click on the Lock Transparent Pixels checkbox for your shadow layer. Drag the Gradient tool from one end of your shadow to the other. You want the gradient to start with black at the base of your object and change to white as the shadow extends away from the object.

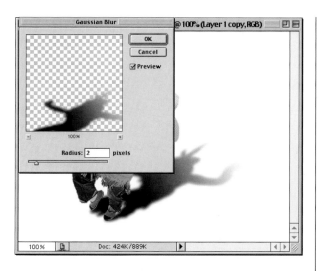

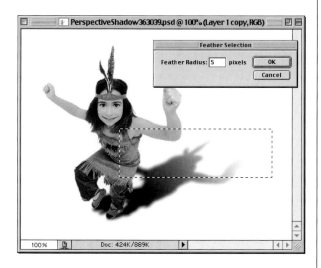

STEP SIX: Turn off the transparency lock on your shadow layer in the Layers palette. Go under the Filter menu, under Blur, and choose Gaussian Blur. When the dialog box appears, enter 2 for Blur Radius, and click OK. In the Layers palette, drag Layer 1 copy below Layer 1. This puts the shadow behind your object.

STEP SEVEN: To add more realism, you can create a perspective blur, where the shadow is less blurry near the object and becomes softer the farther away it gets (like in real life). To do this, use the Rectangular Marquee selection tool to draw a rectangle that covers the top one-quarter of your cast shadow. Go under the Select menu and choose Feather. Add a 5-pixel feather to soften the transition. Then go under the Filter menu, under Blur, and choose Gaussian Blur. Add a 2-pixel blur, and then Deselect by pressing Command-D (PC: Control-D).

STEP EIGHT: With the Marquee selection tool, draw a selection that covers the top half of your cast shadow. Apply another 3-pixel Gaussian Blur, and then deselect. Draw a new Marquee tool selection that covers three-quarters of your shadow (almost to the base) and apply another Gaussian Blur to finish the effect. This creates a 10-pixel blur around the farthest areas of the cast shadow, an 8-pixel blur around the top half, a 5-pixel blur around one-quarter of the distance away from the base, and only a slight 2-pixel blur up close.

Quick Tip:
Making selections in a straight line
In this example, we used the Rectangular Marquee tool, but if you need to draw a selection that includes straight lines but is not a rectangle or a square, you can use the Polygonal Lasso. It draws straight lines from point to point as you click. To access the Polygonal Lasso tool, simply press the letter "L" (which switches you to the regular Lasso tool). Click-and-hold in the document where you want your selection to start, press the Option key (PC: Alt key), and then release the mouse to temporarily switch to the Polygonal Lasso. Just click in your document where you want to create a straight line. As long as you hold the Option/Alt key, it remains the Polygonal tool. When you release the Option key, it turns into an active selection. If you want to continue drawing with the regular Lasso tool without closing the selection, click-and-hold before releasing the Option/Alt key.

Quick Tip:
Easy to remember keyboard shortcuts

In the technique shown on this page, you wind up using Group with Previous to keep your shadows within the layer directly beneath them. The keyboard shortcut is easy to remember because it uses the same keyboard shortcut almost all other Adobe products use to "Group" objects together. It's Command-G (PC: Control-G). Adobe has gone to great lengths to keep you from having to learn a new set of keyboard shortcuts for each Adobe application, so once you learn one application's shortcuts, chances are you can apply them to other Adobe applications. Many of Photoshop's shortcuts are based on Adobe Illustrator shortcuts, so if you know those, you're well on your way. So keep that in mind when working in Photoshop. If you don't know the keyboard shortcut, ask yourself what that shortcut would be in Illustrator, and chances are you'll be right. However, if you're used to CorelDRAW … you're about out of luck.

Grouping Shadows Effect

This trick enables you to control where your shadow falls in a multi-layered document by taking the shadow and masking it into the object on the layer directly beneath it. This is helpful if your shadow winds up casting on something it shouldn't (like the sky).

STEP ONE: Open a background image as the base of your collage.

STEP TWO: Now open two other images that you want to add to the collage. Drag them onto your background image, giving you three layers: a Background layer, an object just above it (in this case, a clock), and another object above that (in this case, a cute little girl).

STEP THREE: In the Layers palette choose the front-most image layer (the girl), then choose Drop Shadow from the Layer Styles pop-up menu at the bottom of the Layers palette. Position your shadow so it clearly casts onto the clock. The problem is that it also casts onto the sky and field behind her, which ruins the collage.

STEP FOUR: The Layer Effects Drop Shadow is attached directly to the layer where you applied it, but you'll need to remove the shadow and put it onto its own separate layer. To do that, go under the Layer menu, under Layer Style, and choose Create Layer. This puts the drop shadow on its own layer. (Note that the shadow is still casting onto the clock and the field.)

STEP FIVE: To mask this shadow into the sign on the layer beneath it, go to the Layers palette, click on the shadow layer, and press Command-G (PC: Control-G), which is the shortcut for Group with Previous. This forces the shadow to appear just within the clock and keeps it from casting onto the background.

STEP SIX: Press the letter "v" to switch to the Move tool, and drag the clock around (here I dragged it upward and to the left). Notice how the shadow stays within the clock, regardless of where it's moved. You can also adjust the shadow layer's position, too, by switching to the shadow layer and dragging it in your image. To undo this grouping effect, press Shift-Command-G (PC: Shift-Control-G).

Quick Tip: Getting rid of white edge pixels in collaged images

In the technique shown on these pages, when I brought the girl into the image, she had a tiny white halo around her arms and hair. This leftover fringe came with the original image that I took her from, which had a white background. When I selected her, it brought some of the fringe along too.

I was able to quickly get rid of that white fringe around the edge by going under the Layer menu, under Matting, and choosing Defringe. I used the default 1-pixel setting, clicked OK, and it immediately removed the white edge fringe. It does this by creating a new edge pixel that is a combination of the background and the edge of your object. If you try a 1-pixel Defringe and it's not enough, undo it, and try a 2-pixel Defringe.

Quick Tip:
Dragging layers between documents

Ever since the introduction of Layers (back in Photoshop 3.0) you've been able to drag-and-drop layers between documents. When you do this, the image you're dropping lands wherever you release your mouse (by default). So if you drag it over and let go of the mouse button right away, chances are your image will be off to the left or right a bit.

    To get your image to be perfectly centered when you drag from one document to another, all you have to do is hold the Shift key as you drag. Your dragged layer will then appear centered within your target document.

Shadow in Motion

This is another popular technique for giving your shadow some motion and adding visual interest to your type. You'll see this technique used in print in posters and logos, and often on the Web or in motion graphics as well.

STEP ONE: Open a new document in RGB mode at 72 ppi. Press "d" to set your Foreground color to black, and fill the Background layer with black by pressing Option-Delete (PC: Alt-Backspace). Set your Foreground color to a medium gray color, switch to the Type tool, and set your type (large type works best).

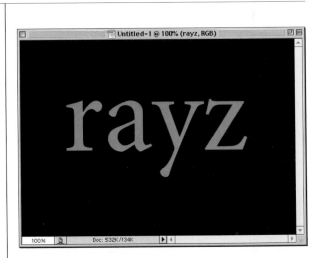

STEP TWO: Make a duplicate of your Type layer by pressing Command-J (PC: Control-J). Hold the Control key (PC: Right-click), click on the layer's name of the copy (in the Layers palette), and in the resulting pop-up menu, choose Rasterize Layer to convert your Type layer into a regular image layer.

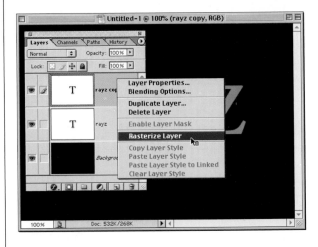

STEP THREE: Go under the Filter menu, under Pixelate, and choose Fragment. After applying the Fragment filter, apply it again by pressing Command-F (PC: Control-F). Apply it one last time using the same keyboard shortcut (for a total of three times).

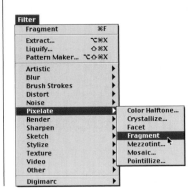

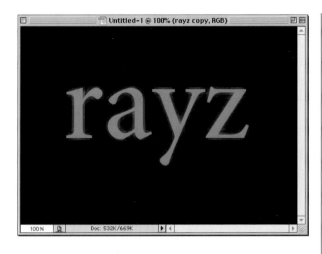

STEP FOUR: After applying the filter three times, the effect still doesn't come through with the intensity we're looking for, so we'll scale the filtered layer up in size to bring it out.

STEP FIVE: Press Command-T (PC: Control-T) to bring up the Free Transform bounding box. Up in the Options Bar, on the far left, there is a matrix of nine dots that indicate from which point on the Free Transform bounding box the transformation will originate. Click the center dot. Then, in the Options Bar, you'll see fields for Width and Height (marked W: and H:). Enter 130 in each field and press Return (PC: Enter) to scale your shadow up.

STEP SIX: Last, click on your original Type layer and rasterize this layer as well (using the same technique we used in Step Two). Click on the top layer (the shadow layer) and press Command-E (PC: Control-E) to merge the two layers together. To colorize your type, press Command-U (PC: Control-U) to bring up Hue/Saturation. Click the Colorize checkbox and move the Hue slider to the color you'd like.

Quick Tip:
Which tool are you using?

If you're new to Photoshop, here's a tip that might make learning Photoshop's tools easier: In the bottom left-hand corner of your document window, there's an Info bar that can display file size information, scratch disk space, or other details about your document. While you're still learning, you may find it helpful to change the readout in this Info bar to give you the name of the tool you're using. This is especially helpful when you're trying to locate specific tools to use for the projects in this book.

To change your Info bar readout, click-and-hold on the right-facing triangle to the right of the Info bar and a pop-up list will appear with your choices. Choose Current Tool from the list, and it will now display your currently chosen tool. As you click through the tools in the Toolbox, each tool's name will appear in the Info bar.

Quick Tip: Avoiding pixelation

When you're resizing images, there's a simple rule of thumb: making your image smaller is good, making it larger is bad. That's a huge oversimplification of the wild and woolly subject of resolution, but in general, scaling an image down in size increases the resolution of the image, and generally doesn't do the image much harm. (The resampling sometimes makes it lose a little clarity, but the amount varies from image to image.) However, increasing the size of an image, especially a low-res image (72 ppi), is generally a recipe for disaster, creating images that are blurry and pixelated. Therefore, starting with a large image and scaling down is far preferable to starting with a small image and scaling up. If you must start with a small image, if you're scanning it, try to scan it at a high enough resolution to keep the image from falling apart (e.g., 600 dpi). If you're shooting digitally, try a minimum, 3-megapixel camera so you start with a large image that you'll likely want to scale down.

Mapping Your Shadow

This is an advanced shadow technique that's ideal to use when you've got a background image that has levels of depth to it, such as fabric, water, sand, or features where objects are on different levels. What you'll do is apply a filter effect that maps the shadow to the "terrain" upon which it will sit and the effect can add a nice extra dose of realism to your project.

STEP ONE: Open the background image upon which you'll be casting a shadow. Press "d" to set black as your Foreground color.

STEP TWO: Press "t" to get the Type tool and create your type. (Although we're using type in this example, this technique works equally with an object.)

STEP THREE: Choose Drop Shadow from the Layer Styles pop-up menu at the bottom of the Layers palette. Increase the Distance setting to 20 and click OK to apply an offset shadow to your type. Then, go under the Layer menu, under Layer Style, and choose Create Layer. This removes the drop shadow from your Type layer and creates a new separate layer below with just the shadow.

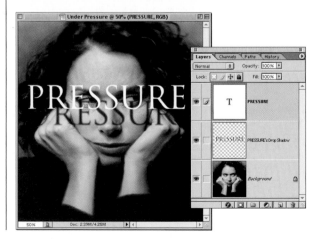

STEP FOUR: In the Layers palette, click on the Background layer, press Command-A (PC: Control-A) to Select All, then press Command-C (PC: Control-C) to copy the Background layer. Then go to the Channels palette and click on the New Channel icon. When the new channel appears, press Command-V (PC: Control-V) to paste your background into this new channel (as shown).

STEP FIVE: Deselect by pressing Command-D (PC: Control-D). Go under the Filter menu, under Blur, and choose Gaussian. Enter 2 pixels (enter 6 for high-res, 300-ppi images), and click OK to blur the channel a bit. Then, press Command-L (PC: Control-L) to bring up Levels. In the Levels dialog box, drag the top left and top right Input Levels sliders toward the center to increase the contrast of the image (as shown in the inset) and click OK.

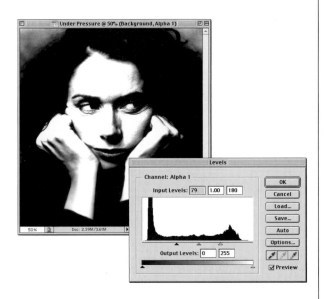

STEP SIX: In the Channels drop-down menu, choose Duplicate Channel. When the dialog appears, from the Destination Area, under Document, choose New to copy this channel into a new separate document. Click OK and the new document will appear onscreen. Save this file in Photoshop's native format and name it Map.psd.

continued

Quick Tip:
Ways to create Styles

You can create a new Style by choosing New Style from the Styles palette's drop-down menu. But you can also create Styles directly from the Layer Effects dialog box (it's actually called the Layer Style dialog box, but I didn't want you to confuse it with the Styles palette. Though, in rereading my last sentence, I probably did just that—made it confusing. Sorry 'bout that). Anyway, as I said, you can create Styles from the Layer Style (Effects) dialog box. After you've created your combination of effects (styles, whatever), click on the New Style button in the upper right-hand corner (just below Cancel) and the New Style dialog box will appear where you can name your style. This new style will be added to the Styles palette just as if you created it from the Styles palette itself.

Quick Tip:
Opening multiple images at once

If you're going to open more than one image from the same folder, Photoshop will allow you to open them all at the same time (rather than choosing one, opening it, and then choosing another, etc.). While in the Open dialog box, click on the first image you want to open, then hold the Shift key, and click on any other images you want to open. When you click OK, Photoshop will open all the Shift-clicked images.

STEP SEVEN: Return to the Layers palette and click on the Drop Shadow layer.

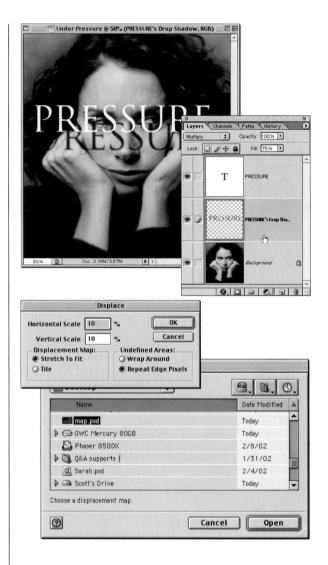

STEP EIGHT: Go under the Filter menu, under Distort, and choose Displace. When the dialog box appears, enter 10% for both Horizontal and Vertical Scale. For Displacement Map, choose Stretch to Fit, and for Undefined Areas choose Wrap Around. When you click OK, Photoshop's Open dialog will appear. Choose the file you saved earlier named Map.psd.

STEP NINE: Click OK to apply that file as a displacement map to your shadow layer, and the shadow will now warp to fit the contours of the background upon which it was placed (as shown here).

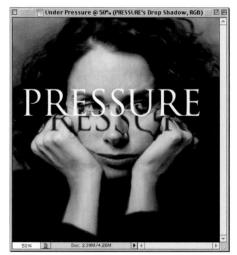

Transparent Glow Type

This is a technique you could actually do back in Photoshop 6.0, but the layer Fill command used here was buried in the Layer Style dialog under Blending Options, and as best as I can tell, nobody ever found it (well, they say one guy in Canada found it, but I wasn't able to verify that). In Photoshop 7, Adobe put it right on the Layers palette, almost daring us to use it.

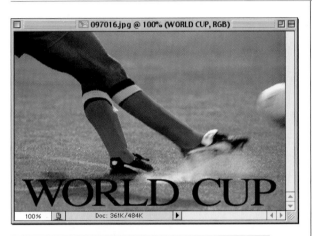

STEP ONE: Open a new document in RGB mode. Press the letter "d" to set your Foreground color to black. Press "t" to get the Type tool and create your type.

STEP TWO: Choose Outer Glow from the Layer Style pop-up menu at the bottom of the Layers palette (it's the first icon from the left). When the dialog box appears, change the Blend Mode from Screen to Normal. Click on the square beige Color Swatch and choose black as your glow color. Increase the Size to 10 and click OK to apply a black glow to your type.

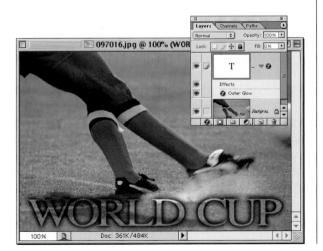

STEP THREE: In the Layers palette, lower the Fill amount to 0%. This makes the black type transparent, but leaves the Outer Glow Layer Style at 100% Opacity (as shown), completing the effect.

Quick Tip:
Easy background transparency in Photoshop 7

Remember back in the old days when you wanted a background color to be transparent in a GIF Web graphic, you'd use GIF89a and click on the color you wanted transparent? Well, those good ol' days are back, but you don't have to suffer through GIF89a again because in Photoshop 7, you can choose a background color to be transparent right from within the Save for Web dialog box. Just use the Eyedropper tool to click on the color you want to appear transparent, then at the bottom of the Color Table, click on the first icon from the left to make that color transparent. See, good things have a way of coming back once again.

3

This chapter is a nice change because you generally get to start each project with a photograph, and then

Maximum Exposure
Photographic Effects

you'll just add cool effects to it. This is a bigger advantage than it might first seem. I mean think about it—if you don't start with a photo, you're starting off with a blank canvas. There's nothing more terrifying than staring at a blank page and trying to come up with an awesome effect entirely from scratch. So, in essence, this chapter is kind of like cheating, and that's good. Unless of course, you live in Vegas where apparently cheating is frowned upon. In fact, if you're caught cheating in a Vegas casino, I've heard they make you use Corel PhotoPaint or PaintShop Pro as punishment, so if you live out that way, you don't want to chance it. In fact, in the interest of personal safety, I'd recommend that all Nevada residents skip this chapter entirely, and always start each Photoshop project with a blank page. Hey, the last thing you want is some angry pit boss chasing you around threatening you with lesser products. It's just not worth it.

Quick Tip:
Quick Tip:
Getting better results from the Eyedropper tool

There's one setting you should change immediately that will give you better results from your Eyedropper tool. Click on the Eyedropper, and in the Options Bar, change the Sample Size from Point Sample to 3 by 3 Average. This helps keep you from getting erroneous readings when using the Eyedropper, because when it's set to Point Sample, you get the reading from one single pixel, which may not be representative of the colors in the area where you're clicking. Set to 3 by 3 Average, it averages the color of the pixels surrounding the area that you clicked, which is considered by many to provide a much more usable reading when doing color correction.

Visual Color Change

If there's one thing clients love to do, it's change the color of the product in their product shots, but luckily for you (a) it's easy, and (b) it creates billable work. Here's one of the easiest ways to change the color of just about anything.

STEP ONE: Open a color image that contains an object or part of an object whose color you want to change.

STEP TWO: Select the object you want to apply a quick color change to (in this example, we used the Lasso tool to select the woman's blouse).

Hue/Saturation

Edit: Master

Hue: 0

Saturation: 23

Lightness: 0

OK
Cancel
Load...
Save...

☑ Colorize
☑ Preview

547046A.jpg @ 50% (Layer 1, CMYK)

50%   Doc: 3.13M/5.15M

STEP THREE: Go under the Image menu, under Adjustment, and choose Hue/Saturation. When the Hue and Saturation dialog box appears, check the Colorize box in the lower-right corner.

STEP FOUR: Now, simply grab the Hue slider (the top one) and drag it until your image has changed to a color you like (of course, make sure the Preview box is checked in this dialog box, or you'll be doing this blind). When it looks good, click OK.

Quick Tip:
Better-looking color-to-grayscale conversions

If you have a color image that you want to convert to a grayscale image, you can choose Grayscale from the Mode menu, but Photoshop just throws away the color, and you generally end up with a pretty bland-looking grayscale image. Here's a tip for getting a better color-to-grayscale conversion: Rather than choosing Grayscale, go to the Channels palette and click on each individual color channel (the Red, Blue, and Green). These channels appear in grayscale mode by default, and more often than not, one of those channels (by itself) makes a pretty good-looking grayscale image. Keep that one, and drag the other two to the trash. Now, when you go under the Image menu, under Mode, and choose Grayscale (it doesn't have any color to throw away, you already did that), you wind up with a great-looking grayscale conversion.

Quick Tip:
Getting around your image, one button at a time

There are a dozen or so keyboard shortcuts for zooming in and out of your image: switching to the Zoom tool, zooming to Fit on Screen, and a bunch more. But there are some lesser-known navigation shortcuts that can be helpful when you're working on large, high-res images. These are mostly one-button wonders that are available to anyone with an extended keyboard (which is just about everybody not using a laptop). Here goes: To jump up one full screen in your image, press the Page Up key. To jump down one full screen, press the Page Down key. To move to the left one full screen, press Command-Page Up (PC: Control-Page Up). To move right one full screen, press Command-Page Down (PC: Control-Page Down). To jump to the upper-left corner of your image, press the Home key. To jump to the lower-right corner of your image, press the End key.

Depth of Field Effect

This effect imitates a shot taken with a camera very close to the subject. This causes the area closest to the lens to be in very sharp focus, but the image immediately starts to go out of focus as the depth of field changes.

STEP ONE: Open the image you want to apply the effect to. Switch to Quick Mask mode by pressing the letter "q." Press the letter "d" to set your Foreground color to black. Click on the Gradient tool and in the Options Bar, make sure the gradient chosen is Foreground to Background.

STEP TWO: Using the Gradient tool, start approximately at the area that you want to be in focus and click-and-drag about 2" toward the area that you want out of focus. (In the example shown here, I started at the bottom right side of the man's face and dragged diagonally up to the left). When you do this, a red-to-transparent gradient will appear across your image.

STEP THREE: The red portion of your gradient should appear over the area you want to remain in focus. Switch back to normal mode by pressing the letter "q" again. Go under the Select menu and choose Feather. Enter a value of 20 and click OK (use a higher number for high-res images). Don't Deselect yet.

STEP FOUR: Go under the Filter menu, under Blur, and choose Gaussian Blur. As you drag the Radius slider to the right, you'll see your selected area start to blur. Choose the amount of blur that looks good to you and click OK. Deselect by pressing Command-D (PC: Control-D) to complete the effect.

Quick Tip:
Navigating with the Navigator palette

Yet another option you have for getting around your document is the Navigator palette. It's kind of a one-stop-shop for navigating your document. It shows you a little thumbnail version of your image in which you can drag a view box to display the part of the image you want to work on. To create your own view box (at the size you want), hold the Command key (PC: Control key) to change your pointer into a magnifying glass. Now, you can click-and-drag within the thumbnail preview window and when you release the key, you have a new view box.

Other ways to navigate inside this palette include dragging the slider to zoom in and out, typing in the exact percentage of zoom you want, or clicking on the tiny mountain icons to zoom either in or out. I don't use the Navigator palette myself; I prefer to use just keyboard shortcuts, but I know some people who use the Navigator palette exclusively, and they seem to be perfectly nice and well-adjusted.

Quick Tip:
Layer Masks tips

The tutorial on the right uses my favorite layers feature—Layer Masks. Here are a few tips for working with Layer Masks that you'll enjoy (okay, I don't know if you'll actually "enjoy" them, but they might come in handy).

• To delete your Layer Mask, drag just the Layer Mask thumbnail into the Trash icon at the bottom of the Layers palette.

• You can view the Layer Mask as a red rubylith. Hold Shift-Option (PC: Shift-Alt) and click on the Layer Mask thumbnail (if you don't already know what a rubylith is, then you probably won't care about this feature).

• You can disable the Layer Mask by holding the Shift key and clicking on the thumbnail.

• You can move the image independently of the mask by clicking directly on the Link icon between the layer thumbnail and the mask thumbnail.

Blending Images for Instant Collages

This is one of the fastest and most fun ways to blend (or collage) two images together. It uses Photoshop's Layer Mask command. This is so easy to do, yet so effective, that it opens up a whole new way for many people to collage multiple images.

STEP ONE: Open a background image (either RGB or Grayscale). Press the letter "d" to set your Foreground color to black.

STEP TWO: Open a second image that you want to use in your collage. Press the letter "v" to switch to the Move tool and drag this image on top of the background image in your original document. Make sure this dragged layer covers (or at least significantly overlaps) the background layer.

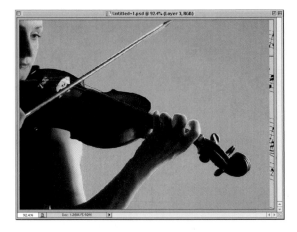

STEP THREE: Go to the Layers palette, and at the bottom of the palette, click on the Layer Mask icon (it's the second one from the left). The image doesn't change, but if you look in the Layers palette, you'll see another thumbnail icon added to the right of your top layer's thumbnail icon. This represents your Layer Mask.

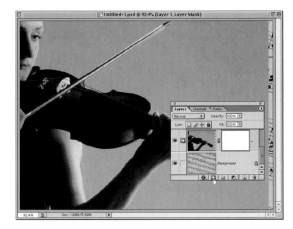

STEP FOUR: Click on the Gradient tool and in the Options Bar, click on the down-facing triangle and the flyout Gradient Picker will appear. Make sure the selected gradient is Foreground to Background, then take the Gradient tool and drag it through the image on the top layer, stopping before you reach the edge of that image. You'll notice that the images blend together.

STEP FIVE: You can continue to drag the Gradient tool over and over again, until the blend looks just the way you want. If you see the edge of your image, you've dragged too close to the edge or past it. Try re-dragging the Gradient tool, stopping about 1" before the edge of your image.

STEP SIX: If you want more control over how your images blend, you can paint directly on the mask by pressing the letter "b" to switch to the Brush tool, choosing a large, soft-edged brush, and painting. When you paint with black as your Foreground color, the background image paints in. When you paint with white, the top image paints over the background. That's all there is to it.

Quick Tip:
If you don't like your Layer Mask, start over

If you applied a Layer Mask to your image and you can't get it to look quite right, sometimes the best thing to do is just start over. There are a couple of ways to do this. You can click directly on the Layer Mask thumbnail and drag it into the Trash icon at the bottom of the Layers palette, but there's another way that may be quicker because you don't have to create a new mask in the Layers palette. Hold the Option key (PC: Alt key) and click on the Layer Mask icon (this displays the mask), then press Option-Delete (PC: Control-Backspace), which fills your Layer Mask with white; and you're "reset" and ready to start over. Option-click (PC: Alt-click) on your Layer Mask thumbnail again, then drag a gradient through your image, or start painting directly on your image (of course, you're really painting on the mask).

Quick Tip:
Merging your visible layers in one shot

In many of the effects in this book, you wind up with three or more separate layers. If you merge these layers one-by-one, the effect may wind up changing or disappearing altogether, because as you merge down, the order of your layers changes (as they're combined) and that changes the blending. Instead, there's a keyboard shortcut you can use that will get around this problem. It's Command-Shift-E (PC: Control-Shift-E). This is the keyboard shortcut for Merge Visible, and it takes all the currently visible layers and flattens them into one layer (it's like having a keyboard shortcut for Flatten Image).

Adding Motion Effects

If you've ever tried to add a sense of motion to an image using Photoshop's Motion Blur filter, you've probably already noticed that the effect is often too intense and tends to overwhelm the image. Here's how to apply a Motion Blur and then selectively decide how much blur and where you want it to appear.

STEP ONE: Open the image that you want to apply a Motion Blur effect to. Make a copy of the Background layer by dragging it to the New Layer icon at the bottom of the Layers palette.

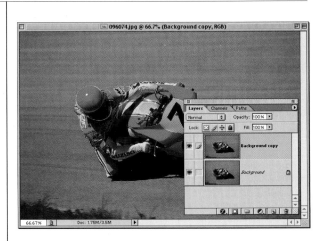

STEP TWO: Go under the Filter menu, under Blur, and choose Motion Blur. Enter an Angle for your blur matching the direction of the object (in this case, it's around −11°). Choose between 40 and 50 pixels for your Distance. Click OK.

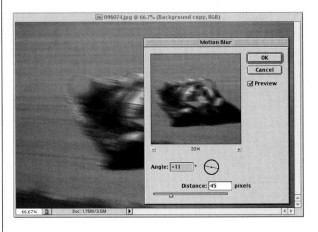

STEP THREE: Press the letter "d" on your keyboard to reset your Foreground color to black (the default). Click on the Layer Mask icon at the bottom of the Layers palette (the first icon from the left). This will not affect your image but it will add a second icon next to your Background copy layer in the Layers palette. Switch to the Brush tool and make sure that your Foreground color is still set to black.

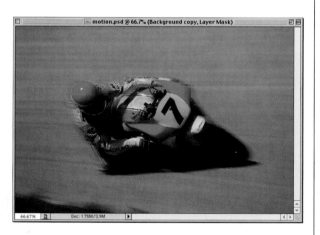

STEP FOUR: Choose a large, soft brush, and paint over the areas where you DON'T want the Motion Blur effect to appear. (We painted over the cyclist's face, over parts of the handlebars, wheels, and legs). If the effect is too intense, lower the Background copy layer's Opacity. The lower you go, the less effect is applied. Also, if you erased too much motion and need to add some back in, switch your Foreground color to white and paint the motion back in.

Quick Tip: Erasing back your original image

If you're working on an image and things start to look bad, you have a few choices. You can go under the File menu and choose Revert, which reverts your image to how it looked when you opened it. But what if you like some of the things you've done thus far and don't want to revert the whole image back to the original? What you can do is switch to the Eraser tool, hold the Option key (PC: Alt key), and start erasing over the areas that you don't want to keep. Usually, the Eraser tool erases your image, but when you hold the Option key (PC: Alt key), it erases back to how the image looked when you originally opened it. Kind of a revert in a brush. This is called the History Eraser, and it works much like the History Brush, but for some reason, many people seem to be more comfortable using the Eraser tool in this capacity rather than using the History Brush.

Quick Tip:
The express lane to backscreening

If you're not too fussy about the exact percent-age of backscreening, there's a faster way to backscreen an image. Make your selection and then press Command-L (PC: Control-L) to bring up the Levels dialog box. Drag the left bottom Output Levels slider to the right to instantly backscreen your selected area.

Backscreening Effect

This is a popular effect in print and multimedia, and it's used when the background image is very busy or very dark (or both) and you want to place ad type over your image that can easily be read. Although we're using the technique with a white-screened effect here, it's just as popular using a dark-screened effect.

STEP ONE: Open a background image that you want to put type over.

STEP TWO: Using the Rectangular Marquee tool, make a selection of the area where you want your type to appear.

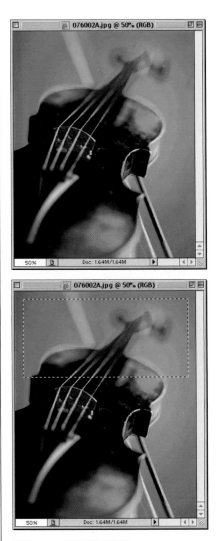

STEP THREE: While this area is still selected, create a new layer by clicking on the New Layer icon at the bottom of the Layers palette.

STEP FOUR: Press the letter "d," then the letter "x" to set your Foreground color to white. Then fill your selection with white by pressing Option-Delete (PC: Alt-Backspace). Deselect by pressing Command-D (PC: Control-D).

STEP FIVE: Lower the Opacity of this layer to create the amount of backscreen effect you'd like. A 20% screen is a very popular choice for backscreening, and to achieve a 20% screen you'd lower the Opacity to 80% on this layer. In this example, I actually lowered the Opacity to 60%. This lets a bit more of the background show through, but because the black text is so large, it's still very readable.

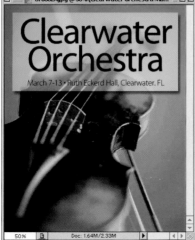

STEP SIX: To add more depth to your backscreen effect you can add a drop shadow behind it. Just click on Layer 1 (the backscreened layer) in the Layers palette to make it active, click on the little *f* icon at the bottom of the Layers palette for a pop-up menu of Layer Effects, and choose Drop Shadow. Click OK in the Drop Shadow dialog to complete the effect.

Quick Tip:
Backscreens aren't just white
Depending on the image, sometimes when you attempt a backscreen effect, a light backscreen won't work. If the image is already of a lighter nature, a light backscreen can get lost, so instead, try a dark backscreen. You can do this in the Levels dialog. Press Command-L (PC: Control-L) to bring up the Levels dialog box, and drag the right Output Levels slider to the left. This will darken your selected area. If you prefer to use Curves, you can add a light backscreen by dragging the bottom point of the curve straight upward. To add a dark backscreen, drag the top-right point straight downward.

Quick Tip:
Color correction for dummies

I know, I know, there should be a book with that title, but until one comes out, Photoshop has the next best thing. It's called Variations. You can find it under the Image menu, under Adjust, and what it does is display your original image and half a dozen different color variations of that image. All you have to do is decide which variation looks better than the original. It also shows you a lighter and darker version of your image, and if one or the other looks better than your original, pick it. Every time you click on one of these thumbnails, it updates your current pick. Your original is always displayed at the top of the dialog, along with your current pick right alongside, so you can easily compare the two. This is a very basic correction tool, and frankly, it's not the greatest, but if you have no color correction experience, this is the place to start. The best part is, when you open the dialog box, you'll realize that it's so easy, that you really need no instructions to use it (even though I just gave them to you).

Studio Tarp Technique

This is an ideal way to create a quick background image for portraits, and works especially well for executive portraits. I've used this technique numerous times when someone's given me a snapshot taken in their kitchen, backyard (insert your own unfortunate location for a photo shoot) and I remove them from that background (using Extract) and put them on a new one.

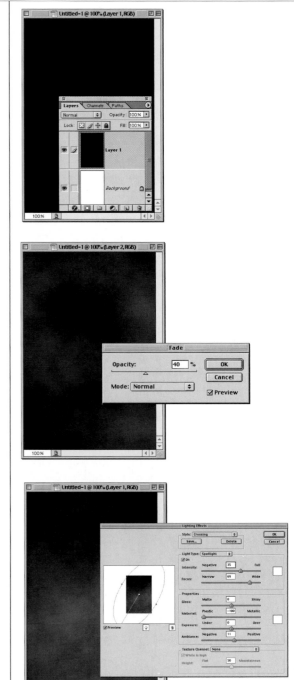

STEP ONE: Open a new document in RGB mode. Press "d" to make black your Foreground color, and then click the New Layer icon at the bottom of the Layers palette to create a new layer. Fill this new layer with black by pressing Option-Delete (PC: Alt-Backspace).

STEP TWO: Create another new blank layer above your black-filled layer. Go under the Filter menu, under Render, and choose Clouds. Go under the Edit menu and choose Fade Clouds. When the Fade dialog box appears, lower the Opacity to 40%, and click OK to lessen the effect of the Clouds filter.

STEP THREE: Press Command-E (PC: Control-E) to merge your clouds layer with the black layer below it. Go under the Filter menu, under Render, and choose Lighting Effects. When the Lighting Effects dialog box appears, choose Crossing from the Style menu, and click OK to apply a soft lighting effect to your layer.

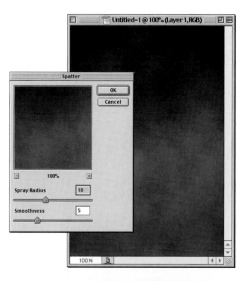

STEP FOUR: Go under the Filter menu, under Brush Strokes, and choose Spatter. When the dialog box appears, set the Spray Radius to 10 and the Smoothness to 5. Click OK. Go under the Edit menu and choose Fade Spatter. When the Fade dialog box appears, lower the Opacity to 50%, and click OK to lessen the effect of the Spatter filter by half.

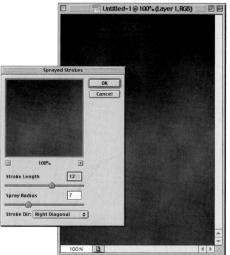

STEP FIVE: Go under the Filter menu, under Brush Strokes, and choose Sprayed Strokes. When the dialog box appears, set the Stroke Length to 12, the Spray Radius to 7, and the Stroke Dir to Right Diagonal. Click OK. Go under the Edit menu and choose Fade Sprayed Strokes. When the Fade dialog box appears, lower the Opacity to 50%, and click OK to lessen the effect of the Sprayed Strokes filter to half.

STEP SIX: To complete the effect, open the image containing a person that you want to put on the new background that you just created. Select them with the tool of your choice (Lasso tool, Extract filter, etc.) and use the Move tool to drag-and-drop them into the new background.

Quick Tip:
How to get an undo, three days after you closed your document

You're probably already familiar with Photoshop's History feature, which by default lets you undo your last 20 steps. Unfortunately, when you quit Photoshop, those undos go away. But there is a way to undo color or tonal corrections days, weeks, or months later. Here's how: The next time you're going to apply a tonal change of some sort (using either Levels, Brightness/ Contrast, Curves, Hue/ Saturation, Color Balance, or a few others), don't just choose them from the menus. Instead, go to the bottom of the Layers palette and click on the New Fill or Adjustment Layer icon. It's the little circle that is half black and half white. A pop-up menu will appear and you can choose which tonal change (or fill) you want to apply. A special layer will appear in your Layers palette with the name of your tonal change (e.g., Color Balance). After you save your *layered* document, when you reopen it, the Color Balance layer will still be there. To edit your original Color balance adjustment, double-click on it. To undo your color balance change, drag the Color Balance layer into the Trash.

Quick Tip:
Making precise-sized selections, method #1

If you know the exact size you want to make a selection, there are a couple of things you can do to get there. The quickest and easiest is to switch to the Rectangular Marquee tool, open the Info palette (shortcut: press F8), and as you start dragging your selection, glance in the bottom right-hand corner of the Info palette and you'll see a W (for Width) and an H (for Height) reading. As you drag, you'll see (in real time) the size of your selection, displayed in your current unit of measurement (inches, pixels, or whatever you have it set to).

Mapping a Texture to a Person

You may have heard of this technique as a Displacement Map technique because it uses Photoshop's Displace filter to map a texture from one object onto another object. This has become particularly popular in the past couple of years and fortunately it's quite easy to do, yet it looks as if you worked on the image for hours.

STEP ONE: Open the image that you want to apply texture to. (In this example, we're using a photograph of a woman, and we're going to apply the texture to her skin.)

STEP TWO: Make a duplicate of your image by going under the Image menu and choosing Duplicate. Then, go under the Image menu, under Mode, and choose Grayscale to convert this duplicate image into a Grayscale image.

STEP THREE: Go under the Filter menu, under Blur, and choose Gaussian Blur. Apply a 2-pixel blur to your grayscale image and click OK. (Note: 2 pixels is okay for low-res, 72-ppi images; for high-res, 300-ppi images, try 4 or 5 pixels.) Now, go under the File menu and save this blurry grayscale image. Name this file "Map" and save it in Photoshop's native format (making it a .psd file). This is the file we'll need when we apply the Displace filter in Step Six.

STEP FOUR: Open the image you want to use as a texture. Use the Move tool to drag this texture image on top of your original image.

STEP FIVE: Press Command-A (PC: Control-A) to put a selection around the entire image area. Then, go under the Filter menu, under Distort, and choose Displace. When the Displace dialog box appears, enter 10% for Horizontal Scale, and for Vertical Scale. Under Displacement Map, choose Stretch To Fit, and for Undefined Areas, choose Repeat Edge Pixels. Click OK.

STEP SIX: When you click OK, the standard "Open File" dialog box appears, prompting you to "choose a displacement map." Locate the grayscale file you saved earlier (in Step Three), click the Open button, and the Displace filter will use this map file to "map out" the texture to fit your image. You'll see your image area warp a bit when you apply this filter, but to see the full effect, there's still a little more work to do.

Quick Tip: Precise-sized selections— method #2

Another way to make a selection in the exact size that you need is to click on the Rectangular Marquee tool and change the style in the Options Bar Style pop-up menu. By default it's set to Normal, but if you choose Fixed Size, you can type in your desired size in the Width and Height fields just to the right of the pop-up menu in the Options Bar.

Now, when you click the Rectangular Marquee tool anywhere within your image, a selection in that fixed size (and only that size) will appear.

continued

Quick Tip:
What to check if you can't save your file in the format you want

If you try to save your Photoshop document and you get a warning in the dialog saying that "Some of the document's data will not be saved using the chosen format," here's what to check for:

(1) Layers: If you have layers in your document, you can only save in Photoshop or TIFF format without losing data.

(2) Check for extra channels: If you have an extra channel (perhaps a saved selection), you cannot save in the EPS format without losing data. Go to the Channels palette, drag the channel to the Trash, and then you can save as an EPS.

(3) You need a Background layer: If your only layer is named Layer 1 or Layer 0, Photoshop treats it as a layered document. You first have to go under the Layers palette's pop-down menu and choose Flatten Image.

(4) Check your color mode: Some file formats aren't available for certain color modes; for example, BMP doesn't show up as a choice when you're in CMYK mode.

STEP SEVEN: Press Command-D (PC-Control-D) to deselect. In the Layers palette, click on the Eye icon in the first column beside the texture layer to hide it. Return to your original image layer (the woman) and select the background area behind her. (Note: Since the background behind the woman is a solid color and easy to select, we used the Magic Wand tool.)

STEP EIGHT: In the Layers palette, click on the texture layer to make it the active layer (your selection should still be in place). Press Delete (PC: Backspace) to leave a silhouette of the texture in the shape of the woman's head. Deselect by pressing Command-D (PC: Control-D).

STEP NINE: At the top left of the Layers palette, change the Blend mode of this texture layer to Soft Light to make it look as if it has been painted onto her skin. Notice how the texture follows the contours of her face as if it were tattooed on. If the Soft Light Blend mode seems too soft, try Overlay or even Multiply for a darker effect. Lower the layer's Opacity if the effect seems too intense (we lowered it to 60%). To complete the effect, on the texture layer use the Eraser tool with a small, hard-edged brush to erase over her eyes, lips, eyebrows, and her blouse so that the effect just appears on her skin.

Montage from One Image

This is a technique I saw years ago, and not since then, until I saw it pop up recently in a print ad in *Entertainment Weekly* for the VH1® original movie, *The Way She Moves*, and I remembered how slick it was, because it lets you create a montage effect by using only one image. It's a great way to add some quick visual interest to an otherwise static photo.

STEP ONE: Open an image that you want to apply this effect to. In the Layers palette, double-click on the Background layer (your image layer) to bring up the New Layer dialog box. Name this layer "Image Layer" and click OK to convert your Background layer into a regular Photoshop layer.

STEP TWO: Next, create a new blank layer by clicking on the New Layer icon at the bottom of the Layers palette. Then, go under the Layer menu, under New, and choose Background From Layer (which converts your new layer into a Background layer).

STEP THREE: Press the letter "d" then the letter "x" to make your Background color black. Go under the Image menu and choose Canvas Size. When the Canvas Size dialog box appears, enter a dimension that is about 25% larger than your current image size, and click OK to put a black canvas area around your image.

continued

Quick Tip:
Getting rid of blemishes and scratches on your image

If you have an image with blemishes, spots, or scratches (generally called "artifacts"), here's a little trick that will help. Click on the Blur tool. In the Options Bar, lower the tool's Opacity setting to 20%, change the blend Mode to Lighten, and start painting over your scratches. In just a few strokes you'll see your scratches start to disappear.

STEP FOUR: In the Layers palette, click on your "Image Layer." Press the letter "m" to get the Rectangular Marquee tool and draw a small rectangular selection in one part of your image (as shown), but don't select the main focus of the image—choose outer areas for the most part. Cut this selected area from your "Image Layer" and put it on its own layer by pressing Command-J (PC: Control-J).

STEP FIVE: Press "v" to switch to the Move tool, and move this new layer either slightly up, down, to the left or to the right (your choice) about 1/2".

STEP SIX: At the bottom of the Layers palette, click on the Add a Layer Style icon (the black circle with an "*f*" in it), and choose Outer Glow. When the Outer Glow Layer Style dialog box appears, click on the tiny beige Color Swatch and change the Glow color to black. Change the Blend Mode to Normal, and adjust the Size upward until your black glow is visible onscreen. Click OK.

STEP SEVEN: In the Layers palette, click on your "Image Layer" again, draw a rectangular selection in a different area, and put it on its own layer again by using the Command-J (PC: Control-J) shortcut. You're going to use the same concept of slightly moving the rectangle for each selection.

STEP EIGHT: Once you make a selection into a layer, you'll need to apply the glow you made to your first layer to all subsequent layers. To do that, just click on the Outer Glow effect and drag-and-drop it (within the Layers palette) on the layer you want the effect applied to.

STEP NINE: Once you've applied the glows to all your layers, you can use the Move tool to position your rectangular layers into a pleasing layout, and then add any type to complete the effect.

Quick Tip:
Resizing by the numbers

Instead of using Free Transform, holding the Shift key (to constrain its proportions), and dragging a corner handle, there's a much more precise way to resize objects on a layer, and this way lets you input a variety of measurement values to get the exact size you want. Here's how:

Press Command-T (PC: Control-T) to bring up the Free Transform function. Now, look up in the Options Bar and you'll see fields where you can increase/decrease the Width and Height. By default, these fields are set up to increase/ decrease by percentages (200%, 300%, etc.), so you can type in any percentage resize you'd like. However, you can also type in other measurement units. For example, if you wanted your image to be 3" x 3", in the Width field type "3 in" (for inches), and in the Height field type "3 in." If you want your resize to be in pixels, type "px" after your value (i.e., "468 px").

Quick Tip:
Put that new layer underneath

By default when you click the New Layer icon (in the Layers palette, it creates a new blank layer directly above your current layer. But if you want the new layer to appear directly below your current layer, all you have to do is hold the Command-key (PC: Control-key) while pressing the New Layer icon and the new layer will appear below your current layer.

Focusing Attention

I saw this technique used very effectively on a menu cover for the Olive Garden® restaurant. It's a take-off on the classic vignette effect, but rather than just softening the edges, it also focuses the attention on the subjects of the image, while adding a soft border technique at the same time.

STEP ONE: Open the image you want to apply the effect to (in this case it's a 72-ppi color image in RGB mode). Make a selection around the area you want as the focal point of your effect using the selection tool of your choice (in this case I used the Rectangular Marquee tool).

STEP TWO: Go under the Select menu and choose Feather. Enter 5 for the Radius and click OK. (Note: For high-res images, use 15 instead.)

STEP THREE: While your selection is still in place, press Command-J (PC: Control-J) to put the selected area on its own separate layer, above your Background layer.

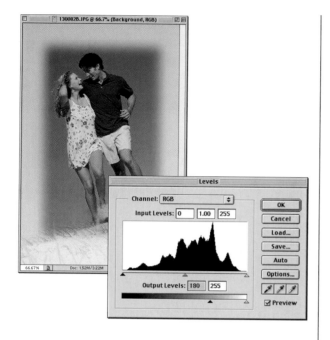

STEP FOUR: In the Layers palette, click on the Background layer to make it the active layer. Then, go under the Image menu, under Adjustment, and choose Levels. When the Levels dialog appears, click on the bottom-left Output Levels slider and drag it to the right, about two-thirds of the way to the opposite end to lighten the background image. (The Output field should read somewhere around 175.)

STEP FIVE: To complete the effect, click on Layer 1, then press Command-E (PC: Control-E) to merge this layer with the Background layer. Now you can add type to finish off the design. (The typeface I used here was Apple Garamond Light Italic, with the Tracking set at 600, and the type was set using all lowercase letters.)

Quick Tip:
Make that guide jump!

If you have a horizontal guide visible in your Photoshop document, you can instantly make that guide become a vertical guide by simply holding the Option key (PC: Alt key) and clicking on the guide. It will immediately jump to a vertical guide (and vice versa).

Quick Tip:
Setting paragraph attributes

By now you probably know that you can create text that will flow within its own "text box" by clicking-and-dragging the Type tool to create a text box in the size you'd like, before you actually enter text. But a lesser-known tip is that if you hold the Option key (PC: Alt-key) while you drag, it will bring up the Paragraph Text Size dialog where you can enter a specified Width and Height for your text box. Pretty slick!

Soft-edged Portrait Background

This is a technique that I started showing in my live seminars as a 30-second portrait or product shot background. Basically, it adds a quick "burned in" effect around the edges of your image, and although the background looks pretty bland when complete, as soon as you put an object or person on it, it instantly "makes sense."

STEP ONE: Open a new document in RGB mode. Choose a light Foreground color that you want to appear in the center of your background. Press Option-Delete (PC: Alt-Backspace) to fill your Background with this color.

STEP TWO: In the Layers palette, create a new blank layer by clicking on the New Layer icon at the bottom of the palette. Set your Foreground color to a darker shade of the color you used earlier (in other words, if you started with a light blue, now pick a dark blue). Then press Option-Delete (PC: Alt-Backspace) to fill your layer with this color.

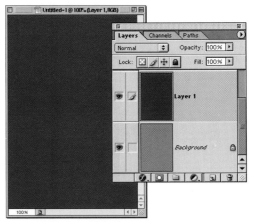

STEP THREE: Press "m" to switch to the Rectangular Marquee tool, and draw a rectangular selection about 1/2" to 1" inside the edges of your image (as shown).

STEP FOUR: Go under the Select menu and choose Feather. When the Feather dialog box appears, enter 25 pixels (for low-res images) or 60 pixels for 300-ppi, high-res images. Click OK, and the feathering will soften the edges of your selection (you'll see the edges of your selection round on screen).

STEP FIVE: Press Delete (PC: Backspace) to knock out a soft-edged hole in your top (darker) layer.

STEP SIX: Open the head shot of the person you want to place on this background. Select just the person (leaving their old background behind) and drag it on top of your original document to give a studio backdrop look to your head shot.

Quick Tip:
Not sure what size view you need? Try this tip.
You probably know that you can view your Photoshop document at almost any percentage view (96%, 115%, 120%, 135%, etc.) by typing in the View field at the bottom left-hand corner of your document window, but here's a cool tip to speed things up. If you don't know exactly which size you want, you can keep that field highlighted and ready as you enter another view size. Here's how: instead of just pressing the Enter key to see your new size, press Shift-Enter, and your new view will be displayed, but the view field is still high-lighted, enabling you to immediately type in a new view percentage.

Quick Tip:
Drawing straight lines

If you've ever had a problem drawing a straight line with a Photoshop tool, here's a little tip that will help. Instead of dragging the tool, just click once at the point where you want to start, then move to the point where you want your straight line to end, hold the Shift key, click, and Photoshop will automatically draw a straight line between the two points.

Photoshop Tattoos

This is a slick technique for adding tattoos to people without having to get your client drunk and dragging them to an unsavory part of town after midnight. Although this version of adding a tattoo is relatively painless for the client, you should definitely charge as though it was a real tattoo. Maybe more.

STEP ONE: Open the RGB image where you want to apply the tattoo.

STEP TWO: Open the image of the tattoo you want to use for the effect. My Creative Director Felix Nelson designed the tattoo shown here (which you can download from the book's companion Web site), and his "tattoo design tip" is to use the Airbrush tool with a small soft-edged brush, and don't use 100% fills—leave the area patchy and don't completely fill it in for a more realistic tattoo.

STEP THREE: Drag the tattoo image onto the photo where you'll be adding the effect. Then press Command-T (PC: Control-T) to bring up Free Transform. Control-click (PC: Right-click) and choose Rotate 90° CW from the pop-up menu of transformations. We do this to set up the image for the filter we'll run in the next step.

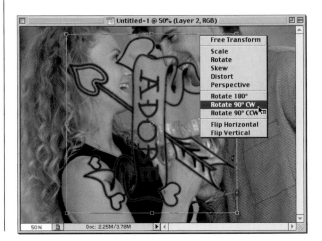

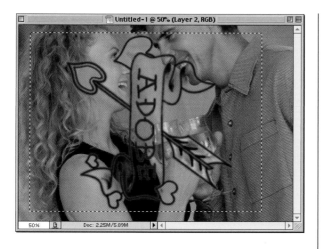

STEP FOUR: Press "m" to get the Rectangular Marquee tool and draw a selection around your tattoo. Make sure it's a bit wider and taller than the tattoo image (as shown).

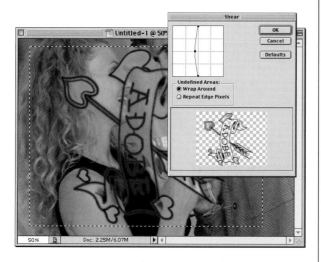

STEP FIVE: Go under the Filter menu, under Distort, and choose Shear. When the Shear dialog box appears, click in the middle of the grid to add an adjustment point. Click-and-drag this point to the left (as shown) to put a slight bend in your tattoo (see why we had to rotate the image before applying the bend?). Click OK to apply the Shear.

STEP SIX: Press Command-T (PC: Control-T) to bring up Free Transform. We're going to Scale the tattoo down to the size of her arm and rotate it slightly to fit the angle of her arm. Grab the top-right corner point, hold the Shift key, and drag inward to scale the image down in size. When the size looks right, move your pointer outside the bounding box and click-and-drag to rotate it into position. Press Return (PC: Enter) to apply the transformation.

continued

STEP SEVEN: Go under the Filter menu, under Blur, and choose Gaussian Blur. Apply a 0.5-pixel blur to soften the appearance of the tattoo and to make it look more realistic.

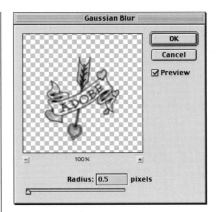

STEP EIGHT: In the Layers palette, change the Layer Blend Mode of the tattoo layer from Normal to Multiply to make the tattoo appear as if it's been burned into the skin.

STEP NINE: Lastly, to complete the effect, go to the Layers palette and lower the Opacity setting of the tattoo layer to 75%, which further helps the tattoo look more natural.

Faking Transparency

My creative director Felix Nelson came up with this technique for making a transparent part of your photo maintain that transparency when placed on another background. It's the best technique I've seen for this type of photo trickery and my hat's off to Felix for not only coming up with it, but making it so easy that anyone can do it. Felix rocks!

STEP ONE: Open the image that contains transparent areas. In the example shown here, the base of the monitor is transparent and that will present a problem when we put this monitor on a different background. (You can download the same image from our Web site.)

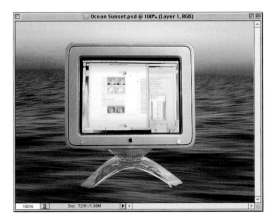

STEP TWO: Select the object using Photoshop's selection tools (or you can use the Path we included in the monitor file. Go to the Paths palette and Command-click [PC: Control-click] on Path 1 to load it as a selection). When the monitor is selected, drag it onto the background image as shown.

STEP THREE: Select just the bottom of the monitor (the areas that you'll want to look transparent). As you can see, the brownish color from the original photo shows through the transparent areas and is a dead giveaway that it was pasted from a different background onto this image.

continued

Quick Tip:
The hidden Fill Dialog shortcut

Although there doesn't seem to be a keyboard shortcut for bringing up the Fill dialog box, there actually is; it's just kind of buried in Photoshop folklore (whatever that is). To open the Fill dialog box, just press Shift-Delete (PC: Shift-Backspace). Freaky.

STEP FOUR: Once you have the bottom of the monitor selected, press Shift-Command-J (PC: Shift-Control-J) to cut the stand off the layer and put it on its own separate layer. Now press Shift-Command-U (PC: Shift-Control-U) to remove the color from the base. Now press Command-J (PC: Control-J) two times to make two duplicate layers of your base, as shown at right.

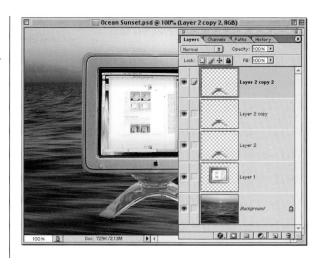

STEP FIVE: On the Top Layer (Layer 2 Copy 2) change the Layer Blend Mode to Screen, and then press Command-L (PC: Control-L) to bring up Levels. Type in 128 in the first Input Levels field to darken the shadows on this layer. Then, click on the layer just below it (Layer 2 copy) and change the Layer Blend Mode to Overlay.

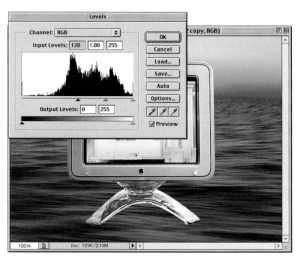

STEP SIX: Now, click on Layer 2 (your original base layer) and change the Layer Blend Mode to Multiply. Press Command-L (PC: Control-L) to bring up Levels. Type in 128 in the third from the left Input Levels field to blow out the highlights in this layer and complete the transparent effect (as shown). We also added a new image in the computer monitor window, just for looks.

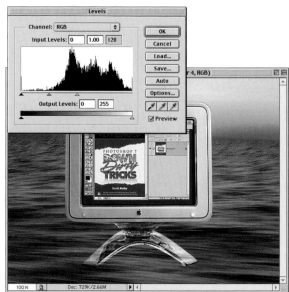

From Snapshot to Car Ad

Next time you're thinking of selling your car through AutoTrader®, you might try this effect on the photo and ask at least $800–$900 more. You've seen this technique numerous times in print ads for the big carmakers, and we blow the cover off how it's done.

STEP ONE: Take a photo of your car (okay, this isn't my car; I stole it, but I did take the photo on a street near our office). To make the shot look a bit more like a car ad, I took it from a low angle (I got down on one knee in the street, mind you) and I used a Nikon Coolpix 990.

STEP TWO: Use the Selection tool of your choice to put a selection around the car. (You can download the car from the book's companion Web site, and I saved the selection for you. To load it, go under the Select menu and choose Load Selection. Choose Alpha 1 from the Channel pop-up menu, and click OK to load the selection.)

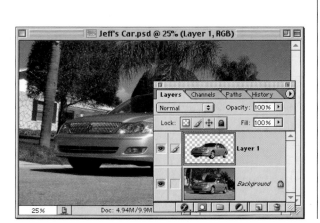

STEP THREE: Once the Selection is in place around your car, press Command-J (PC: Control-J) to put a duplicate of the car on its own layer

continued

Quick Tip:
Make that Curves dialog HUGE!

Since everybody's using these huge monitors set at large resolutions (like 1280 x 1024), it can make the Curves dialog box really tiny, which makes working with curves sometimes a bit frustrating. That's probably why Adobe added a little button in Photoshop 7 that, well…makes the Curves dialog box much bigger. It's in the bottom right-hand corner of the Curves dialog, just below the Preview checkbox. Click on it, and the size will "jump up."

Quick Tip:
The Layer Styles trap

This is more of just a "heads-up" than a tip, but if you create a custom Layer Style (a combination of different Layer Effects) and save it to the Styles palette, the settings saved will only give the desired effect if you apply the style to images that have the same resolution as the image you created the style within. In other words, if you create a custom Layer Style, while working in a 72-ppi document, and then later apply that style to a 300-ppi image, the effect will look different—in many cases much less intense, and in some cases it might not look right at all. The tip here is: if you find a combination of styles you like, create that style in both low-res, and high-res versions, so you always get the same effect, no matter what the resolution of your image.

STEP FOUR: In the Layers palette, click on the Background layer. Then go under the Filter menu, under Blur, and choose Motion Blur. When the dialog box appears, set the Angle to 0° and the Distance to 214, and then click OK to apply a motion blur to the Background layer (as shown).

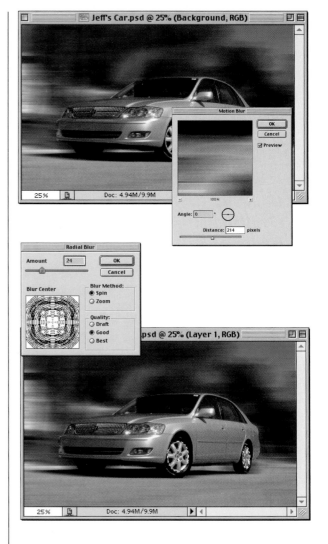

STEP FIVE: In the Layers palette, click on Layer 1 (the copy of the car). Press Shift-M to get the Elliptical (round) Marquee tool. Draw an Elliptical selection around the front wheel. (Tip: Hold the Spacebar to reposition the ellipse as you're drawing it.) Then, go under the Filter menu, under Blur, and choose Radial Blur. For Blur Method, choose Spin, enter 24 for Amount, and click OK to put a "spin" on the wheels.

STEP SIX: Repeat the process on the back tire. (You can't select both tires at the same time and apply the Radial Blur filter because the center of the blur won't fall in the right place.)

STEP SEVEN: Lastly, we'll darken the windows to hide the fact that if you look through the back windows, the background doesn't appear motion blurred. Make a selection of the window areas of the car, then press Command-J (PC: Control-J) to put the windows on their own separate layer.

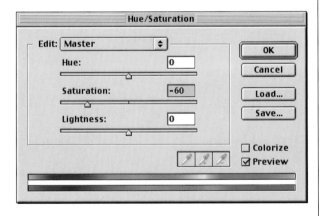

STEP EIGHT: The windows in this particular picture look very green, so we'll remove the saturation from the windows before we darken them. Press Command-U (PC: Control-U) to bring up the Hue/Saturation dialog. Lower the Saturation to –60 and click OK to reduce the green in the windows.

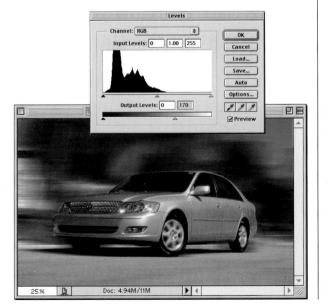

STEP NINE: To complete the effect, press Command-L (PC: Control-L) and when the Levels dialog box appears, drag the lower-right Output Levels slider to around 170 to create a tinted windows effect.

From Snapshot to Movie Poster

This technique lets you take a few snapshots and use a popular Hollywood technique employed in countless movie posters. The technique is actually very simple; the hard part may be making selections of the people in your snapshots—so make your job easy—shoot them on easy-to-mask backgrounds (in other words, don't do what I did).

STEP ONE: Open the images you want to collage into your movie poster. In this instance, I'm using three shots taken with my Nikon Coolpix 990 in front of our offices. The photos are (left to right): Ted LoCascio our Associate Designer; Chris Main our Managing Editor; and Felix Nelson, our Cabana Boy.

STEP TWO: Open an image that's large enough to accommodate the three images collaged together, and make sure it's the same resolution and color mode as your original images. In this case, I used an image that was 7.833" x 9.042". Why that particular size? I have no idea, that's just what I used. Go figure.

STEP THREE: Return to one of your snapshots and make a selection of the person (I used Photoshop's Extract filter, under the Filter menu, to remove the person from the background). To make things easier, I've already selected each person for you and saved Alpha Channels for you to load—just go to the book's companion Web site to download these images.

STEP FOUR: After your selection is in place, drag the person on top of your large background image (as shown). Press Shift-Command-U (PC: Shift-Control-U) to remove the color from the image. (We do this for effect as we'll add a blue tint to all three images, but it also makes it easier because matching the skin tones is no longer really an issue. There's a technical term for this—cheating).

STEP FIVE: Next, go under the Image menu, under Adjustment, and choose Hue/Saturation. Click the Colorize button, and then move the Hue slider to 216 to add a blue hue to the black-and-white image. Go under the Filter menu, under Noise, and choose Add Noise. For Amount enter 3, for Distribution choose Gaussian, and turn on Monochromatic. Click OK to apply some noise to the person.

STEP SIX: Repeat Steps Three, Four, and Five for the other two persons (select each one, drag it into the other image, remove the color, tint them blue, and Add Noise). In the Layers palette, position the second person behind the first one, and the third person behind the second (as shown). Also, to hide the edges of each person, go under the Layer menu, under Matting, and choose Defringe.

continued

Quick Tip:
Unlinking layers the fast way

If you have a number of layers linked together and you want to quickly unlink them, you'll love this tip—just hold the Option key (PC: Alt key) and click directly on the tiny Brush icon in the 2nd column beside your current layer. This will immediately unlink all layers linked to your current layer.

STEP SEVEN: Now it's time to add some dramatic shadows to the images, to…well, add some drama. Hold the Command key (PC: Control key) and in the Layers palette, click on the layer of the first person you added to your background image to put a selection around that person. Next, press the letter "L" to switch to the Lasso. Press "d" to set your Foreground color to black.

STEP EIGHT: While you have the Lasso tool, hold the Option key (PC: Alt key) and drag over the center of your subject's face, following the contours of the face. This will be the dividing line for your shadow area. By holding the Option (PC: Alt) key, you're subtracting from your existing selection. When you're done, what you should have is half the person selected (as shown). Create a new layer by clicking on the New Layer icon at the bottom of the Layers palette.

STEP NINE: Go under the Select menu and choose Feather. When the Feather dialog appears, enter 5 to soften the edges. Press "g" to switch to the Gradient tool. Up in the Options Bar, click on the down-facing arrow next to the Gradient Thumbnail to bring up the Gradient Picker. Choose the second gradient (Foreground to Transparent). Take the Gradient tool and drag from the right side of your selection to the left to create the shadow.

STEP TEN: If your shadow doesn't look right, you have to press Delete (PC: Backspace) and try again—don't just drag a new gradient over the old gradient. When it looks right, press Command-D (PC: Control-D). You'll have to repeat Steps Seven through Nine on the other two persons in your poster. Because the third person is facing the opposite direction, you'll have to deselect the other side (as shown).

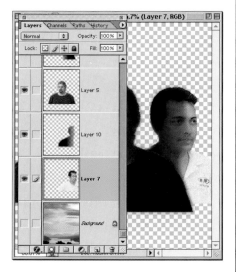

STEP ELEVEN: Once all your shadows are in place, we're going to merge all the persons and their shadow layers together into one layer. In the Layers palette, hide the Background layer by clicking on the Eye icon next to it. Then, go under the palette's pop-down menu and choose "Merge Visible" to merge the layers you have left visible into one single layer. Now you can make the Background layer visible again.

STEP TWELVE: Click on the New Layer icon to create a new blank layer and drag it beneath the layer with your heads. Press "m" to switch to the Rectangular Marquee tool and draw a selection from just below their shoulders to the bottom of the image.

continued

Quick Tip:
Hide that path!

If you've been tromping over to the Paths palette every time you want to hide a path from view, there's actually a quicker way—just press Shift-Command-H (PC: Shift-Control-H) and your path will be temporarily hidden. To make it visible again, just press the same shortcut.

Quick Tip:
Change the size of your palette thumbnails in one click

You can quickly change the size of the thumbnail previews in any of Photoshop's palettes that display thumbnails by Control-clicking (PC: Right-clicking) outside the thumbnail in a non-used area. For example, if you drag downward on the Layers palette, with only one or two layers you'll see the gray open area I'm talking about. Control-click (PC: Right-click) there and a pop-up menu with thumbnail sizes will appear.

STEP THIRTEEN: Press Option-Delete (PC: Alt-Backspace) to fill the selected area with black. Deselect by pressing Command-D (PC: Control-D). Press "g" to switch to the Gradient tool.

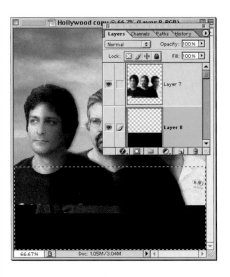

STEP FOURTEEN: Go up to the Options Bar and click on the down-facing arrow next to the Gradient Thumbnail to reveal the Gradient Picker. Click on the first gradient (Foreground to Background). In the Layers palette, click on your people layer. Click on the Layer Mask icon at the bottom of the Layers palette, then drag the Gradient tool from near the top of the black up toward the faces to blend them with the black area below them.

STEP FIFTEEN: The final step is to add type to help give the "movie-poster" effect. In this case, the type at the top is Minion (kind of like Times) set in all caps with +1000 tracking to add lots of space between the letters. The movie title is the same font, but for the line of credits just below it, I needed a tall thin typeface, so I used Bodega Serif (it was the only tall thin face I had on hand). The very bottom line is Minion, again in all caps.

Colorizing Black & White Images

This is a technique for colorizing grayscale images that's great for getting that hand-tinted effect. This particular version uses Photoshop's Hue/Saturation command to add color to selected areas.

STEP ONE: Open a grayscale image that you want to colorize. You have to be in a color mode to colorize a grayscale image, so go under the image menu, under Mode, and choose RGB to put your image into a color mode.

STEP TWO: Using one of Photoshop's selection tools, select the first area that you'd like to colorize (in this example, I used the Lasso tool to select an area).

continued

Quick Tip:
When to use Colorize

The only time you really need to check (turn on) the Colorize box in the Hue/Saturation dialog is when the image or selected area you're working on doesn't already contain color. Turning this checkbox on adds color to the image. If your image is already in color, and you want to change the color, you don't need to click Colorize, just move the Hue slider to pick a new color.

Quick Tip:
Getting realistic colors

One trick you can use to get more realistic colors for critical areas like flesh tones, grass, hair, sky, etc., is to open a full-color image at the same time that you're trying to colorize your grayscale image. That way, when you're in the Color Picker, you can move your cursor outside the dialog to sample real colors right from the color image, and then return to your image and paint with those colors.

STEP THREE: Go under the Image menu, under Adjustment, and choose Hue/Saturation, or press Command-U (PC: Control-U). When the dialog box appears, check the Colorize box. Now you can move the Hue slider to choose the color you'd like. If the color seems too intense, lower the Saturation slider.

STEP FOUR: Continue this process of selecting areas, going to Hue/Saturation, checking the Colorize box, and moving the Hue slider to add color to your image.

If you were one of those people who bought previous versions of this book (I call these people "my very best

Full Metal Jacket
Metal and Chrome Effects

friends in the whole wide world"), then you'll probably remember its chrome chapter. (I did ask you to commit the entire chapter to memory, didn't I?) Well, this chapter is vastly different. It's much "chromier," "metallic-er" and even a bit "goldified." If you take the time to learn the techniques in this chapter, and one day you get a call from Snoop Doggy Dogg to design the logo for his new CD, you'll have paid for the cost of this book many times over, and before you know it, it'll be "raining Benjamins." This works equally well if someone like…say, General Motors calls to have you design a new GM logo (the current form of which features the tasteful use of chrome around the edges). If that should happen, you'll probably be taking a limo to work from now on. Now, what happens if, instead of General Motors calling, it turns out to be General Mills? Then turn to my chapter on Photoshop Cereal Design. I think it starts on page 322.

Quick Tip:
Change contours for a new effect

On the third page of this chrome tutorial, I give you two different options for effects. (The second one is what we used on the cover for the word "Dirty," but we added some bolts on top of the chrome, as any self-respecting "Photoshop-er" might do.) If you like to experiment and create options of your own, changing the current contour of your Bevel and Emboss, or Satin effect, is a great way to tweak an existing effect and give it a totally different look. Just double-click on the effect, then click the down-facing triangle next to the current Contour thumbnail. A library of contours will appear, and you can just start clicking on each contour until you see an effect you really like. It sounds simple, and it is.

Cover Chrome

This version of chrome uses nothing but Photoshop's built-in Layer Styles, and I call it "Cover Chrome" because it's the basis of the chrome effect we used on the cover (actually it's based on Option #2 at the end of this tutorial). I know, the name "Cover Chrome" is pretty lame, but hey…I needed a name for this effect and all the good chrome names had already been taken.

STEP ONE: Create a new blank document in RGB mode. Set black as your Foreground color by pressing the letter "d", then create some type (in this example, we used the Rapier font). This effect is designed for very large display-sized type (such as 220 points or more), so make sure your type is fairly big. Go to the Layers palette and at the bottom of the palette, choose Satin from the Layer Styles pop-up menu.

STEP TWO: When the dialog box appears, change the Blend Mode to Screen, click on the black Color Swatch, and change the color to white. Increase the Distance to 14 and lower the Size to 7. Turn on the Anti-aliased checkbox and leave the default Contour as is. Don't click OK yet. In the list of Styles in the left-hand side of the Layer Styles dialog box, click on the name Bevel and Emboss.

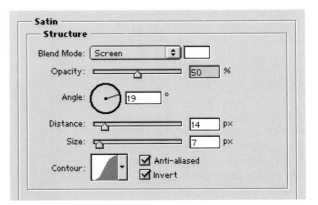

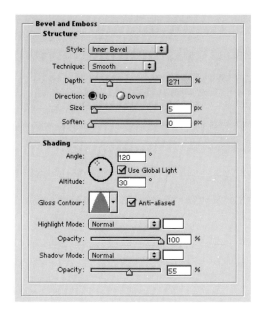

STEP THREE: In the Bevel and Emboss dialog, increase the Depth to 271%. Under the Shading section, set the Altitude to 30°. Click on the down-facing triangle next to Gloss Contour and choose the default contour that looks like one hill (as shown). Change the Highlight mode to Normal and increase the highlight Opacity to 100%. Change the Shadow mode to Normal, decrease the Opacity to 55%, and change the shadow color to white. Don't click OK yet.

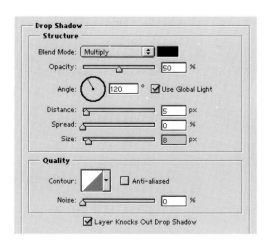

STEP FOUR: In the list of styles in the left-hand side of the Layer Styles dialog box, click on the name Drop Shadow to make its options visible. Lower the Opacity to 50% and increase the size to 8.

Quick Tip:
Changing your units of measurement

A trick for quickly changing your unit of measure (say, from inches to pixels) is to open the Info palette and click on the little crosshairs in the lower left-hand corner of the palette. A pop-up list of measurement units will appear, and you can choose the one you want directly from there.

continued

Quick Tip:
High-powered chiseling

Photoshop allows you to create a hard-edged chisel effect via the Bevel and Emboss Layer Effects by changing the Technique to Chisel Hard.

Another way to create a hard-edged chisel effect is to use Alien Skin's Inner Bevel plug-in from their Eye Candy collection of Photoshop plug-in filters. For more information on their way-crazy, cool plug-ins, visit them at www.alienskin.com.

STEP FIVE: Click OK to apply your combination of Layer Styles to produce the effect you see (right). That completes the effect, but since we've come this far, there are a couple of minor things you can change that will give you an entirely different effect, so I thought I'd throw those in as well. Rather than calling them Steps Six and Seven, because they're not really steps, we'll call them Option 1 and (you guessed it) Option 2.

OPTION 1: In the Layers palette, double-click on the Satin effect to bring up its options. Click on the down-facing triangle next to Gloss Contour and when the Contour Picker appears, click on the last of the default contours (it looks like two upward-facing triangles, as shown). This gives a brighter, more detailed chrome with inset lines that looks pretty sweet!

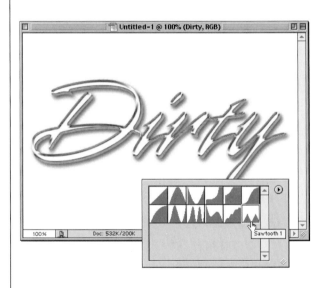

OPTION 2: If you've already created Option 1, then you can add this on top to create another nice metallic twist. This time in the Layers palette, double-click on the Bevel and Emboss effect to bring up its options. Click on the down-facing triangle next to Gloss Contour and when the Contour Picker appears, choose the one with one hill, and this gives you yet another version to choose from.

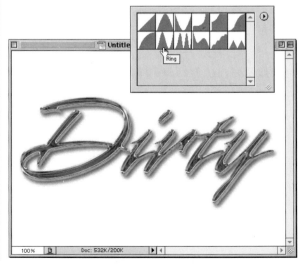

White Chrome

This is a quick Type effect that uses a combination of three Layer Effects to create 95% of it and at the end, we add a quick Curve and Hue/Saturation adjustment just for kicks. You don't need to add the Curve, but honestly, what you're going to do using Curves is so easy that even if you've never tried Curves before, you'll be able to do this.

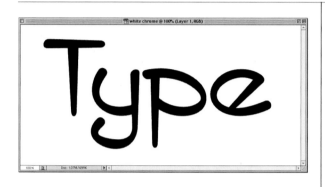

STEP ONE: Set some display type at a very large point size (this technique is designed to be used only on very large type. In the example shown here, we used the font ITC Styleboy set at 350 points in a 12x6" document set to low-res at 72 ppi).

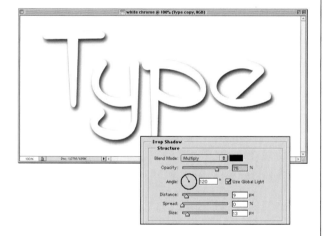

STEP TWO: After your type is set, choose Drop Shadow from the Layer Styles pop-up menu at the bottom of the Layers palette. Set the Distance to 9, Size to 13, and click OK to apply a drop shadow to your black type. Press "d" then "x" to set your Foreground color to white, then press Option-Delete (PC: Alt-Backspace) to fill your type with white, leaving only the drop shadow visible (as shown).

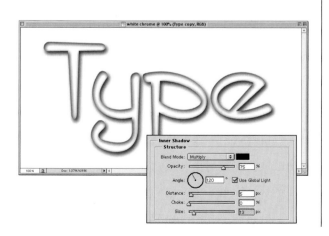

STEP THREE: This time from the Layer Style pop-up menu, choose Inner Shadow. When the dialog box appears, increase the Size to 13 to apply a shadow on the inside of your type. Don't click OK yet.

continued

Quick Tip:
How to find the Chrome gradient

When you select the Gradient tool, the Options Bar immediately displays the Gradient tool options. If you click on the down-facing triangle immediately to the right of the Gradient thumbnail of your currently selected gradient, a flyout Gradient Picker will appear with all the gradient presets you have loaded. Now, how do you know which one is the Chrome gradient? Well, if you have the Tool Tips preference turned on (it's on by default), just hold your cursor over any gradient swatch and its name will appear. If you've turned off Tool Tips (frankly, they drive me crazy, except for finding gradients), then you can choose to view your gradients by name rather than by thumbnails. You do that by clicking on the right-facing triangle in the Gradient Picker to display a pop-up menu where you can choose Text Only to display the gradients by name. This makes finding the Chrome gradient a snap.

Quick Tip :
Creating another document with the same exact specs as your current document

If you do much collaging of images, this tip will save you boatloads of time (meaning a cargo bay of cheap watches). To create a new document with the same size, resolution, and color mode as your current document, go under the File menu and choose New. While the New dialog box is onscreen, go under the Window menu, under Documents. There you'll see a list of all your currently open documents. Choose the one you want, and Photoshop will automatically load its size, resolution, and color mode into your open "New" dialog box. All you have to do is click OK.

STEP FOUR: From the list of Styles on the left side of the Layer Styles dialog box, click directly on the word Satin to make its options visible. Lower the Distance setting to 4 and the Size setting to 5, then click on the down-facing triangle next to the Contour setting to bring up the Contour Picker. Choose the contour (from the default set) that has two steep hills. Then turn on the Anti-aliasing checkbox, and turn off the Invert checkbox. Now, you can click OK, and both effects will be applied to your type.

STEP FIVE: Just applying those three effects gives you a pretty good-looking white chrome effect and you can stop this technique here and use the type as is. However, I'm going to take it a step further by adding some color. Again, this is totally optional. We'll start by choosing a Hue/Saturation Adjustment Layer from the Adjustment Layer pop-up menu at the bottom of the Layers palette (as shown).

STEP SIX: When the Hue/Saturation dialog box appears, click on the Colorize checkbox, increase the Hue to 232, decrease the Saturation to 22, and then click OK to apply a blue tint to your chrome. You'll also see an Adjustment Layer added to your Layers palette (which is handy in case you want to edit this color later— you can just double-click on the Adjustment Layer and it will bring up the Hue/Saturation dialog box with the previous settings you applied).

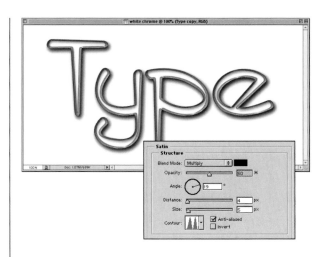

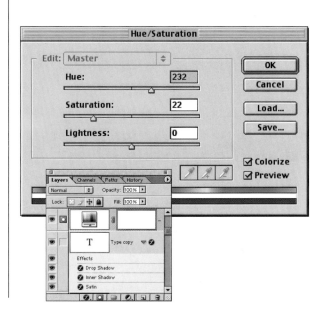

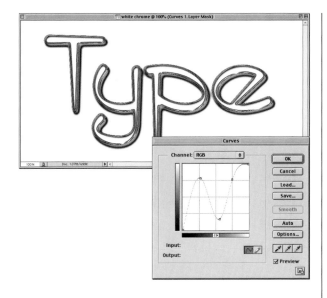

STEP SEVEN: Choose a Curves Adjustment Layer from the pop-up menu at the bottom of the Layers palette. When the Curves dialog box appears, create the Curve shown left by clicking once on the left side of the curve line (which adds a point) and then dragging that point upward to form the first "hill". Then click at the top of the Curve to add a point and drag that one down. Lastly, add one more point to the right and drag it upward, re-creating the curve shown, then click OK.

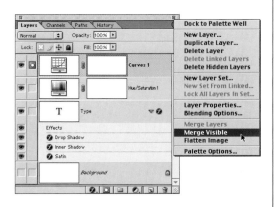

STEP EIGHT: Hide the Background layer from view by clicking on the Eye icon in the first column to the left of the Background layer. Go under the Layers palette's drop-down menu and choose Merge Visible to merge all these layers into one. Now you can make the Background layer visible again to complete the effect (shown below).

Quick Tip:
**Using big effects
at small sizes**

In a number of places in
this book I mention that
you need to create the
effect at a large size. For
example, if it's a Type
effect, I might tell you to
create the effect at 200- or
300-point size so the
effect looks right. But
don't let that tie your
hands if you need to use
that big effect at a small
size—just create it at the
larger size, then use either
the Image Size command,
or Free Transform to scale
it down to the size you
really need later. The
effect will usually hold
when scaled down but if
you start at that smaller
size, oftentimes the effect
won't look right, so you're
better off to start off
big, and shrink it down
later. This is a very
common technique with
pro Web designers.

Ultimate Chrome

This is a chrome technique that I learned from *Photoshop User* magazine's original creative director. It's based on a cover design he did for the magazine, but he created the original cover using Photoshop 5.5, and since then we've found even easier ways to create the same effect using Photoshop 7's features.

STEP ONE: Open a new document in RGB mode. Make light gray your Foreground color. Create your type (you'll need to use very large type for this effect; ideally, 200-point or more). I used the Webdings typeface at 300 points.

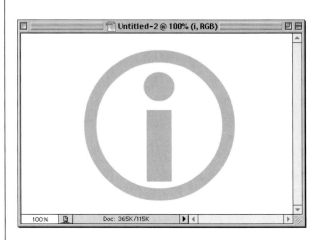

STEP TWO: Rasterize this Type layer by going to the Layers palette and Control-clicking (PC: Right-clicking) on the Type layer and from the pop-up menu that appears, choose Rasterize Layer. At the bottom of the Layers palette, choose Bevel and Emboss from the Styles pop-up menu. When the dialog box appears, you can use the default settings, so just click OK.

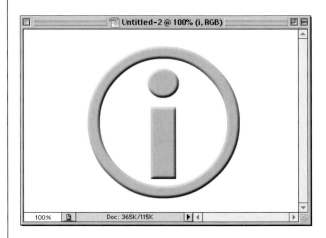

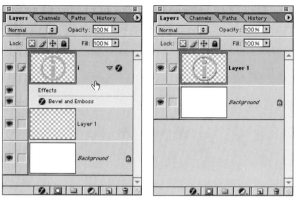

Figure A   Figure B

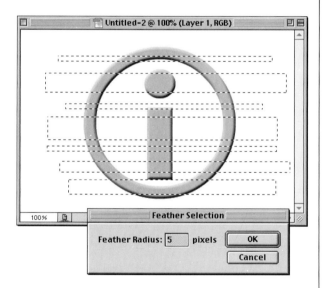

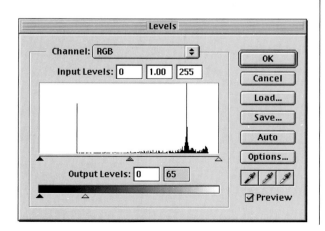

STEP THREE: We're going to remove the Layer Style from this layer, while leaving the bevel still applied. To do this , create a new blank layer by clicking on the New Layer icon at the bottom of the Layers palette, and then drag this blank layer below your Type layer; but then click back on your Type layer (as shown in Figure A). Press Command-E (PC: Control-E) to merge these two layers together (as shown in Figure B).

STEP FOUR: Press the letter "m" to switch to the Rectangular Marquee tool. Draw a series of rectangular selections across your text. Start by drawing one, then hold the Shift key to add other rectanglar selections. Vary the height of each selection (as shown at left). Go under the Select menu and choose Feather. Enter 5 pixels for low-res, 72-ppi images or 20 pixels for 300-ppi, high-res images, and click OK.

STEP FIVE: Press Command-L (PC: Control-L) to bring up the Levels dialog box. Grab the bottom right Output Levels slider and drag it all the way over to the left until the readout shows 65, and then click OK.

Quick Tip:
How to see feathering before you apply it

One of the downsides of the feathering feature is that you can't see how much you're really feathering; it's pretty much a guess because there's no preview. Here's a cool trick that many people use to see a feathered edge effect before they apply it: First, make a selection (inside the edges of your image) and then press the letter "q" to enter Quick Mask mode (your selection will appear as a red box by default). Go under the Filter menu, under Blur, and choose Gaussian Blur. When you apply the blur, you'll see the edges become very soft. When the softness of the edges looks right, press the letter "q" again to return to Normal mode and make your selection active. Go under the Select menu and choose Inverse to choose the background edges, rather than the inside of your selection, and press Delete (PC: Backspace) to feather the edges softly at the exact amount you saw in the Quick Mask preview.

continued

Quick Tip:
Crop and straighten at the same time

When you're using the Crop tool, you can rotate your selected area before you crop by moving your pointer outside the bounding box that appears around your image where you dragged the Crop tool. You'll see that your pointer temporarily changes into a double-headed arrow, which enables you to freely rotate your object. When it's rotated just the way you like it, you have two choices: Double-click inside the bounding box or press Return (PC: Enter) to make the rotation permanent. If you're using the Crop tool and you decide that you don't want to crop the image after all, click once on the Crop tool icon in the Toolbox. A dialog box will appear giving you the option to Crop or Don't Crop.

STEP SIX: Press the Down Arrow key on your keyboard eight times to move the selection downward. Then press Command-I (PC: Control-I) to invert the selection. Press Command-L (PC: Control-L) to bring up Levels again. Grab the TOP right *Input* Levels slider, and drag it over to the left until the readout up top shows 140, and then click OK.

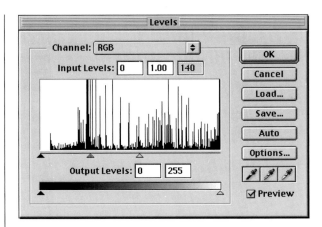

STEP SEVEN: Your image should look like the one shown here. Deselect by pressing Command-D (PC: Control-D).

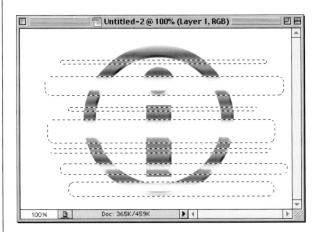

STEP EIGHT: At the bottom of the Layers palette, choose Bevel and Emboss from the Styles pop-up menu. When the dialog box appears, increase the Depth to 200% and the Size to 7 (for high-res images, increase the Depth to 800% and the Size to 25), click OK to apply another bevel to your image.

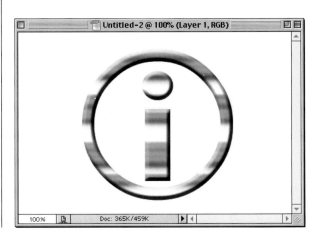

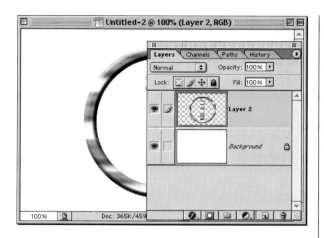

STEP NINE: Again we're going to remove the Layer Style from the layer. Create a new blank layer, and drag this blank layer below your Type layer. Click on your type layer, then press Command-E (PC: Control-E) to merge these two layers together.

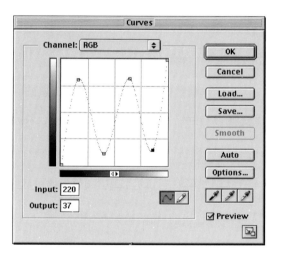

STEP TEN: Press Command-M (PC: Control-M) to bring up the Curves dialog box. You'll see a straight line (the curve) at a 45° angle. Click once about 25% from the bottom left to add a point, and drag it upward (you're going to add four points to create the curve shown here). When your curve looks like this, click OK.

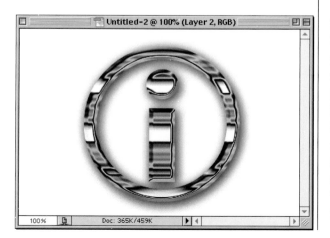

STEP ELEVEN: Lastly, add a Drop Shadow from the Layer palette's Layer Style pop-up menu. Increase the Size to 18 pixels (40 for high-res, 300-ppi images), and then apply the Unsharp Mask filter (found under the Filter menu, under Sharpen) with the Amount set at 100%, Radius at 1, and Threshold at 5, to complete the effect.

Quick Tip:
If it's metal, sharpen the living heck out of it

First off, I had to say "heck," because there could be kids reading this book—and some of them might be really smart toddlers, so you can never be too careful. One thing I've found, and that *you* might find helpful is that when you have a chrome or metallic image, you can apply the Unsharp Mask filter with very high settings for Amount settings (such as 300 to 500) and it looks just fine. In fact, sometimes I'll apply Unsharp Mask to chrome type three or four times in a row (with Amount settings around 100 to 150). Those hard edges just soak up the sharpening.

The main things you need to look out for are halos or weird unwanted colors that can start to creep into your edges. Otherwise, sharpen till the cows come home (if you don't have cows, just keep sharpening until someone yells, "Stop!").

Quick Tip:
Adding glints
to chrome

The type of effect shown at right is often accented with "glints" (little sparkles of light). Check out page 153 for one technique for adding glints to your images.

Chrome Double Stroke Effect

I first saw this effect in a print ad for "Cocky," the album from hip-hop and rock rapper Kid Rock. I loved the effect of having one stroke layered on top of another with chrome contours on both strokes. It makes use of Bevel and Emboss contours, and it's actually pretty simple to pull off.

STEP ONE: Create a new document in RGB mode at 72 ppi. Press the letter "d" to set your Foreground color to black, then set some type at a very large point size (in the example shown here, I used the font Aachen Bold set at 80 points, and I increased the width in the Character palette to 130%).

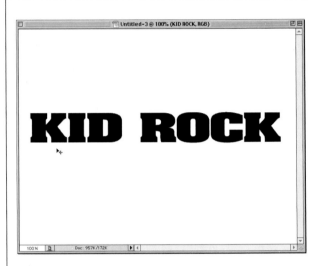

STEP TWO: From the Layer Styles pop-up menu at the bottom of the Layers palette, choose Inner Shadow. When the dialog box appears, lower the Opacity to 40%, increase the Size setting to 10, and click OK to apply a soft shadow on the inside of your type. When you click OK, you won't see the shadow yet because your type is black.

STEP THREE: Press the letter "x" to change your Foreground color to white. Press Option-Delete (PC: Alt-Backspace) to fill your type with white. Now you should see the inner shadow you created in the previous step (as shown at right).

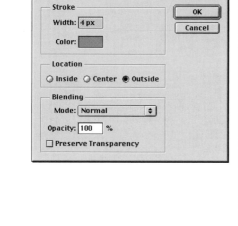

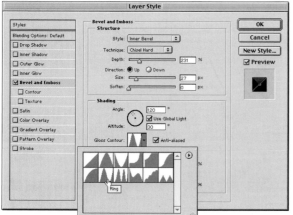

STEP FOUR: Go to the Layers palette and Command-click (PC: Control-click) on your Type layer's name to put a selection around your type. While your selection is in place, add a new blank layer above your type layer by clicking on the New Layer icon at the bottom of the Layers palette.

STEP FIVE: Go under the Edit menu and choose Stroke. When the dialog box appears, click on the Color Swatch and change your stroke color to gray. For Width enter 4 pixels, for Location choose Outside, and then click OK to put a gray stroke around your selection. Don't Deselect yet. From the Layer Style pop-up menu (at the bottom of the Layers palette), choose Bevel and Emboss.

STEP SIX: When the dialog box appears, change the Technique to Chisel Hard. Increase the Depth to 231% and increase the size to 27. In the Shading section, click on the down-facing triangle next to Gloss Contour. In the default set of contours, choose the second contour on the second row (it's named Ring) as shown at left. Then, click on the Anti-aliased checkbox to smooth the contour. Change the Shadow mode from Multiply to Lighten, then click OK to apply this effect to your stroked layer.

continued

Quick Tip:
Fill shortcuts
Here are some quick shortcuts that can be real timesavers for filling selections or layers. For example:

• To fill an entire layer with your Foreground color, press Option-Delete (PC: Alt-Backspace).

• To fill just an object on a layer (not the entire layer), press Shift-Option-Delete (PC: Shift-Alt-Backspace).

• To fill with your Background color, press Command-Delete (PC: Control-Backspace).

• To fill your layer with black, press the letter "d," then Option-Delete (PC: Alt-Backspace).

• To fill your layer with white, press the letter "d," then the letter "x," then press Option-Delete (PC: Alt-Backspace).

Quick Tip:
Horizontal scaling without the palette

In the project we're working on here, when we set the type we increased the amount of Horizontal Scaling (the thickness of the letters) by increasing the Scaling amount to 130% in the Character palette. But there's another way to edit the Horizontal Scaling of your image without typing numbers in the Character palette. Just set your type, then press Command-T (PC: Control-T) to bring up Free Transform. Then click-and-drag the right center adjustment point (on the Free Transform bounding box) to the right. As you do, it will stretch the type (scaling it horizontally) and will give you the same effect as if you had typed a percentage in the Character palette in the first place. This is a much more visual way to scale your type horizontally.

STEP SEVEN: Since you haven't deselected, your selection should still be in place. Go under the Select menu, under Modify, and choose Expand. When the Expand dialog box appears, enter 4 and click OK to expand your selection by 4 pixels.

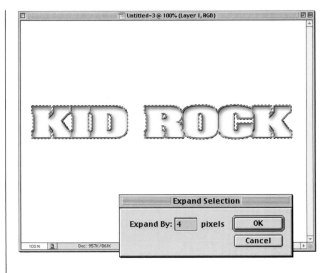

STEP EIGHT: Go under the Edit menu and choose Stroke. When the dialog box appears, your previous setting should still be in place, so just click OK to put a gray stroke around your expanded selection.

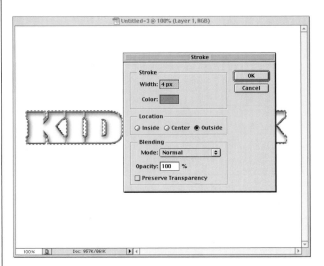

STEP NINE: Since you applied this stroke to the same layer that you beveled earlier, this new stroke is automatically beveled, and the contour you applied gives it a chrome look. To complete the effect, simply Deselect by pressing Command-D (PC: Control-D), then switch to the Background layer, press "d" to make your Foreground color black, then press Option-Delete (PC: Alt-Backspace) to fill the background with black.

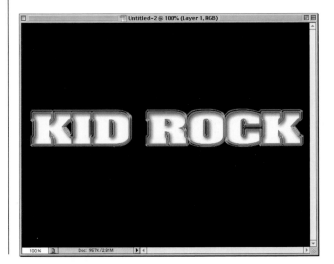

Going for the Gold

This is a great technique for creating elegant gold type. Don't be put off by the fact that this technique uses Curves—what we do in Curves is so easy, even if you've never used Curves before, you'll have no trouble doing what you have to do here.

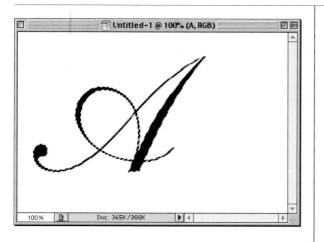

STEP ONE: Open a new document any size in RGB mode. Click on the Type tool and create some text (I typed the letter "A" using the Shelley Allegro Script font from Adobe). Hold the Command key (PC: Control key) and click once on your Type layer in the Layers palette to put a selection around your text (as shown).

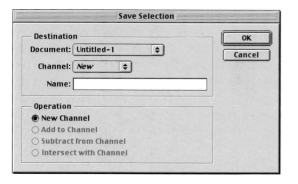

STEP TWO: Go under the Select menu and choose Save Selection to save your selection as an Alpha Channel. When the dialog appears, just click OK. Press Command-D (PC: Control-D) to Deselect. Now, delete your Type layer by dragging it into the Trash icon at the bottom of the Layers palette.

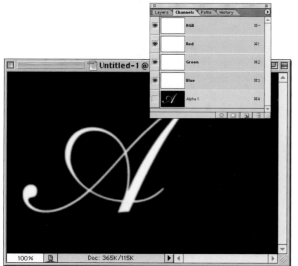

STEP THREE: Go to the Channels palette (under the Window menu, choose Channels) and click on Alpha 1 (as shown). Go under the Filter menu, under Blur, and choose Gaussian Blur. Enter 1 pixel and click OK to apply a slight blur to this channel. (For high-res images try a 3-pixel blur. The more blur, the wider the bevel will appear later.)

continued

Quick Tip:
Saving time when creating custom gradients

If you're creating custom gradients and the colors you need for your gradient appear in the image you currently have open, you can really save yourself some time when changing the color of existing Color Stops. (Does that make any sense? Well, read on, and hopefully it will.) Here's how: Click on the Gradient thumbnail (in the Options Bar) to open the Gradient Editor. Then, click on the Color Stop you want to edit (don't double-click, just click once), then move your pointer out over your image. Your pointer immediately changes into an Eyedropper tool and you can sample a color directly from that image. Your Color Stop will change to that color—all without opening the Color Picker. Pretty neat! (Do people still say "neat"?)

Quick Tip:
Try different curve settings for different metallic effects

The curve setting shown in Step Five will do a good job of producing metal, but this is one area where you can experiment and have some fun. The curve shown in this example has just one hill, then it heads back up. For a more dynamic effect, try a curve with two or three hills. The more hills, the wilder it gets. If your curve starts introducing all sorts of weird colors, don't sweat it. When you're done with your curve, press Shift-Command-U (PC: Shift-Control-U) to take all the color out of your image, leaving just the shiny metal. The point is that there are no "right" curves; just move the points until something looks good to you.

STEP FOUR: Return to the Layers palette and click once on the Background layer to make it active. Go under the Filter menu, under Render, and choose Lighting Effects. When this dialog box appears, you only have to make one small change. At the bottom of the palette, where you choose the Texture Channel, choose Alpha 1 from the pop-up menu, and then click OK.

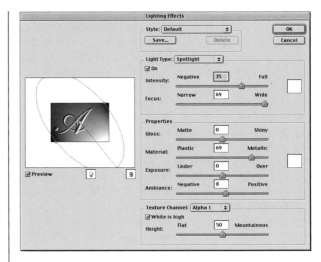

STEP FIVE: Go under the Image menu, under Adjustments and choose Curves. Create a curve that looks like the one shown here by clicking on the lower left-hand side of the curve and dragging upward. Release the mouse button, then click on the right-hand side and drag downward. As you drag the second point downward, you'll see the chrome effect start to appear. When your curve looks somewhat similar to the one shown here, click OK.

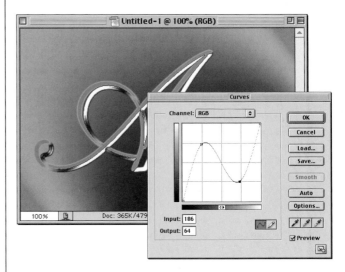

STEP SIX: Go under the Select menu and choose Load Selection. When the dialog appears, choose Alpha 1 from the Channel pop-up menu and click OK. This reloads a selection around your type, but you'll notice it's too small to encompass the entire beveled type. Go under the Select menu, under Modify, and choose Expand.

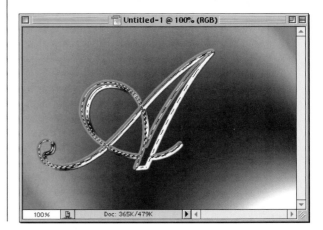

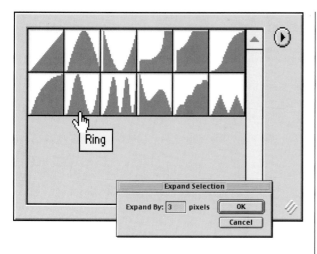

STEP SEVEN: When the Expand dialog appears, enter 3 and click OK to expand your selection by 3 pixels (if 3 is too much, or too little, choose Undo and try a higher or lower number—the goal is to select all the way to the edge of the bevel).

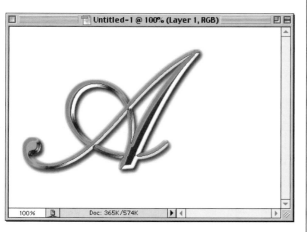

STEP EIGHT: Press Shift-Command-J (PC: Shift-Control-J) to put your selected type up on its own layer. In the Layers palette, click on the Background layer to make it the active layer. Press Command-A (PC: Control-A) to Select All, then press Delete (PC: Backspace). Deselect by pressing Command-D (PC: Control-D). Click on your text layer, choose Drop Shadow from the Layer Styles pop-up menu at the bottom of the Layers palette, and click OK.

STEP NINE: Last, choose Color Overlay from the Layer Styles pop-up menu at the bottom of the Layers palette. In the dialog, change the Blend Mode to Overlay, then click on the Color Swatch and choose a gold color (I used this gold build of R=208, G=165, B=16). Click OK to complete the effect. I added some extra type to finish off the project.

Quick Tip:
The "make anything chrome" trick

If there's anything that you want to turn into chrome, there's just one trick you have to know (besides the curve shown): You've got to bevel the object first. The chrome won't work on a non-beveled object. That's why we use the Lighting Effects filter on a blurred channel—it creates a beveled effect. The rest is simple enough—just draw a hill in the curves window.

So, the next time you want to turn something into chrome, think first about how to bevel or emboss it, then think chrome. Tip #1: The Bevel and Emboss Inner Bevel Layer Effect will usually do the trick, but right after you apply it, you have to create a new blank layer, drag it below your beveled and embossed layer, click on your beveled layer, and choose Merge Down from the Layers palette's drop-down menu. Otherwise, the chrome curve interacts with the live bevel effect and it looks …well, bad.

Tip #2: Alien Skin's Inner Bevel plug-in from their Eye Candy collection also works like a charm.

Quick Tip:
Finding out which gradient is which

Photoshop's gradients all have names and even if you create your own, you're prompted to create a name for it. The problem is that the Gradient Picker shows thumbnails, so how do you know which gradient is which? There are two quick ways to make sure you're choosing the gradient you're looking for: (1) Go under the Edit menu, under Preferences, and choose General. In the General Preference dialog box, turn on the checkbox for "Show Tool Tips." With this preference turned on, if you rest your pointer over a gradient in the Gradient Picker, its name will "pop-up"; and (2) You can change the Gradient Picker to display the gradient names by choosing "Text Only" from the Picker's drop-down menu. However, the ideal solution may be to choose "Small List" from the drop-down menu, which gives you a small thumbnail followed by the gradient's name.

Terminator Titanium

This is a technique I've been using for a while to create a metallic liquid titanium effect, similar to the one used in the movie *Terminator 2* (hence the name). I first picked up the technique from a tutorial by Rick Hutchinson, from his *Bright Ideas* PDF-based magazine, and the technique shown here is very similar, with just a few minor changes to make it easier.

STEP ONE: Create a new document in RGB at 72 ppi. Place the logo into your document that you want to convert to "Terminator Titanium" so that it appears on its own layer above the Background layer. In the example here, we used the the letter "f" from Webdings. *(Note: this technique seems to work best with images that have a lot of solid black areas.)*

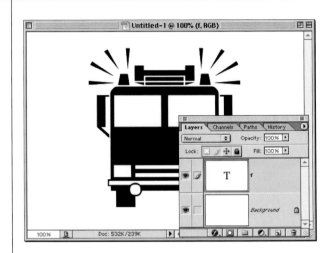

STEP TWO: Hold the Command key (PC: Control key) and in the Layers palette, click on your Type layer (or icon layer) to put a selection around your image. When the selection appears, go under the Select menu and choose Save Selection. When the dialog box appears (shown at right), click OK to save your selection as a channel.

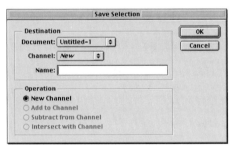

STEP THREE: Deselect by pressing Command-D (PC: Control-D). Go to the Channels palette and you'll see a new channel named Alpha 1 (as shown). Click on this channel and press Command-A (PC: Control-A) to Select All, then press Command-C (PC: Control-C) to Copy this channel into your Clipboard memory. Deselect by pressing Command-D (PC: Control-D).

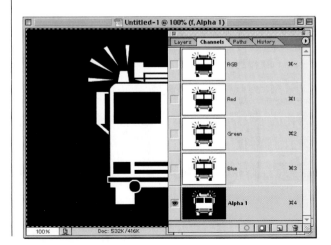

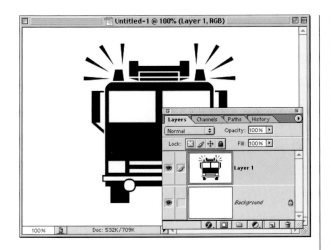

STEP FOUR: Go to the Layers palette, click on your icon layer, then drag it into the Trash icon to delete this layer. Now, click on the New Layer icon at the bottom of the palette to create a new blank layer. Press Command-V (PC: Control-V) to paste the channel held in your Clipboard memory into this new blank layer. Press Command-I (PC: Control-I) to Inverse this layer. (Your image should look the one shown at left.)

STEP FIVE: Make a copy of this layer by dragging it to the New Layer icon at the bottom of the Layers palette. Lower the Opacity of this copied layer to 40%. Press Command-A (PC: Control-A) to Select All, then go under the Edit menu, under Transform, and choose Flip Horizontal. Deselect by pressing Command-D (PC: Control-D).

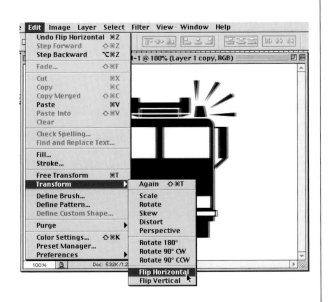

STEP SIX: Once your image is flipped, go under the Filter menu, under Blur, and choose Gaussian Blur. Enter 6 (try 12 for high-res, 300-ppi images) and click OK to apply a blur to your flipped layer. Then press Command-I (PC: Control-I) to invert your layer.

Quick Tip:
When to Merge Down and when to Merge Visible

There are times when it's better to Merge Visible (which combines all visible layers into one new layer) rather than simply merging down. The main reason you'd want to Merge Visible, rather than Merge Down, is that by merging Visible you retain the way the image looks at the current time (i.e., as the layers collapse into one another, the Blend Modes don't change). However, if you Merge Down one layer at a time, the new layer takes the Blend Mode of the lower layer. This means that if you used Blend Modes, your image may look very different each time you Merge Down. So, if you're using any Blend Modes at all, you're better off to hide any layers you don't want affected, then choose Merge Visible from the Layers palette's pop-down menu.

continued

Quick Tip:
Gradients

• To bring up the Gradient Editor, switch to the Gradient tool and in the Options Bar up top, click once on the Gradient thumbnail.

• To add a new Color Stop to your gradient, click anywhere below the Gradient Editor Bar.

• To remove a Color Stop, click-and-drag downward.

• To edit the color of any Color Stop, double-click directly on the Color Stop.

• To change the Opacity setting for the Gradient tool, press the 1–9 number keys on your keyboard (2=20%, 3=30%, etc.) while the Gradient tool is selected.

• To step through the Blend Modes in the Gradient's palette, press Shift-+ while you have the Gradient tool.

• To delete a gradient, hold the Control key (PC: Right-click) and in the Gradient Picker or Editor click-and-hold on the gradient you want to delete, then choose Delete Gradient from the pop-up list.

STEP SEVEN: Go under the Filter menu, under Distort, and choose Wave. When the Wave dialog box appears, lower the Number of Generators to 2. Lower the Wavelength Min. to 1, and set the Max. at 140. For Amplitude use 1 and 12. Leave all the other settings at their defaults (as shown) and click OK to apply this filter to your blurred layer.

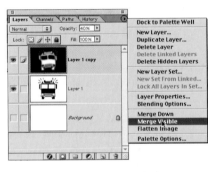

STEP EIGHT: Go to the Layers palette, and click the Eye icon next to the Background layer to hide it from view. Then, in the palette's pop-down menu, choose Merge Visible to merge the other two layers into one.

STEP NINE: Go under the Filter menu, under Sketch, and choose Chrome. When the dialog box appears, set the Detail to 7, Smoothness to 7, and click OK. Then press Command-I (PC: Control-I) to invert the image (as shown).

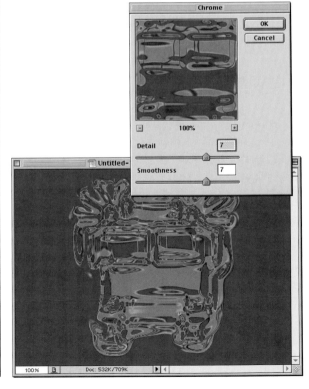

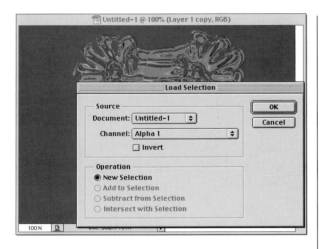

STEP TEN: Remember that Alpha Channel we created at the beginning of this tutorial? Now we're going to put it to use. Go under the Select menu and choose Load Selection. When the dialog box appears, from the Channel pop-up menu, choose Alpha 1, then click OK to load this channel as a selection.

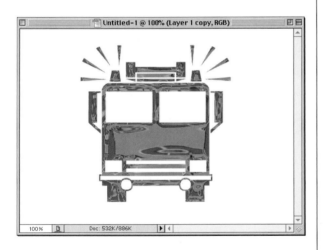

STEP ELEVEN: Once the selection appears on screen, press Shift-Command-I (PC: Shift-Control-I) to Invert the selection. Next, press Delete (PC: Backspace) to remove all the excess area around your icon, leaving you with just the icon. You can now make the Background layer visible again by clicking in the first column where the Eye icon usually appears.

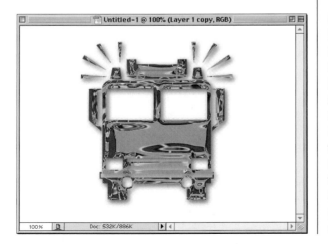

STEP TWELVE: Duplicate your icon layer by dragging it to the New Layer icon. Change the Blend Mode of this copied layer to Vivid Light (if you're still using version 6.0, use Hard Light instead), then lower the Opacity of this layer to 50%. Press Command-E (PC: Control-E) to merge these two layers. Last, add a Drop Shadow from the Layer Style pop-up menu at the bottom of the Layers palette.

Quick Tip:
Want some cool metal gradients? You've already got 'em!

If you need a metallic gradient, you don't have to build one from scratch—you've already got a collection of cool preset metallic gradients just waiting for you to load. Fortunately, loading them into your flyout Gradient Picker is a breeze. Here's how: First, switch to the Gradient tool, then, up in the Options Bar, click on the down-facing triangle right next to the Gradient thumbnail. This brings up the Gradient Picker. In the upper-right side of this menu is a right-facing triangle, which is a pop-up menu. Click on it, and at the bottom of the menu, you'll see a list of gradient presets you can load just by choosing them from the menu.

To load the metallic gradients, choose the ones named "Metals" from the pop-up list, and Photoshop will ask if you want to replace your current gradients with this set or append (add) them to your current set. It's that easy.

Quick Tip:
Bending the horizon of the Chrome gradient

In the project we're working on here, we create a custom gradient to simulate the chrome effect used by traditional airbrush artists. One of Photoshop's default gradients has a somewhat similar chrome gradient, and it shares a common problem with the custom gradient we created—its "horizon line" is perfectly straight. Most airbrush artists vary this horizon line slightly to make the gradient look more natural. You can do the same thing in Photoshop (vary the horizon line) by using Photoshop's Wave filter (found under the Distort submenu). Use this filter to create a slight rolling effect along the horizon line. A good place to start is to lower the Number of Generators to 1. Set the Wave Length Min. to 1 and Max to 100. Set the Amplitude to 1 and 6, and click OK, This should add a slight roll to your horizon line.

Reflective Chrome Gradient

This technique, a take-off on the chrome effects created by traditional airbrush artists, uses a gradient that mimics the ground and the sky that would be reflected by real chrome. In this example, we'll create a custom gradient to simulate that style of chrome, but the gradient alone isn't enough—it's the other elements that you add to it that give the impression of chrome.

STEP ONE: Create a new document in RGB mode at 72 ppi. Press "d" to make black your Foreground color, then press Option-Delete (PC: Alt-Backspace) to fill the Background layer with black. Add a new blank layer by clicking on the New Layer icon at the bottom of the Layers palette. Hide the black background by clicking on the Eye icon in the first column beside the Background layer.

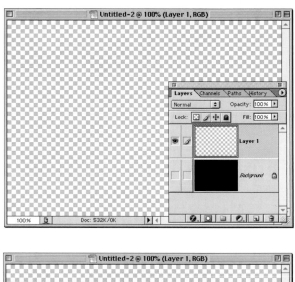

STEP TWO: Create the shape you want for your metal console. In this example, I changed the Foreground color to gray and used the Rounded Rectangle tool to create, well…a rounded rectangle (as shown at right).

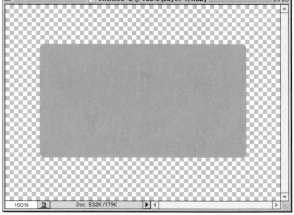

STEP THREE: Next, switch to the Gradient tool and its Options will appear up top in the Options Bar. Click on the Gradient thumbnail to bring up the Gradient Editor. When the Editor appears, click on the third gradient from the left on the top row (it's the Black to White gradient).

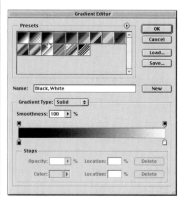

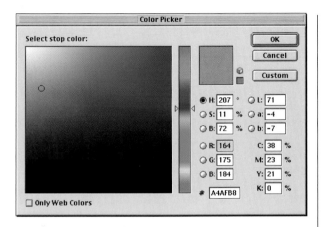

STEP FOUR: We're going to create our own custom gradient using the Black to White gradient as a starting point. First, double-click on the far left-hand side Color Stop, located directly below the Gradient Editor Bar. This brings up the Color Picker prompting you to "Select stop color." In the RGB fields, enter: R=164, G=175, B=184 to set this first stop to a light "sky" blue. Click OK.

STEP FIVE: Next, slide the far right Color Stop over to the center of the Gradient Editor Bar. Double-click on it to set its color. This time in the RGB fields, enter: R=226, G=227, B=226 to set this middle stop to an almost white color. Click OK.

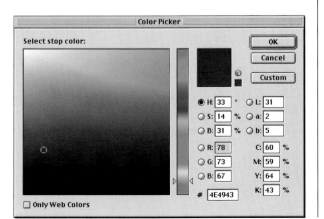

STEP SIX: Click immediately to the right of your middle Color Stop under the Gradient Editor Bar to add a new gradient Stop. Slide this Stop almost right up against the middle Stop. Double-click on this new Stop to set its color. In the RGB fields, enter R=78, G=73, B=67 to set this new stop to a brownish color. Click OK.

Quick Tip:
Which gradient should you edit?

When you're creating custom gradients, you always have to start with a gradient (by that I mean, when you open the Gradient Editor, it opens with a gradient already loaded into the editor). This is weird because it works in about exactly the opposite way you'd think it would. You'd imagine you'd click the "New" button, and it would give you some default starting point, but it doesn't. Instead, it works like this—you open the Editor, the last gradient you used is already there waiting to be edited, and when it looks the way you want it to, you put a name in the Name field, and only then do you click the "New" button. (I know, it's weird but that's the way it works.) So which gradient should you use? Who knows for sure, but I always start by clicking on the third default icon in the top row. It's the Black to White gradient, which is easier to edit than the Foreground to Background gradient (the first in the list) for a variety of reasons that I don't have the space to explain here. Just trust me, give the "edit the Black to White gradient" thing a try.

continued

Quick Tip:
Don't use the Delete button

That's right, don't use that Delete button in the Gradient Editor dialog box. Well, you can use it if you're charging by the hour, but outside of that, it's much faster to click on the gradient you want to delete and drag downward. It will immediately disappear (become "deleted").

STEP SEVEN: We're going to add two more Stops: One halfway between the middle and the end (set to R=224, G=221, B=87 for a beige) and then one at the very right-end of the Gradient Editor Bar (set to R=226, G=225, B=198 for a very light, almost white stop). Your gradient should look like the one shown at right. Name this gradient "metal sky" and click the New button. Press OK to save it.

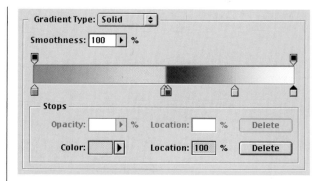

STEP EIGHT: Now we add the fluff stuff that helps sell the effect. Hold the Command key (PC: Control key) and in the Layers palette click on the layer with your rounded rectangle to put a selection around it. Then, go under the Select menu, under Modify, and choose Contract. Enter 6 pixels and click OK to shrink your selection by six pixels. Grab the Gradient tool, and drag it from the top of your selection to the bottom (as shown at right).

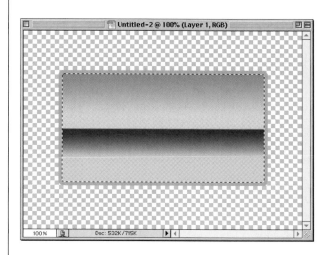

STEP NINE: While your selection is still in place, add a new blank layer above your current layer by clicking on the New Layer icon at the bottom of the Layers palette. Go under the Edit menu and choose Stroke. When the Stroke dialog box appears, make sure the stroke color is set to black, and enter 2 pixels for the stroke Width. Set your Location to Center and click OK to apply a 2-pixel stroke around your selection. Don't Deselect yet.

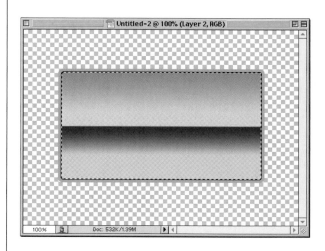

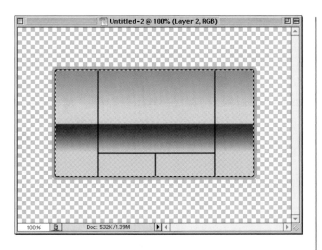

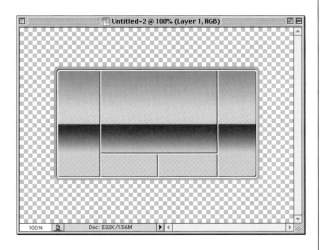

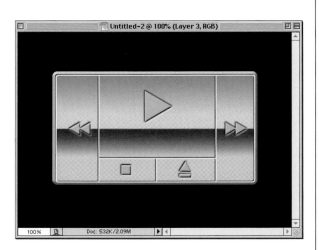

STEP TEN: Now switch to the Line tool (it's one of the Shape tools in the Toolbox). When you get the Line tool, up in the Options Bar, click on the third icon from the left to enable you to draw just lines, without adding a special shape layer. We're going to visually divide our console using lines, so create the lines shown at left. Since the selection is still in place, you can drag past the borders, but the lines will stop at the edge of your selection.

STEP ELEVEN: Deselect by pressing Command-D (PC: Control-D). Make a duplicate of this Line layer by dragging it to the New Layer icon in the Layers palette. Press "d" then "x" to set white as your Foreground color. Press Shift-Option-Delete (PC: Shift-Alt-Backspace) to fill your lines with white. Press "v" to switch to the Move tool, then press the Right Arrow key once and the Down Arrow key once to offset your white lines from your black lines, giving the impression of an indentation.

STEP TWELVE: Make your black Background layer visible again (click where the Eye icon used to be). Click on the gradient layer, and add a Bevel and Emboss Layer Style with the Depth set to 300%, and lower the Shadow opacity to 33%. Last, create a new blank layer on top. Get the Polygon tool, set its Sides to 3 (in the Options Bar) and use it to add naviga-tion buttons (as shown). To give the buttons the "sunken-in" look, add a Bevel and Emboss, but change the Style to Pillow Emboss.

Quick Tip:
Getting back to the tool's default settings

Each tool in Photoshop has its own set of Options, and chances are that you're going to be constantly changing them. For example, in Step 10 of this project, you're changing the option for the Line tool. You never have to worry about messing these tool options up, because you're always just one click away from resetting the tool to its default settings. Up in the Options Bar, on the far left side of the bar, Control-click (PC: Right-click) once on the icon for the tool you're using. Choose Reset Tool from the pop-up menu and that resets the tool to its default settings so you can play to your heart's content.

Quick Tip:
The advantage of loading the layer's transparency

In Step Two in the example shown at right, I have you hold down the Command key (PC: Control key) and click on the layer. This puts a selection around everything on the layer (in this instance, it's a Type layer, so it puts a selection around your type). What you're doing (in technical terms) is loading the layer's transparency (which you can do manually by going under the Select menu, choosing Load Selection, and then choosing to load the channel named "transparency"). What most people do who need to put a selection around their type, but don't know this trick, is use the Magic Wand tool to select each letter individually. It works—it does put a selection around the type—but if you move that type, it leaves little specs (well, pixels) behind that the Magic Wand misses. The advantage of loading the transparency instead is that it doesn't leave any little stray pixels behind. That's why we always choose to load transparency.

Liquid Metal

This time we're using a filter to create the metallic effect, instead of embossing and using Curves to create the look. We use the Find Edges filter to create the highlight and shadow areas of our metal to give us a more rounded liquid style effect as opposed to the hard metal most traditional methods create.

STEP ONE: Open a new document in RGB mode at 72 ppi. Create some large bold type.

STEP TWO: Go to the Layers palette, hold the Command key (PC: Control key), and click once on your Type layer's name to put a selection around it.

STEP THREE: Go under the Select menu and choose Save Selection. When the dialog box appears, click OK to save your selection as an Alpha Channel. Now that you've saved it, you can Deselect by pressing Command-D and in the Layers palette, drag the Type channel into the Trash at the bottom of the palette to delete it.

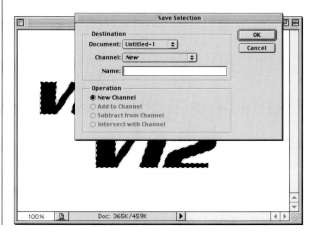

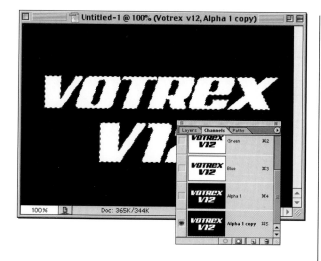

STEP FOUR: Go to the Channels palette and click on Alpha 1. Make a copy of this channel by dragging it to the New Channel icon at the bottom of the Channels palette. This creates a new channel called Alpha 1 copy.

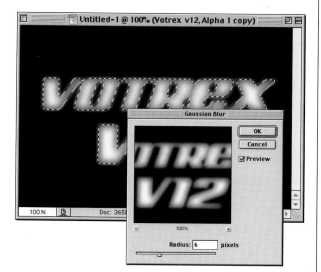

STEP FIVE: Go under the Filter menu, under Blur, and choose Gaussian Blur. For Radius enter 3 and click OK. Hold the Command key (PC: Control key) and click once on Alpha 1 copy to put a selection around the type. Go under the Filter menu, under Blur, and choose Gaussian Blur. This time for Radius, enter 6 and click OK to blur the inside of the type. Now go to the Layers palette, and click once on the Background layer. Don't deselect yet.

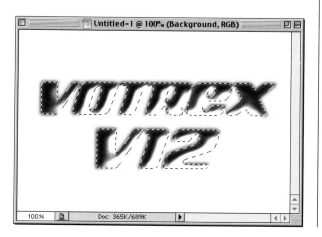

STEP SIX: Go under the Filter menu, under Render, and choose Lighting Effects. In the Light Type pop-up menu, choose Directional. You only have to make a couple of other changes here: Under Properties, set the Gloss to 100 (Shiny), set the Material to –100 (Plastic), then skip down to the Texture Channel and choose Alpha 1 copy from the pop-up menu. Click OK.

continued

Quick Tip:
You can load Channels just like a layer's transparency

This is a follow-up to the tip on the opposite page, where we showed the advantage of loading a layer's transparency to put a selection around any object on the current layer. You do that by holding the Command key (PC: Control key) and clicking on the layer's name in the Layers palette. Well, you can do the same thing in the Channels palette—you can load the Alpha Channel as a selection by holding the Command key (PC: Control key) and clicking on the Alpha Channel you want to load, and it will instantly load as a selection.

Quick Tip:
Another use for the Find Edges filter

In the project at right, we use the Find Edges filter. Another thing I often use the Find Edges filter for is converting a photograph into a line drawing. Just apply the Find Edges filter and it does a pretty nice job of tracing the edges of your photo. It does create a slight problem in that it often introduces a number of weird colors to the resulting line art, but all you have to do is go under the Image menu, under Adjustment, and choose Desaturate to remove the extra colors and return it to a black and white line drawing.

STEP SEVEN: Don't Deselect yet. Go under the Filter menu, under Stylize, and choose Find Edges to begin bringing in the liquid metallic look. Deselect by pressing Command-D (PC: Control-D). Now go under the Select menu and choose Load Selection. When the dialog box appears, choose Alpha 1 (your clean type channel) from the pop-up menu, and click OK to load that as a selection. Press Shift-Command-I (PC: Shift-Control-I) to Inverse your selection, and then press Delete (PC: Backspace) to delete the background area, cleaning up your edges. Then press Shift-Command-I (PC: Shift-Control-I) to reselect your type.

STEP EIGHT: While your selection is still in place, press Shift-Command-J (PC: Shift-Control-J) to put your selected area on its own layer. Then, go under the Filter menu, under Sharpen, and choose Unsharp Mask. For Amount choose 200%, for Radius choose 1, for Threshold choose 15, and click OK to enhance the metallic look. Next, choose Drop Shadow from the Layer Style pop-up menu at the bottom of the Layers palette and click OK. Last, go under the Image menu, under Adjustments, and choose Hue/Saturation. Click the Colorize button, then drag the Hue slider over to 214 and lower the Saturation to 20 to complete the effect.

Remember that scene in the movie Dirty Dancing—*the big dance at the end of the movie? At one point, Patrick*

Dirty Dancing
Down and Dirty Tricks

Swayze comes dancing down the center aisle toward the stage where Baby (yes, parents can be so cruel) stands there waiting for him, while swaying the hem of her skirt to and fro? Do you remember that part? Seriously, did she look incredibly gawky and awkward? I think it was at that moment when the director decided to change her name in the movie from Angela to "Baby," as a way of publicly shaming her for not having a cool dance move of her own. Now, you're probably wondering what all this has to do with Photoshop? Plenty—because before you read this chapter I strongly urge you to go out and rent the Dirty Dancing video and tell me if you, as a Photoshop user, would freeze up the way Baby did at one of those "all-eyes-on-you" moments. If you see this movie and feel certain that you could come up with a more compelling "come hither" dance than Baby did, then and only then should you read this chapter.

Giving Depth to a Page

This is a technique that first caught our attention when we saw it used in some of the UK computer magazines (like *Computer Arts*) in their subscription ads, and then it started catching on in the states. It's ideal for giving some depth to a cover design, a page from a newsletter, magazine, etc.

STEP ONE: Open a new blank document (here, it's a 72-ppi RGB image, but all you have to make sure of is that your new document is the same resolution as the object to which you want to apply the effect). Then, open your object (in this case, a cover of the book), select it, and drag it into your blank document.

STEP TWO: Press "m" to switch to the Rectangular Marquee tool, and draw a rectangular selection around the bottom quarter of your cover (as shown). Next, create a new blank layer by clicking on the New Layer icon at the bottom of the Layers palette. Then, go under the File menu and choose New.

STEP THREE: When the dialog box appears, enter 1 pixel for Width, 2 pixels for Height, and enter the same Resolution as your original cover document. Click OK to create a very tiny new document. Press Command-+ (PC: Control-+) about nine times to zoom in on your document. Switch to the Pencil tool (it's behind the Brush tool in the Toolbox) and paint the top half of your document black.

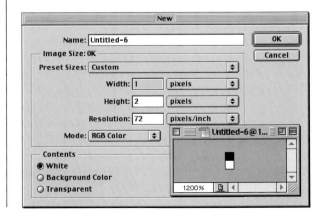

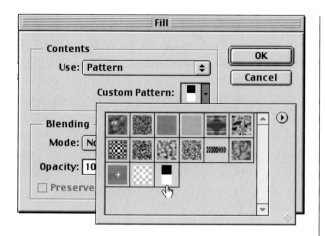

STEP FOUR: Press Command-A (PC: Control-A) to Select All. Go under the Edit menu and choose Define Pattern. Name your pattern and click OK. Then, switch back to your original document. Your selection should still be in place, so go under the Edit menu and choose Fill.

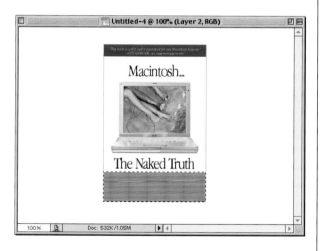

STEP FIVE: In the Fill dialog, for "Use" choose Pattern. Click the down-facing triangle next to the Pattern thumbnail to bring up the Pattern Picker. Choose the very last pattern in the Picker (it's the one you just created, which is very similar to the TV scan lines effect later in this chapter, except that we used a smaller scan line). Click OK to fill your selection with horizontal white and black lines.

STEP SIX: Press Command-T (PC: Control-T) to bring up Free Transform. Drag the top center point downward to shrink your black and white lines. This will act as the book's pages. Next, hold the Command key (PC: Control key), click the bottom left-hand corner point and drag upward to pinch the left side of the pages. Press Return (PC: Enter) to lock in your changes.

continued

Quick Tip: Changing Image Size? Let Photoshop do the math

In Photoshop's Image Size dialog box, there's a button that most people ignore. It's called Auto, and here's how it works: You tell Photoshop what line screen you need to output your file at and what level of quality you're looking for (Draft, Good, or Best), and it will do the math, calculating the proper resolution for you based on your choices.

Here's what it does: If you enter 133 line screen and choose Best quality, it doubles that figure and sets your resolution at 266. At Good quality, it gives you 1.5 times the line screen, and at Draft it gives you 72 ppi.

When using this feature, be careful to start with a 300-dpi scan or higher. If you start with a 72-dpi scan, and choose 133 line with Best quality, it'll jump you up to 266 ppi; but it doesn't warn you that your image will look so pixelated when printed that it will trash your whole project, because you can't add resolution that's not really there to begin with.

STEP SEVEN: Press "v" to switch to the Move tool, then drag this "book pages" layer down until the top of the pages touches the bottom of your cover. In the Layers palette, drag this layer beneath your cover layer, then click on the cover layer to make it active. Press Command-E (PC: Control-E) to merge the cover with the pages layer directly beneath it. Deselect by pressing Command-D (PC: Control-D). Press Command-T (PC: Control-T) to bring up Free Transform.

STEP EIGHT: Move your pointer outside the bounding box and click-and-drag up and to the left to rotate the cover a little. Next, hold Shift-Option-Command (PC: Shift-Alt-Control), grab the top-right corner point and drag inward quite a bit to add the perspective effect (as shown). The cover will look pixelated and distorted, but don't sweat it.

STEP NINE: Grab the top center point, and drag quite a bit downward to remove the "stretched looked" from the book cover. This works well because it maintains the perspective effect, without all the distorted stretching (as shown). Press Return (PC: Enter) to lock in your transformation. Last, choose Drop Shadow from the Layer Style pop-up menu at the bottom of the Layers palette. Increase the Size to 10, and click OK to complete.

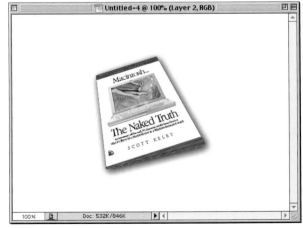

Wrapping Type Around a Globe

This was a technique for which I had a lot of requests, because normally this sort of thing would be achieved using a 3D application, but since a lot of us don't have 3D apps (I sure don't), here's a way to get a similar effect.

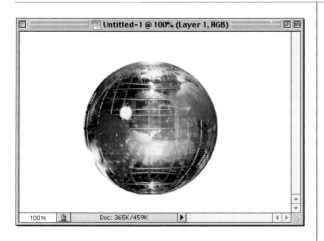

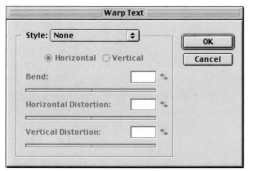

STEP ONE: Open a new document, and then open the object where you want to wrap type. Select the object and drag it into your new document. In this case, I used a globe as my object, but you can use any round or cylindrical object. In fact, you can just draw a black circle if you'd like.

STEP TWO: Press "t" to switch to the Type tool, and then create your type (this effect seems to work best if you use all caps in a tall, thin typeface, but it's not absolutely necessary). When you've entered half your type, click on the Warp Text button that appears in the Options Bar, just to the right of the type Color Swatch. This will bring up the Warp Text dialog box.

STEP THREE: When the Warp Text dialog box appears, choose Arc from the Style pop-up. Drag the Bend slider to the right until it reads +100%. This may make your type arc outside of your image window, but you can move your pointer outside the dialog box into your image window to reposition your type. It's going to look a little too large and too wide right now, but we'll deal with that later. For now, just click OK.

continued

STEP FOUR: Make a duplicate of your arced Type layer by dragging it to the New Layer icon at the bottom of the Layers palette. Click on the Warp Text button again in the Options Bar. Arc will already be selected as your Style in the dialog box, but this time you're going to drag the Bend slider all the way to the left until it reads -100%. Click OK.

STEP FIVE: Press "v" to get the Move tool and reposition the bottom half of your circular type to make it as close to a circle as possible. I've noticed that it rarely makes a perfect fit, so sometimes, you'll have to press Command-T (PC: Control-T) to bring up Free Transform to resize your text. Grab one of the side handles and slightly resize your entire bottom text block to make it fit. If it requires too much resizing, you may have to go to the Character palette and add some vertical scaling to thicken the type back up. Once it looks right, press the Return key (PC: Enter) to lock in your transformation.

STEP SIX: Go under the Layer menu, under Rasterize, and choose Type. Click on your original Type layer and rasterize that as well. Now, click back on your Type copy layer and press Command-E (PC: Control-E) to merge it with the original text layer.

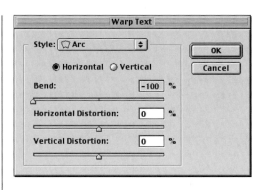

STEP SEVEN: Press Command-T (PC: Control-T) to bring up Free Transform. Hold the Shift key, grab one of the corner points, and drag it inward to shrink the type to size (as shown). (Note: It may not make a perfectly round circle, but in most cases, it won't matter, just get it reasonably close.) Press Return (PC: Enter) to complete the transformation.

Quick Tip:
**How to view
at just the right
percentage**

If you want to view your document at a specific percentage, you can jump right to that view by highlighting the view percentage (in the lower left-hand corner of your document window), typing in the exact percentage you want, and then pressing the Enter key.

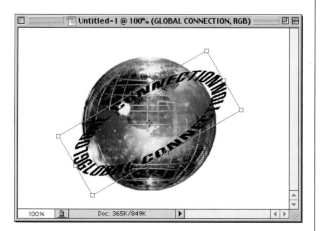

STEP EIGHT: Press Command-T (PC: Control-T) to bring up Free Transform around your text again. Next, go up in the Options Bar and in the H: field (Height), enter 40%. Then, in the field immediately to its right (the Rotate field), enter –30°. Click OK to scale and rotate your type (as shown).

STEP NINE: Finally, go to the Layers palette, hold the Command key (PC: Control key), and click on the globe layer to put a selection around it (don't actually change layers—you should still be on the text layer). Press "e" to switch to the Eraser tool and erase the type at the top of your arced text that appears inside the circular selection. Press Command-D (PC: Control-D) to Deselect and view the final image.

Quick Tip:
Getting rid of onscreen jaggies

Have you ever noticed that sometimes when you're viewing your Photoshop document, some edges, or even type, can look jaggy? That happens when you view your document at sizes other than 100%, 50%, 25%, or 12.5%. For example, when you view your document at 66.67% (a common size when you zoom in and out), Photoshop's display can look jaggy. To see the clean, crisp look of your image, make sure you view it at 100% (or 50%, or 25%, or 12.5%). By the way, do you know why Adobe lets these other sizes look jaggy? To speed things up, that's why. When you zoom out to 16.67% on a 100-MB image, do you really want to sit there while this tiny postage stamp of an image redraws at high-res? Didn't think so. That's why Adobe uses a low-res redraw on these zoomed-out images. Pretty smart, those Adobe folks.

Halftone "Pop Dots" Effect

This effect has been gaining popularity over the past year, and I was reminded of it recently when I got a direct mail piece from a nationally known music club, and the envelope used a similar effect to tell me that if I "Buy one, I get two for $3.99 each!" Here's how it's done:

STEP ONE: Open a new image in RGB mode at 72 dpi. Open the document that has the image to which you want to add this effect. Select the object and use the Move tool to move it into your new document, creating a new layer.

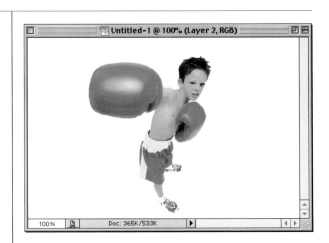

STEP TWO: Create a new layer by clicking on the New Layer icon at the bottom of the Layers palette. Hold the Command key (PC: Control key) and in the Layers palette, click on the image layer to put a selection around your image. Now, go under the Select menu, under Modify, and choose Expand. Enter 10 pixels and click OK to expand your selection by 10 pixels.

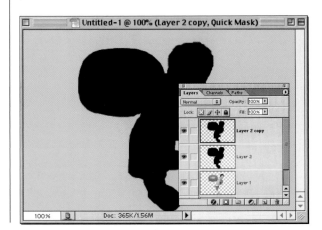

STEP THREE: Press "d" to switch your Foreground color to black, and fill your selection with black by pressing Option-Delete (PC: Alt-Backspace). Next, while it's still selected, make a duplicate of this layer by dragging it to the New Layer icon at the bottom of the Layers palette, and then press the letter "q" to enter Quick Mask mode. By default, the area around your image will change into a red tint, so don't let that freak you out.

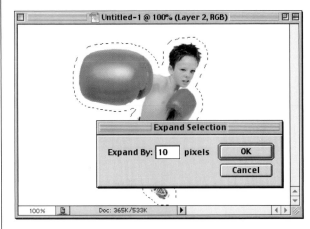

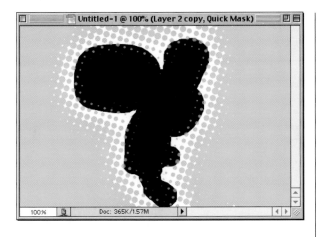

STEP FOUR: Go under the Filter menu, under Pixelate, and choose Color Halftone. When the dialog box appears, just use the default settings and click OK. You'll need to apply this filter numerous times to get the effect around the image we're looking for. Once you've applied it, you can apply it again by pressing Command-F (PC: Control-F). In the example shown here, I applied it eight times.

STEP FIVE: Press the letter "q" again to leave Quick Mask mode. This creates a selection on your image. Press Option-Delete (PC: Alt-Backspace) to fill your selection with black. Deselect by pressing Command-D (PC: Control-D). In the Layers palette, click on Layer 2, go under the Filter menu, under Blur, and choose Gaussian Blur. For Amount enter 6, then click OK to apply a soft blur to your black image.

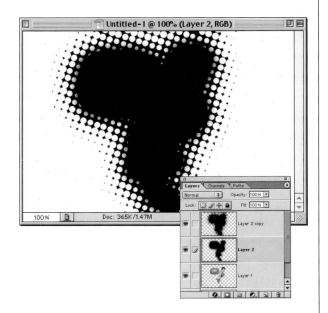

STEP SIX: Click on your original image layer (it should be just above the Background layer) and drag this layer to the top of the Layers palette, making it the topmost layer. You can leave the effect on a white background, or you can fill the background layer with a solid color (as shown).

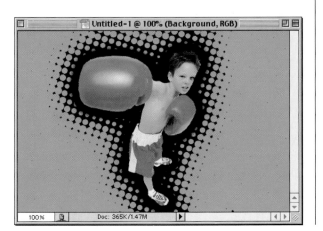

Quick Tip:
Resizing multiple layers at one time

Here's a real timesaving tip that enables you to resize objects or text on multiple layers—all at the same time. Just link together the layers that you want to resize, then press Command-T (PC: Control-T) to bring up the Free Transform bounding box. Hold the Shift key (to constrain proportions), then grab any of the bounding box handles and drag. As you drag, all of the linked layers will resize at the same time.

Quick Tip:
How to switch to the Precise Cursor any time

When using Photoshop's Paint tools, your cursor displays the size of the brush you're using. But if you ever need a more-precise cursor for really detailed work, you can temporarily switch to the "Precise Cursor," which looks like a crosshair. To do this, just press the Caps Lock key on your keyboard and your cursor (not just your Paint cursor, but any cursor) will switch to the crosshair cursor. To switch back, press the Caps Lock key again.

If you don't know about this Caps Lock trick, it can be quite confusing because you could be using the Type tool with the Caps Lock turned on to type some text in all caps, and when you switched to another tool, it would be the crosshair cursor, and you wouldn't know why. Freaky!

Glassy Reflections

This is a nice technique for enhancing a logo or Web button by adding a small reflection in a couple of places to make it seem as if the logo had a glass cover over it and was reflecting the light present when it was photographed. We start with an elliptical logo, but I also show how to apply a similar effect to a round logo.

STEP ONE: Open the logo (or graphic) to which you want to apply the glassy-like highlight reflections. The image needs to be on its own layer so if it's not, select the image and press Shift-Command-J (PC: Shift-Control-J) to put it on its own layer. (Note: If you download the copy of this logo we created, it's already on its own layer for you. See, we care.)

STEP TWO: Hold the Command key (PC: Control key) and in the Layers palette, click on the logo layer to put a selection around it. Go under the Select menu, under Modify, and choose Contract. Enter 12 and click OK. (The goal is to shrink the selection so that it's a couple of pixels inside the inner ellipse. You may have to experiment with the amount of contraction.)

STEP THREE: Press Shift-L until the Polygonal Lasso tool appears in the Toolbox. Up in the Options Bar, click on the third icon from the left (as shown) so that when you're using the Polygonal Lasso, it will subtract from the current selection. Start by creating the v-shaped selection shown here (that will be the area where your reflection will be added).

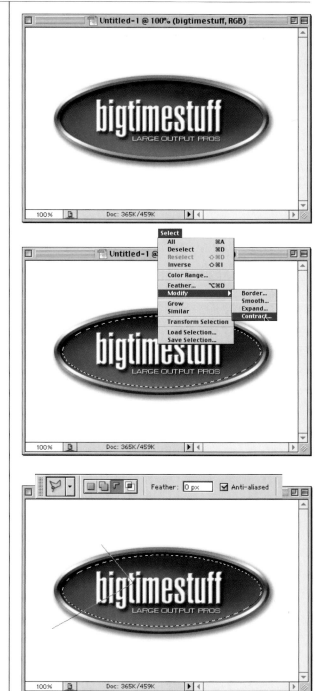

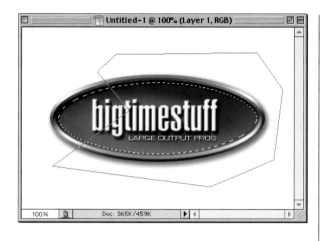

STEP FOUR: Now, continue outside the ellipse, clicking with the Polygonal Lasso tool all the way around (as shown) until you reach the point where you started (remember, you're subtracting from your elliptical selection).

STEP FIVE: When you click on the starting point with your Polygonal Lasso, you'll be left with just the selection shown here. In the next step, we'll knock a little thin triangular hole in your selection for a more-realistic look.

STEP SIX: Using the Polygonal Lasso tool, you're going to subtract a thin rectangular area from your current selection (as shown). Start by drawing a straight line that begins just outside the left side of your ellipse, click again three quarters of the way inside your selection, and continue drawing until you have a thin rectangle cut out (as shown).

Quick Tip:
You can still apply most transformations to editable Type layers

Many people don't realize that while you have an editable Type layer, you can still apply a number of transformations (such as Scale, Rotate, Skew, Flip Horizontal, and Flip Vertical), and your type will remain fully editable (meaning you can change the letters, tracking, leading, etc.). However, to apply Distort or Perspective transformations, you'll first have to Rasterize the Type layer by going under the Layer menu, under Rasterize, and choosing Type.

continued

Quick Tip:
Cropping

Here are some quick tips for getting the most out of Photoshop's Crop tool:

• To rotate the Cropping boundary, move your pointer outside the box and it will change to a two-headed arrow tool. Click-and-drag to rotate.

• To constrain your cropping to a perfect square, hold the Shift key as you drag the cropping box.

• If your cropping boundary snaps to the edge of your image window, hold the Control key (PC: Right-click), and then you can resize the boundary without it snapping.

• To scale your cropping boundary from the center outward, hold the Option key (PC: Alt key) as you drag.

• To move the cropping boundary, click within the boundary and drag.

STEP SEVEN: When you click the Polygonal Lasso tool on the point where you started, you'll have the selection shown here. Next, create a new blank layer by clicking on the New Layer icon at the bottom of the Layers palette.

STEP EIGHT: Press the letter "d" then "x" to set your Foreground color to white. Press "g" to switch to the Gradient tool, and up in the Options Bar, click on the down-facing triangle to the right of the Gradient thumbnail to bring up the Gradient Picker. Choose the second gradient from the left (Foreground to Transparent) as shown here.

STEP NINE: Drag the Gradient tool from the left side of your selection to the right side (as shown), dragging just past the edge of your selection.

STEP TEN: Deselect by pressing Command-D (PC: Control-D) to complete the left-side reflective highlight. If the reflection seems too intense, you may lower the Opacity of this layer to 75%, but that's totally up to you. Now on to the lower right side. First, create a new layer, then hold the Command key (PC: Control key) and in the Layers palette, click on the logo layer to put a selection around it. Under Select, under Modify, choose Contract.

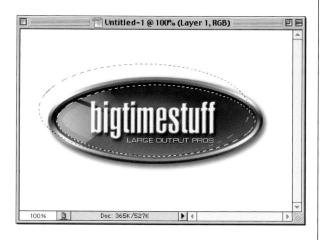

STEP ELEVEN: Enter a number of pixels to shrink the selection to the inner ellipse (10 pixels in this example). Switch to the Elliptical Marquee tool. In the Options Bar, click on the third icon from the left to make the Elliptical Marquee subtract from the current selection. Drag an ellipse that overlaps your current selection so just a small portion the original ellipse will remain on the lower right side (as shown in the next step).

STEP TWELVE: Press "g" to switch to the Gradient tool, and this time drag from just outside the right bottom part of the logo to about $1/4$" past the left side of the selection (as shown). Note: "x" marks the starting point of the gradient.

continued

Quick Tip:
Where has the "Blur" gone?

By now you've probably noticed that starting in Photoshop 6.0, Blur and Intensity have disappeared from some of the Layer Style dialog boxes (Inner Glow, Outer Glow, and Drop Shadow). But never fear; Adobe didn't remove these effects, they simply renamed them.

What used to control the amount of Blur is now controlled by Size, and what used to affect the Intensity is now called Spread.

These effects have also been enhanced. By changing the Spread (formerly Intensity), you can get a completely solid edge with just a small amount of Blur (I'm sorry Size). This is something that previously couldn't be accomplished in these dialog boxes.

The name change is a little weird, but hey, they could have changed the name to "Softening the edges of a predetermined selection in which the amount of said selection can be affected by the front-end user."

Quick Tip:
Quick zoom

In some cases in this book, I mention that you might have to zoom in to your document as much as 1200%. A quick trick for zooming in on your image is to press Command-+ (PC: Control-+). Each time you press this combination, Photoshop zooms in closer, so you just have to press it a few times and you're really zoomed in. To zoom back out, use the same modifier key, but instead of using the plus sign (for zooming in), use the minus sign.

STEP THIRTEEN: Press Command-D (PC: Control-D) to Deselect. Now, go under the Filter menu, under Blur, and choose Gaussian Blur. Enter 1 pixel, and click OK to soften the reflection on this side. Finally, lower the Opacity of this layer to 75% to complete the effect.

OPTIONS: The logo doesn't have to be elliptical to apply this technique. Here's the same technique applied to a round logo—the only difference is that this time we just need one reflection (on the top left) rather than one on each side.

OPTIONS: Here's the final image of the round logo after we added the Foreground to Transparent gradient, and lowered the Opacity to 75%.

TV Scan Lines Effect

This remains one of the most popular effects in print, TV, and the Web; and it simulates the scan lines that a TV produces when photographed with a camera. Also, check out the Quick Tip on the right, which shows another technique for creating scan lines.

STEP ONE: Open the image where you want to apply TV scan lines—either RGB or Grayscale will work.

STEP TWO: Go to the New dialog box (under the File menu) and create a new document 1 pixel wide by 4 pixels high. Choose the same mode as your open image (e.g., if you want to add scan lines to an RGB image, choose RGB).

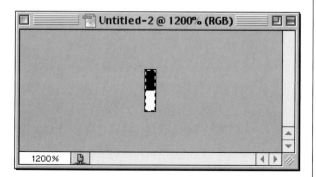

STEP THREE: Zoom in on this tiny document until it's easily seen (you might have to zoom in as much as 1200%). Set your Foreground color to black, then take the Pencil tool and fill in the top half of your image with black (as shown). Go under the Edit menu and choose Define Pattern (this makes your black-and-white document a repeating pattern). A dialog box will appear where you can name your new pattern "Scan Lines."

continued

Quick Tip:
Jump to Overlay mode shortcut
In the TV Scan lines effect, after you create your scan lines and put them on their own layer, you have to change the Blend Mode to Overlay. I show you how to do that by choosing Overlay from the pop-up menu in the Layers palette, but actually, there's a way to change to Overlay mode without going to the Layers palette at all. Just use the keyboard shortcut Shift-Option-O (PC: Shift-Alt-O), and your active layer will switch to Overlay mode. Before you do this keyboard shortcut, make sure you have the Move tool selected (press the letter "v"). The reason is that if you have one of the Paint tools selected, you'll end up changing the Blend Mode for that tool instead, because just like layers, Paint tools have Blend Modes, and they share the same keyboard shortcuts as well.

Quick Tip:
Scan lines filter trick

If you want another way to create scan lines, believe it or not there's a filter you can apply that does a pretty good job at creating them. Here's how to use it:

(1) Open the image to which you want to apply scan lines, then create a new blank layer above it.

(2) Press "d" then "x" to set your Foreground color to white, then press Option-Delete (PC: Alt-Backspace) to fill the layer with white.

(3) Go under the Filter menu, under Sketch, and choose Halftone Pattern. In the dialog box, set the Size to 2, Contrast to 50, and Pattern Type to Line. Click OK to apply vertical black-and-white lines to your layer.

(4) Change the Blend Mode of this layer to Overlay and lower the Opacity to taste.

Give this method a try and see how you like it compared to this technique.

STEP FOUR: Go back to your original document. Click on the New Layer icon at the bottom of the Layers palette to create a new layer. Go under the Edit menu and choose Fill. In the Fill dialog box, for "Use" choose Pattern, then click the down-facing triangle next to the Custom Pattern thumbnail to reveal the Pattern Picker. Click on the last pattern (it will be the Scan Lines pattern you just saved) to choose it.

STEP FIVE: Click OK to fill this layer with your black-and-white scan lines pattern. Your new layer is now filled with a black-and-white pattern (as shown).

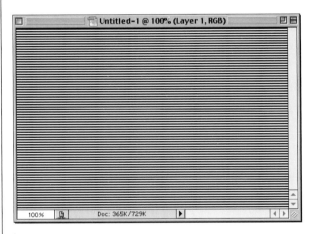

STEP SIX: In the Layers palette change the layer's Blend Mode from Normal to Overlay. Lower the Opacity so that the effect isn't too strong (in other words, adjust to suit your taste) to complete the effect.

Navigation Tabs

As soon as Apple Computer updated their Web site with these cool-looking navigation tabs, the letters started pouring in asking us to figure out how they did it. The job is now easier thanks to the Rounded Rectangle tool, because before, we had to try and draw the tabs with the Pen tool, and now it's about a 15-second job to make the shapes, and the rest is, well…the fun part.

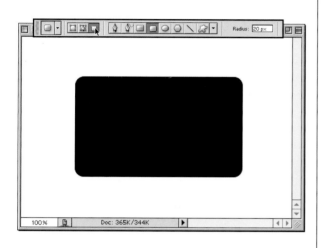

STEP ONE: Open a new RGB document. Press "d" to make your Foreground color black. Create a new blank layer, then press Shift-U until the Rounded Rectangle tool appears in the Toolbox. Up in the Options Bar you have to make two changes: (1) click on the third icon from the left (Fill Pixels), and (2) increase the Radius setting to 20. Then draw your rounded corner box (as shown).

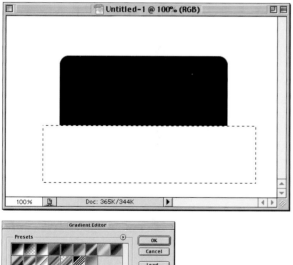

STEP TWO: Press "m" to switch to the Rectangular Marquee tool and draw a rectangular selection around the bottom one-quarter of your rounded rectangle. Press Delete (PC: Backspace) to flatten out the bottom section, giving you the basic shape for your tab. Deselect by pressing Command-D (PC: Control-D).

STEP THREE: Press "g" to switch to the Gradient tool. In the Options Bar, click on the Gradient thumbnail to bring up the Gradient Editor. In the Editor, double-click on the left Color Stop under the Editor Bar. When the Color Picker appears choose 45% black and click OK. Now, double-click on the right Color Stop, and this time choose white (0% black), then click OK.

continued

Quick Tip: Rounding corners

In Step One of the technique on the right, I ask you to create a rounded corner box. If you use the tool with its default settings, you'll probably think the corners aren't rounded enough, so it's helpful to know that the roundness of the corners is controlled in the Options Bar. Increase the Radius size to make them more round and decrease the Radius to make them less round. While we're talking rounded corners, there's a tool in ImageReady that I wish Adobe would move over to Photoshop—it's the Rounded Corner Selection Tool, that makes, well…do I even have to describe it?

Quick Tip:
Makin' copies

Once you've created a Web tab or button (or almost anything else on a layer), you can make duplicate copies superfast by using this shortcut: First, hold the Command key (PC: Control key) and click on the layer you want to duplicate (this puts a selection around everything on the layer). Then, hold Option-Command (PC: Alt-Control) and drag off copies as you need them. Yeah, baby!

STEP FOUR: In the Layers palette, turn on "Lock Transparent Pixels" for your layer (it's the first icon from the left). Using the gradient you just created, draw a gradient from the top of your shape to the bottom (as shown).

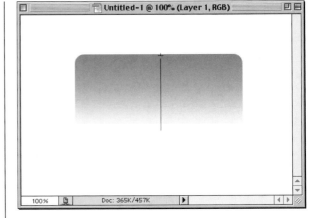

STEP FIVE: Choose Bevel and Emboss from the Layer Styles pop-up menu at the bottom of the Layers palette. For Style choose Inner Bevel, set the Angle to 126, Depth to 2, and Size to 4. Raise the Highlight Opacity to 100% and lower the Shadow Opacity to 50%. Don't click OK yet.

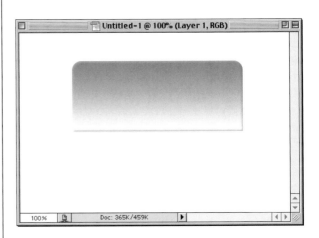

STEP SIX: In the list of Styles on the left-hand side of the dialog box, click on the name Outer Glow to bring up its options. Set the Blend Mode to Normal, then click on the Color Swatch in the dialog and choose 30% black as your glow color. Increase the Spread to 25% and click OK.

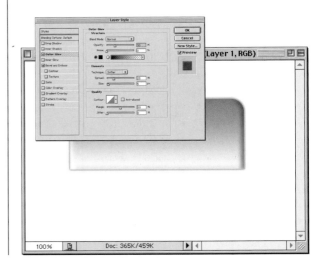

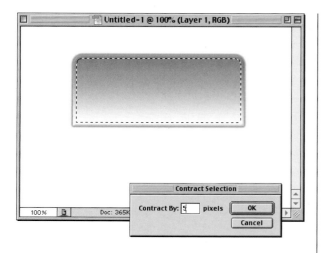

STEP SEVEN: Hold the Command key (PC: Control key) and in the Layers palette, click on the layer that contains the tab to put a selection around it. Then, go under the Select menu, under Modify, and choose Contract. When the dialog box appears, enter 5 and click OK to shrink your selection.

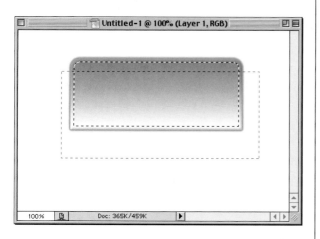

STEP EIGHT: Press "m" to switch to the Rectangular Marquee tool. Now we're going to subtract a large chunk of your selection, leaving just a thin area at the top still selected. Hold the Option key (PC: Alt key) then draw a rectangle starting from below the bottom of your current selection to just a little below the top (as shown). This will leave you with a thin selection across the top.

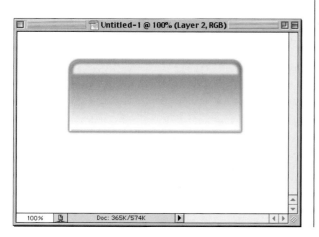

STEP NINE: Click on the New Layer icon in the Layers palette. Press "x" then Option-Delete (PC: Alt-Backspace) to fill with white. Press Command-D (PC: Control-D) to Deselect. Under the Filter menu, under Blur, choose Gaussian Blur, type in 1.5 pixels, and press OK. In the Layers palette lower the Opacity to 75%.

Quick Tip:
How Web browsers display backgrounds

Just about everyone has a different-sized monitor for their computer, and just about everyone sees your Web page in a different-sized browser window. (Some have it fill their entire screen, but most leave it set at the default size the browser manufacturer specified.) The point is that some people have a 21" monitor and some have a 15", and to make sure you never see a huge blank spot, browsers automatically tile (repeat vertically and horizontally) whatever size image you use as a background. They tile like tiles on your kitchen floor. (You do have tile, don't you? That carpet-in-the-kitchen thing gets really messy.)

Because we know the browser is going to tile our background, filling every inch of visible space, we don't need to create huge backgrounds in Photoshop. Instead, we can create tiny little backgrounds that appear seamless when displayed on a page. This helps the file size stay small and helps the page load faster.

continued

STEP TEN: If you add some type and a very light drop shadow, here's what your tab will look like. However, if you want a row of tabs, you might want to do this first: Click on the Eye icon next to the Background layer to hide it, then choose Merge Visible from the palette's pop-up menu. Press Command-T (PC: Control-T) to bring up Free Transform. Hold the Shift key, grab a corner point, and drag inward to scale down the tab's size considerably.

STEP ELEVEN: To really make this technique look right, you need to make more than one copy of the tab and place it with other tabs in a row (as shown here). To colorize a tab, go under the Image menu, under Adjustment, and choose Hue/Saturation. Click the Colorize button and move the Hue slider to choose the color you'd like for your tab.

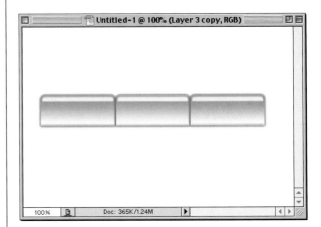

STEP TWELVE: Press "d" to set your Foreground color to black, then press "t" to get the Type tool. Click in the center of the image, type your text in the dialog box, and click OK. (In this instance, I used the Myriad 400 Reg font at 14 points.) Choose Drop Shadow from the Layer Style pop-up menu at the bottom of the Layers palette. Lower the Opacity to 30%, set the Angle to 90°, and click OK to apply a slight drop shadow to your type.

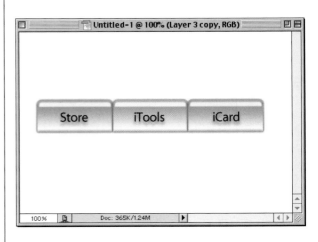

Oscar Starbrights

I call these "Oscar Starbrights" because you see these lens effects used on distant shots of the stage at the Oscar Awards ceremony and a host of other indoor stage events, from boxing matches to rock concerts. The effect is similar to the "Star Effects" filter used with still cameras.

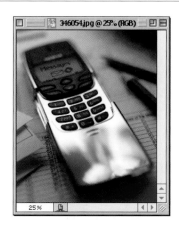

STEP ONE: Open the image where you want to apply starbrights. Press the letter "d" then "x" to set your Foreground color to white.

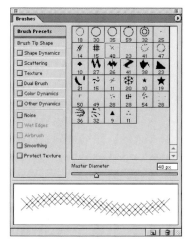

STEP TWO: Go under the Window menu and choose Brushes. In the Brushes palette, click on the right-facing arrow to bring up the pop-up menu. Choose Assorted Brushes from the list of brush sets at the bottom and click on Append to add this set of brushes to your palette. Scroll down and choose the 48-pixel brush that looks like an "X" (as shown).

STEP THREE: Create a new blank layer by clicking on the New Layer icon at the bottom of the Layers palette. Now, click your brush on the first spot where you want a starbright to appear. Next, create another new blank layer.

continued

Quick Tip:
Getting back your last selection

If you make a selection, deselect it, then go on about your business and later realize that you forgot to save that selection, you can get your last selection back, as long as you haven't made another selection. Just go under the Select menu, choose Reselect, and the last selection you made will reappear.

Quick Tip:
Getting your image down to size

When you're dragging Photoshop layers between documents, have you noticed that if part of your layer extends outside the edge of your document window, Photoshop doesn't delete those areas? Yep, it's still there. For example, if you drag an image of a car over to a new document and position it so that only the front half is showing, the back half (even though you can't see it) is still there. If you decide later that you want to show the whole car, you can simply drag the car further into your image window and the parts hidden off screen will appear. That's good, right? Well, sometimes. Actually, it's only good if you think that at some point you might need those parts. Otherwise, you're eating up memory storing stuff that you don't need. Want to get rid of all that excess image data? Press Command-A (PC: Control-A) to Select All, then go under the Edit menu and choose Crop. Everything outside your image window gets cropped off, shrinking your file size in the process.

STEP FOUR: In the Brushes palette click on the 25-pixel brush that looks like an "X". In the list of options on the left side of the palette, click on Brush Tip Shape to bring up those options. Increase the Diameter to 30 and change the Angle to 45°. Click once on the center of your original starbright. Now, choose a 27-pixel, round, soft-edged tip and click once in the center of your original starbright.

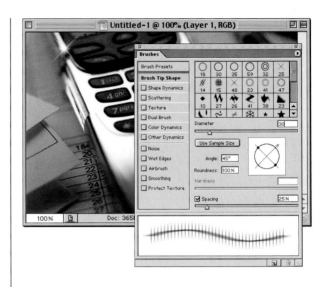

STEP FIVE: Create another blank layer. In the Layers palette, Command click (PC: Control click) on your original starbright layer to put a selection around your starbright. Press "g" to get the Gradient tool and then click on the down-facing arrow next to the Gradient thumbnail (in the Options Bar) to bring up the Gradient Picker. Choose the Spectrum gradient (as shown), and then drag the Gradient tool from the center of your starbright to the right, past the starbright's edge.

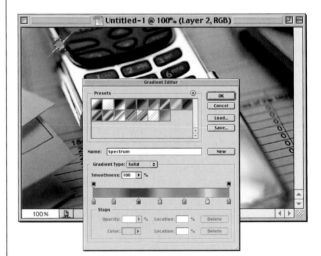

STEP SIX: Deselect by pressing Command-D (PC: Control-D). In the Layers palette, change the Blend Mode to Lighten, then hide the Background layer and choose Merge Visible from the palette's pop-down menu. Now you can press Command-J (PC: Control-J) to create duplicates of your starbright to move to other locations in your image (as shown).

Adding Flames to Anything

This is another technique I learned from the amazing Felix Nelson, who used this effect on marketing materials for PhotoshopWorld, the annual convention of the National Association of Photoshop Professionals (the theme was "Photoshop Rocks!"). We're applying it to a guitar (with the Photoshop palette as its neck), but the technique works equally for cars, toasters, you name it!

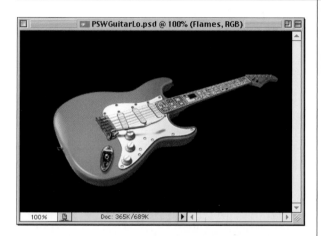

STEP ONE: Open the image where you want to apply flames. The image shown (left) was drawn by Felix in Photoshop, using a low-res photo as a template.

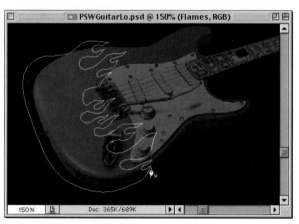

STEP TWO: Press "p" to get the Pen tool and draw a set of flames (as shown). (Note: if you download this guitar from the book's companion site, this path is already drawn for you in the Paths palette.) You may want to lower the Opacity of the guitar layer (as we did here) to make it easier to see where to put your Path as you draw it.

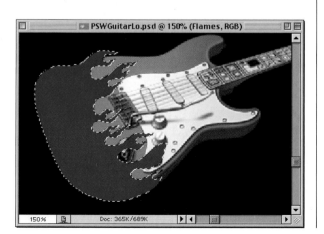

STEP THREE: After drawing the path, raise the Opacity of the guitar layer back to 100%. Create a new blank layer by clicking on the New Layer icon at the bottom of the Layers palette. Press Command-Return (PC: Control-Enter) to turn your path into a selection. Next, click on the Foreground Color Swatch and choose a Teal color (I chose PANTONE 328). Fill your selection with this color by pressing Option-Delete (PC: Alt-Backspace).

continued

Quick Tip:
Where are my Layer Clipping Masks?

If you upgraded to Photoshop 7 from version 6, and you used Photoshop's Layer Clipping Masks, you're probably wondering where they went. Actually, they're still there, but Adobe gave them a new name that's more indicative of what they really are: Now Layer Clipping Masks are named Vector Masks. Were you wondering why you might use a Vector Mask? It's to give your output a sharp edge (vector) when outputting to a PostScript Level 3 printer.

Quick Tip:
Match another open image's size and resolution

If you have an image already open and you want it to be the same size, resolution, and color mode as another open document, here's a quick trick to have Photoshop do all the work for you. While the image is open onscreen, go under the Image menu and choose Image Size. When the dialog box appears, go under the Window menu, under Documents, and choose the name of the open image you want it to match. It will enter all the appropriate information in the Image Size dialog box for you, and as long as you have the Resample Image checkbox turned on, you can click OK and your image will jump to those new specs.

STEP FOUR: Go under the Edit menu and choose Stroke. In the Stroke dialog, for Width enter 2 px, then click on the Color Swatch and choose a dark blue. For Location, choose Center and click OK to apply a 2-pixel stroke to your selected area. Press Command-D (PC: Control-D) to Deselect.

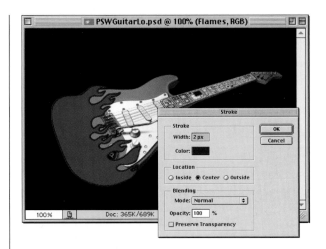

STEP FIVE: Next, Command-click (PC: Control-click) on the guitar layer in the Layers palette to put a selection around the guitar (even though we're still on the flames layer). Press Shift-Command-I to inverse your selection, then press Delete (PC: Backspace) to remove any flames that extend beyond the guitar, then deselect by pressing Command-D (PC: Control-D). To make the highlights and detail in the guitar visible under the flame, change the flame layer's Blend mode to Color.

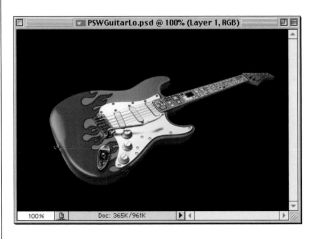

STEP SIX: To complete the effect, press "e" to switch to the Eraser tool, and erase over any areas that shouldn't be covered with flames (such as the pick guard, the input jack, the bridge, and the strap pin at the base of the guitar).

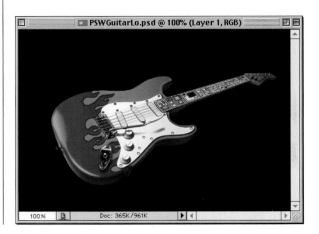

Raised Edge Inner Shadow Effect

This is a technique that I saw on the Q&A background from *Photoshop User's Photoshop 7.0 Special Supplement*. I saw it first in the final proofs and asked Felix how he did it. When he showed me, I said, "We have to put that in the new book." Thanks to Felix, here it is.

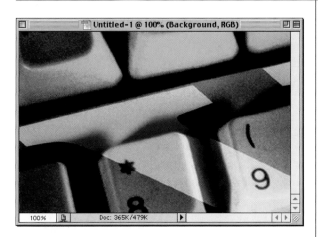

STEP ONE: Open an image to which you want to apply the effect .

STEP TWO: Press "t" to switch to the Type tool and create your Type (in this instance, we used the font Trajan).

STEP THREE: Hold the Command key (PC: Control key) and in the Layers palette, click on your Type layer to put a selection around your text. You can now delete your Type layer by dragging it to the Trash icon at the bottom of the Layers palette.

continued

Quick Tip:
Put your guides right were you want 'em

If you know the exact position where you want a guide placed, you can have Photoshop place it for you by going under the View menu and choosing New Guide. In the dialog box, enter the position you want, click O, and you're in business.

Quick Tip:
Want to bend the top or bottom? Make it vertical first

If you want to put a bend in the top and bottom of an object (or rasterized type for that matter), here's a quick way to do it. Start by using Free Transform and rotate the image 90° CCW. This enables you to use the Shear filter (found under the Filter menu, under Distort) to bend the object to the left or right; but then after running the filter, you'll need to rotate it back 90° CW to make it upright again.

STEP FOUR: Press Command-J (PC: Control-J) to put your selected area up on its own layer, above the Background layer. Press Command-L (PC: Control-L) to bring up Levels. Move the lower left Output Levels slider to 128 (as shown) to lighten your layer.

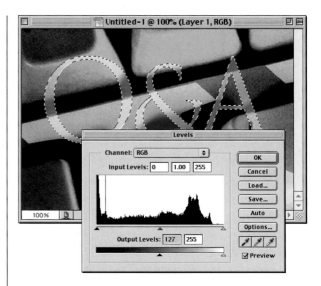

STEP FIVE: Choose Inner Shadow from the Layer Style pop-up menu at the bottom of the Layers palette. In the dialog box, lower the Opacity to 50%, and click OK to apply a shadow inside your text. Command-click (PC: Control-click) on your Q&A layer to select it. Next, go under the Select menu and choose Expand. Enter 3 pixels and click OK to expand your selection (as shown).

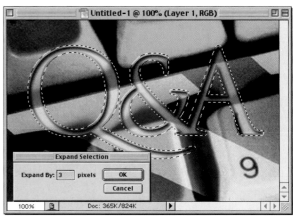

STEP SIX: Click on the Background layer to make it active, then press Command-J (PC: Control-J) to put the selected area on its own layer (as you did earlier, but this time it's expanded by 3 pixels). In the Layers palette, drag this new layer above your original text layer.

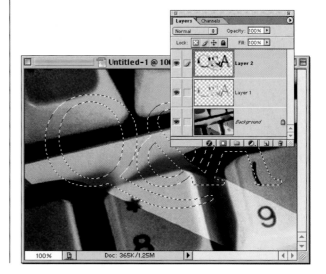

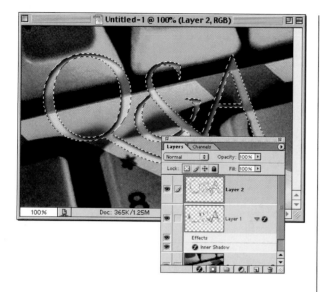

STEP SEVEN: Command-click (PC: Control-click) on your original text layer to put a selection around the type (even though you're still on the top layer). Press Delete (PC: Backspace) to knock a hole in this layer revealing the type on the layer beneath it.

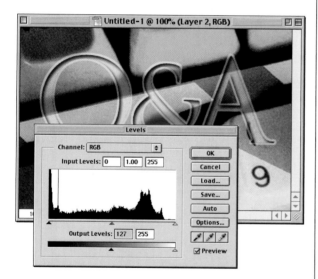

STEP EIGHT: Deselect by pressing Command-D (PC: Control-D). Then press Command-L (PC: Control-L) to bring up Levels. Move the lower left Output Levels slider to 128 (as shown) to lighten your layer.

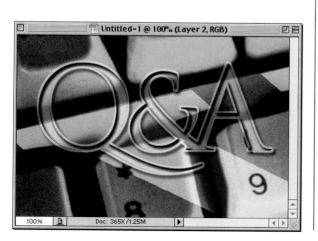

STEP NINE: Choose Drop Shadow from the Layer Style pop-up at the bottom of the Layers palette, and click OK to complete the effect.

Quick Tip: See RGB and CMYK at the same time

If you're working on an RGB document that you know will be converted to a CMYK document for press, there's a way you can see both RGB and CMYK versions of your document while you're working. That way, you can see how changes you make in the RGB image will actually look in your CMYK image—all in real time. Here's how: While your image is open onscreen, go under the Window menu, under Documents, and choose New Window. This opens another view of your existing document. Press Command-Y (PC: Control-Y) to show a CMYK preview of your image, then return to your original document and edit as normal. You'll see your changes updated in the CMYK version as you work. Pretty slick!

Putting an Image in a Monitor

In this technique, we're showing how to use Free Transform to put an image into a monitor. Now I don't want you to think, "Oh, how often will I need that?" because this technique works just as well for fitting any image into other spaces—a window of a house, a TV screen, a billboard, etc. So it's really a handy one to know.

STEP ONE: Open the image that contains the monitor (TV, etc.) where you want to place another image.

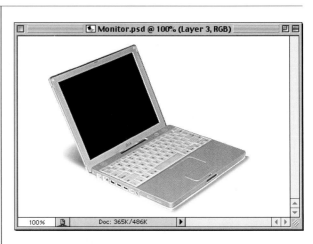

STEP TWO: Open the image you want to place inside the monitor.

STEP THREE: Press "v" to get the Move tool and drag this image into your monitor image. It will appear on its own layer above your image. Press Command-T (PC: Control-T) to bring up Free Transform. Hold the Shift key, grab one of the corner points and drag inward to scale the image down to a size that's close to the size of the monitor (it doesn't have to be exact, but get in the ballpark). Press Return (PC: Enter) to lock in your transformation.

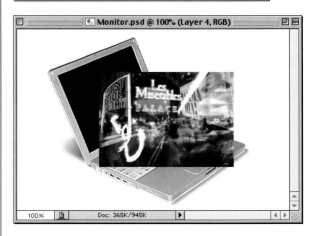

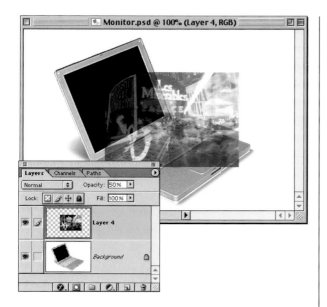

STEP FOUR: In the Layers palette, lower the Opacity of this layer to 50%. This will help when you try to position the image within the monitor area—you'll be able to see the monitor through your photo—a big help.

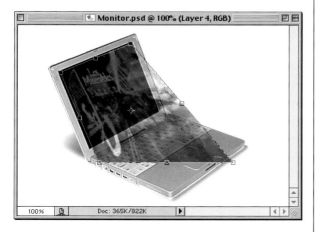

STEP FIVE: Press Command-T (PC: Control-T) to bring up Free Transform again. Hold the Command key (PC: Control key), grab one of the corner points, and drag it to the corresponding corner of the monitor (as shown). You'll have to do this for all four corners.

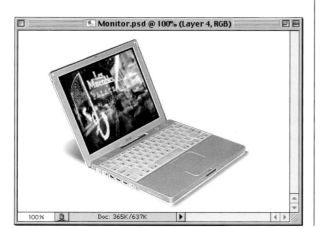

STEP SIX: When you have a perfect fit, press Return (PC: Enter) to lock in your transformation, then in the Layers palette, raise the Opacity of this layer back to 100% to complete the effect.

Quick Tip:
Accurate Unsharp Masking
When applying the Unsharp Mask filter, make sure that your image size is at 100% view, or what you see onscreen will probably be much different than what prints out. Because of the way Photoshop displays your image at smaller views, you might not see little spots and other annoying artifacts that you might be introducing into your document. Therefore, always make sure to apply it at a 100% view and you'll avoid a major case of the "spots."

Quick Tip:
Creating
new layers

There are a number of ways to create new layers. The quickest way is to click on the New Layer icon at the bottom of the Layers palette. No dialog box pops up to slow you down—you immediately get a new blank layer.

You can use the keyboard shortcut Shift-Command-N (PC: Shift-Control-N) to create a new layer and bring up the New Layer dialog box (so you can name your layer as you create it), but that's a bit slower.

If you're looking for the absolute slowest way to create a layer (if you're charging by the hour), you can go under the Layer menu, under New, and choose Layer.

You can also choose New Layer from the Layers palette's pop-down menu if you're charging by the hour, but still have a deadline to meet.

Gettin' "Gelly" with Buttons

This is a "gel design age" thanks to the look of Apple's Aqua interface for Mac OS X and the resulting marketing pieces that sprang forth from it. When we first showed this technique in *Photoshop User* magazine, it took literally twice as many steps, but we've since found an easier way that makes it so easy you can create your own aqua-like button in about 60 seconds.

STEP ONE: Create a new document (RGB, 72 ppi). Create a new blank layer by clicking on the New Layer icon at the bottom of the Layers palette. Set your Foreground color to light blue, then Press Shift-U until the Rounded Rectangle tool appears in the Toolbox. Up in the Options Bar, set the Radius to 40 pixels, click on the third icon from the left (Fill Pixels) and drag out your shape (as shown).

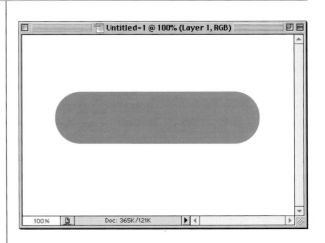

STEP TWO: Command-click (PC: Control-click) on your pill layer to select it. Create another blank layer. Then go under the Select menu, under Modify, and choose Contract. Enter 20 pixels and click OK to contract your selection (as shown). Press the letter "d" then "x" to set your Foreground color to white.

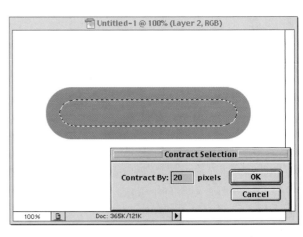

STEP THREE: Press Option-Delete (PC: Alt-Backspace) to fill your contracted selection with white. Press Command-D (PC: Control-D) to deselect. Then go under the Filter menu, under Blur, and choose Gaussian Blur. When the dialog box appears, enter 10, and click OK to apply a blur to your white layer.

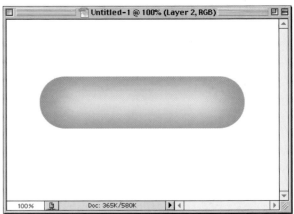

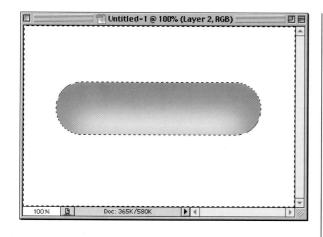

STEP FOUR: Press "v" to switch to the Move tool, and drag your blurry white layer down to where its bottom edge touches the bottom of the pill shape (as shown). Then, hold the Command key (PC: Control key) and click once on the pill layer to put a selection around the pill (but you're still on the white blurry layer). Press Shift-Command-I (PC: Shift-Control-I) to Inverse your selection, then press Delete (PC: Backspace) to remove any spillover from your white blur.

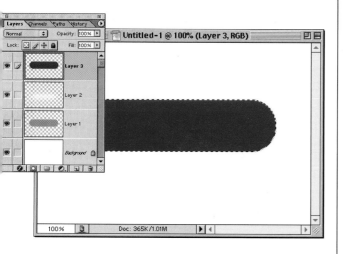

STEP FIVE: Now, press Shift-Command-I (PC: Shift-Control-I) to get your pill selected again. Create a new blank layer by clicking on the New Layer icon at the bottom of the Layers palette. Set your Foreground to a darker blue than your original blue, and fill your selection by pressing Option-Delete (PC: Alt-Backspace).

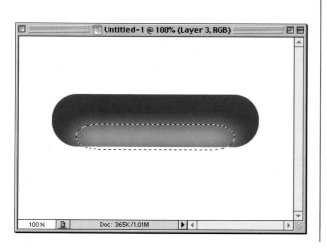

STEP SIX: Deselect by pressing Command-D (PC: Control-D). In the Layers palette, hold the Command key (PC: Control key) and click once on the white blurry layer to put a selection around it (don't change layers, just get the selection in place; you should still be on the dark blue pill layer). Now, press Delete (PC: Backspace) to knock a soft hole out of the blue pill shape (as shown).

Quick Tip:
Hiding the marching ants

If you're working on a project, there are times where you need to have something selected, but it would help if you didn't have to see the "marching ants" selection border on the screen. To keep your selection in place, but to hide those annoying marching ants, press Command-H (PC: Control-H). Adobe now calls this command just "Extras," but it probably should be called "Hide Selection" or "Hide Marching Ants"; but if they did name commands with such obvious names, then you wouldn't need this book, so now that I think of it, I really like that name, Extras. Yep, that works for me.

continued

Quick Tip:
Zooming around the Layers palette

You can jump to the layer directly below your current layer in the Layers palette by pressing Command-Left Bracket (PC: Control-Left Bracket), or you can move to the layer above your current layer by pressing Command-Right Bracket (PC: Control-Right Bracket). Using these keyboard shortcuts, you can quickly step up and down through your Layers palette.

STEP SEVEN: Press "m" to switch to the Rectangular Marquee tool, then place your pointer inside the selected area (that you just knocked out) and drag the selection upward a little bit (maybe one-quarter of the way up) and hit Delete (PC: Backspace) again. Repeat this one or two more times, until you're almost to the top of the pill as shown (make sure you stop just short of the top). Deselect by pressing Command-D (PC: Control-D).

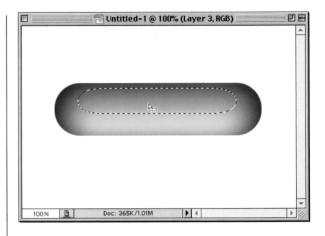

STEP EIGHT: Command-click (PC: Control-click) on your pill layer to select it. Create another new blank layer. Then go under the Select menu, under Modify, and choose Contract. Enter 20 pixels and click OK to contract your selection (as shown). Press the letter "d" then "x" to set your Foreground color to white.

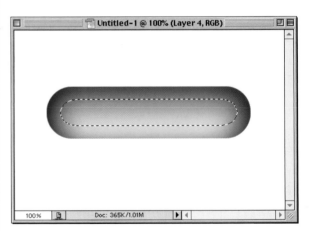

STEP NINE: Press "g" to get the Gradient tool. Up in the Options Bar, click on the down-facing arrow next to the Gradient thumbnail to make the Gradient Picker visible. Choose the second gradient from the left (Fore-ground to Transparent) and drag this gradient from the top of your selection to the bottom (as shown).

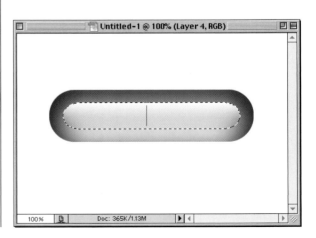

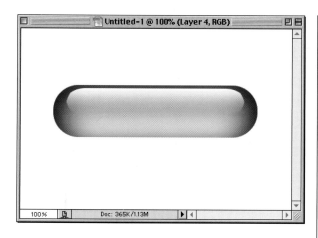

STEP TEN: Deselect by pressing Command-D (PC: Control-D). Press "v" to switch to the Move tool, and drag your white gradient layer upward to where it's almost at the top, but leave a gap of dark blue between your white gradient and the top of the pill (as shown). This creates the highlight area of the pill.

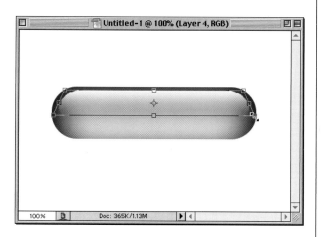

STEP ELEVEN: Press Command-T (PC: Control-T) to bring up Free Transform. Then go under the Edit menu, under Transform, and choose Perspective. Then grab the left bottom corner, and click-and-drag outward just a bit to add a perspective effect to your highlight layer. Press Return (PC: Enter) to lock in your transformation. Hide the Background layer, then choose Merge Visible from the palette's pop-down menu.

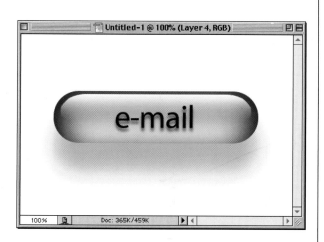

STEP TWELVE: Next, choose Drop Shadow from the Layer Style pop-up menu at the bottom of the Layers palette. When the dialog box appears, click on the Color Swatch. When the Color Picker appears, take your cursor outside the dialog box into your image area, and click on a blue part of your pill shape to colorize the shadow. Lower the Opacity to 50%, set the Angle at 90°, Distance to 45, Size to 32, turn off Use Global Light, and then click OK to complete the effect.

Quick Tip:
Filter repeater!
After you've applied a filter, if you need to repeat the same filter using the exact same settings, it's easy—press Command-F (PC: Control-F). However, there are times where you may need to apply the same filter, but first you need to tweak the settings just a bit. There's a shortcut you can use that will open the dialog box of the last filter you applied, and it will already have your last-used settings in place. It's Option-Command-F (PC: Alt-Control-F).

This is the chapter where it all pays off. This is where we dissect some of the most popular Photoshop advertising

Commercial Break
Advertising Effects

effects and expose them for the cheap tawdry tricks that they are. It's no secret that some big ad agencies spend vast sums of money to find out what motivates people to spend their hard-earned money on a particular product. For example, recent studies have shown that if you use an olive color on the cover of your product, and use a combination of gray, blue, and orange on the inside of your product, people will find the product absolutely irresistible, regardless of the content. Further studies have shown that if you're able to work some suggestive words into the name of your product (for example, the word "Dirty"), then overall sales will increase by nearly 32%. If on top of that, you can somehow apply a metallic effect to the aforementioned word, and at the same time toss a few bolts or rivets on top of it, you'll have a product so compelling that even Hindu priests will abandon their mountaintop spiritual sanctuaries just to buy whatever it is you're selling. This is powerful information. Use it wisely.

Quick Tip:
Turning a path into a selection

Once you have part of a path selected using the Direct Selection tool, you can turn it into a selection by going to the Paths palette and choosing Make Selection from the palette's pop-down menu. The advantage of using this method is that you can add feathering (among other options) in the Make Selection dialog box. The disadvantage is that if you don't want feathering or some of the other path's options, you waste time in a dialog box you don't need.

Another method is to click on the Load Path as a Selection icon at the bottom of the Paths palette. It's the third icon from the left that looks like a circle of dots. Be careful, though, because if you used the Make Selection dialog previously and added feathering, the amount of feathering that you used will be added when you click on the icon at the bottom of the palette. To avoid this, go back to the Make Selection dialog and change the feathering to 0 (zero).

Torn Out of a Photo

I originally saw this technique in a series of print ads for retail giant Best Buy®. In the ads, it looked as if a person had been ripped out of a boring photo and placed in a Best Buy store. What I liked about the technique was how they had two edges—one on the tear, and then the second just outside it that really made it look realistic.

STEP ONE: Open the photo that has the object, or person, that you want to rip out of the image. Double-click on the Background layer and click OK in the dialog to convert it into a regular layer. Create a new blank layer by clicking on the New Layer icon in the Layers palette. Go under the Layer menu, under New, and choose Background From Layer.

STEP TWO: Press "L" to get the Lasso tool, and draw a very loose selection around the person (as shown). Don't try to get too close to the person; it's supposed to look ripped, so make the selection look somewhat arbitrary.

STEP THREE: Once your selection is in place, click on your image layer (Layer 0) in the Layers palette and press Shift-Command-J (PC: Shift-Control-J) to cut your selection out of the image and put it up on its own layer. Hide this new layer by clicking on the Eye icon in the first column beside the layer (as shown).

STEP FOUR: Click back on Layer 0 again in the Layers palette, go under the Image menu, and choose Canvas Size. Click the Relative button, enter 2 inches for both Height and Width and click OK to add 2 inches of white space around your image (as shown). In the Layer Style pop-up menu at the bottom of the Layers palette, choose Drop Shadow, and click OK.

STEP FIVE: Press "L" to get the Lasso tool, and draw another very loose selection around the cutout hole in your photo. Again, this isn't supposed to be precise, so just make a loose selection, and in fact, if you want to make it a bit "jaggy," all the better. Remember, these will represent the rough edges of a tear, so "let it rip" (so to speak).

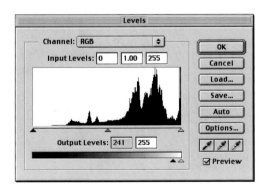

STEP SIX: Press Command-L (PC: Control-L) to bring up the Levels dialog. Grab the bottom left Output Levels slider and drag it nearly all the way to the right to completely blow out the selected area, leaving it white. Click OK, but don't Deselect yet.

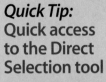

Quick Tip:
Quick access to the Direct Selection tool
When you're using the Pen tool, you adjust points and paths using the Direct Selection tool (which looks like a white hollow arrow). You can temporarily switch to this tool any time you're working with the Pen tool by holding the Command key (PC: Control key), and your current Pen tool will become the Direct Selection arrow. When you're done, release the Command key (PC: Control key), and you'll jump back to the last Pen tool you were using.

continued

Quick Tip: Rotating through the Pens

In Photoshop, you can only toggle between two of the Pen tools found in the Tool palette: the regular Pen tool and the Freeform Pen tool. To toggle between these two, press Shift-P.

However, when a path is selected, you can actually access other pens that don't even have keyboard shortcuts. For example, if you have an active path, and you move the Pen tool over a line segment—look at your pointer—it changes to the Add Anchor Point tool. Then, move the Pen tool over an anchor point and it changes into the Delete Anchor Point tool.

STEP SEVEN: Go under the Filter menu, under Noise, and choose Add Noise. Increase the Amount to around 10%, for Distribution choose Gaussian, and turn on the Monochromatic checkbox. Click OK to apply some noise to your selected area (which adds a slight texture to the white area, helping it look more torn, and distinguishing it from the white background).

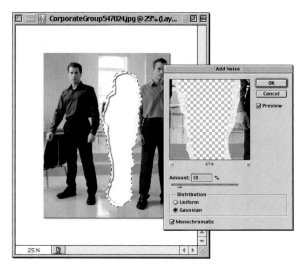

STEP EIGHT: Press Command-D (PC: Control-D) to deselect and complete this phase of the project (that's right, there's more!).

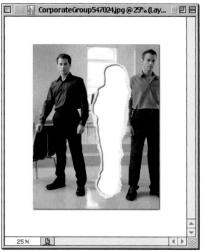

STEP NINE: Open the document that you want to place your cutout person into. Go back to your original image and make the top layer (the person) visible again by clicking in the first column where the Eye icon used to be. Press "v" to switch to the Move tool and drag this layer into your new document (as shown).

STEP TEN: Press "L" to get the Lasso tool, and this time draw a selection that is more accurate—right along the edge of the person (as shown).

STEP ELEVEN: Press Shift-Command-I (PC: Shift-Control-I) to Inverse the selection. Press Command-L (PC: Control-L) to bring up the Levels dialog. Grab the bottom left Output Levels slider and drag it nearly all the way to the right to blow out the selected area (just like last time). Press Command-F (PC: Control-F) to apply the Add Noise filter again, using the same settings as before.

STEP TWELVE: Press Command-D (PC: Control-D) to Deselect. Last, choose Drop Shadow from the Layer Style pop-up menu at the bottom of the Layers palette. Increase the Size to 10, set the Angle to 138°, and click OK to complete the effect (as shown).

Quick Tip:
Jump to the Background layer

To jump instantly to the Background layer in your Layers palette, press Shift-Option-Left Bracket (PC: Shift-Alt-Left Bracket). To jump to the top layer in your layers stack, press Shift-Option-Right Bracket (PC: Shift-Alt-Right Bracket).

You can also jump to the Background layer from within your image itself when you're using the Move tool by holding the Command key (PC: Control key) and clicking on any part of the Background layer in your image.

Quick Tip:
Duplicating is faster than copying and pasting

I use the Option-Command-drag (PC: Alt-Control-drag) to make copies of objects because it's so much faster than copying and pasting. Try it for yourself. Select an object, go under the Edit menu, and choose Copy, then choose Paste (or use the keyboard shortcuts for Copy and Paste). Now, select an object and use the Option-Command-drag (PC: Alt-Control-drag) method and you'll notice that your copy appears immediately. There's no delay whatsoever; it happens in real time. Another benefit is that if you have something saved in your Clipboard memory, using the drag-copy method leaves that Clipboard intact.

Popping from an Image

This is one of those techniques for which I had so many requests that I wanted to include it in the book. It's primarily seen in print ads where a person, a body part, a car, etc. extends out of the photo and into white space where body copy usually resides. It's kind of as if the object is popping out of the photo, and it not only adds visual interest and movement, it also gives you something to wrap type around.

STEP ONE: Open the photo that has the object, or person, that you want to extend from the image.

STEP TWO: Press "L" to get the Lasso tool, and draw a selection around the part of the object you want to extend from the photo (as shown). Press Command-J (PC: Control-J) to put the selected area on its own layer.

STEP THREE: In the Layers palette, click on the Background layer. Press "m" to switch to the Rectangular Marquee tool and draw a selection that starts near the left edge of where you made your original selection on the object and extends to the right side of your document window (as shown). Press Delete (PC: Backspace) to erase part of the background.

STEP FOUR: Press Command-D (PC: Control-D) to Deselect. In the Layers palette, click back on the partial bike copy layer. Choose Drop Shadow from the palette's Layer Styles pop-up menu. In the dialog box, increase the Size to 13 and click OK. Go under the Layer menu, under Layer Styles, and choose Create Layer to remove the Drop Shadow from your bike layer, putting it on its own separate layer below your current layer.

STEP FIVE: It's almost guaranteed that the drop shadow will create a visible seam down the middle of your bike layer. In the Layers palette, click on the Drop Shadow layer below it, then press "e" to get the Eraser tool. Erase any excess drop shadow that appears within the part of your image that's not supposed to stick out.

STEP SIX: Last, add any additional text to complete the effect (as shown here).

Quick Tip:
Defining patterns
In older versions of Photoshop, you could only define one pattern at a time. When you created a new pattern, the old pattern would disappear, never to be found again. Photoshop 6.0 and 7.0 come with a number of preset patterns that you can use time and time again. You can also define your own patterns and add them to the Pattern Picker so that you can go back and use them whenever you want. Just go under the Edit menu, choose Define Pattern, name your pattern, and click OK to add it to the bottom of the Pattern Picker in the Fill dialog.

Creating 3D Packaging

You can use Photoshop's built-in tools to turn a flat image into an object with depth (such as product packaging, a video box, etc.). We'll be adding perspective to an image using Photoshop's transformation tool, but you'll also add shading and highlights to help "sell" the effect that your image has depth.

STEP ONE: Open the image that you want to use as the cover of your product box. Press Command-A (PC: Control-A) to select the entire image, then press Shift-Command-J (PC: Shift-Control-J) to put your cover shot on its own layer. Double-click directly on this layer's name in the Layers palette and rename it by simply typing "Front" right in the palette.

STEP TWO: Go under the Image menu and choose Canvas Size. Enter a value that is a few inches wider and a few inches higher than your current image. This gives some needed work area around the image (as shown). Press the letter "v" to choose the Move tool, and drag your layer named Front to the right side of the screen.

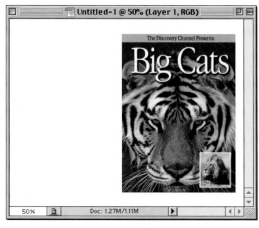

STEP THREE: To build the spine, create a new layer by clicking on the New Layer icon at the bottom of the Layers palette. Double-click on this layer's name and rename it "Spine." Using the Rectangular Marquee tool, draw a rectangular selection to the left of your box front. Choose a Foreground color that will complement the colors in your box front.

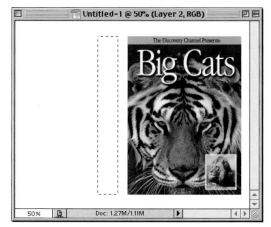

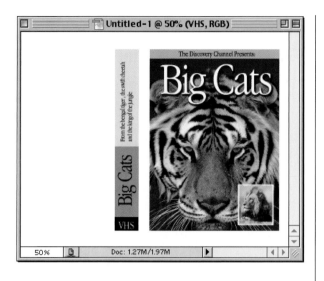

STEP FOUR: Fill this selection by pressing Option-Delete (PC: Alt-Backspace). I recommend adding some text to the spine to help sell the 3D effect, so use the Type tool to create your type, then go under the Layer menu, under Rasterize, and choose Type. Press Command-E (PC: Control-E) to merge this text layer with the Spine layer beneath it.

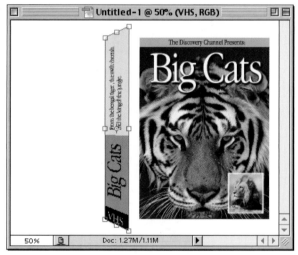

STEP FIVE: On the Spine layer, press Command-T (PC: Control-T) to bring up Free Transform. Hold Shift-Option-Command (PC: Shift-Alt-Control) then click-and-drag the top right handle of the bounding box straight upward about ¹/₂" above the box front (you'll see the spine stretch as you do this).

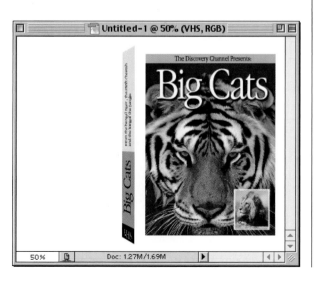

STEP SIX: Keep holding the same keys and grab the lower left handle and drag it upward about the same amount. Release the keys, grab the left middle handle, and drag inward about the same amount to remove the distortion caused by the stretching. Press Return (PC: Enter) when it looks like the spine shown here. Switch to the Front layer.

Quick Tip:
Getting rid of the checkerboard pattern

This should really be called "How to get rid of that annoying checkerboard pattern." I'm talking about the gray-and-white pattern that appears behind transparent layers to let you know which parts of the layer are transparent. In most cases you don't need this pattern, because you already have something that lets you see what's transparent on a layer—they're called your eyes. Because of that, I constantly have people asking me how to turn it off, so I thought I'd better include this information in the book. You go under the Edit menu, under Preferences, and choose Transparency & Gamut. Under Transparency Settings, choose None for Grid Size, click OK, and the pattern will be gone.

continued

Quick Tip: Making Color Overlay work

If you've ever tried Photoshop's Color Overlay Layer Style, you may have been disappointed in how it works (I know I was at first), because rather than overlaying a transparent color over your object, it pretty much puts a solid fill over it. To get this Layer Style to work the way it probably should, all you have to do is change the Blend Mode in the Color Overlay dialog box from Normal to (get this…) Overlay. That way, the color doesn't obliterate the effects you've already applied. Try it and you'll see what I mean.

STEP SEVEN: Press Command-T (PC: Control-T), hold Shift-Option-Command (PC: Shift-Alt-Control), and grab the upper-left handle and drag straight upward until it matches the height of the spine. Then grab the lower-right handle, and drag upward about the same amount. Release the keys and drag the right-middle handle inward about 1". Press Return (PC: Enter) to lock in your transformation.

STEP EIGHT: Switch to the Spine layer. Press "v" to get the Move tool and drag the spine to the right until it touches the left edge of the box. Press Command-L (PC: Control-L) to bring up Levels. Move the right bottom Output Levels slider to the left a bit to darken the spine, then click OK. Next, switch to the Front layer, then press "b" to get the Brush tool. In the Options Bar, click on the Airbrush icon, and lower the Opacity to 20%.

STEP NINE: Choose a small, hard-edged brush, and switch your Foreground color to white. Hold the Shift key and click at the top corner between the box front and the spine and drag down the edge to the bottom to add a highlight to the front edge. Switch to the Background layer and change the Foreground color to black by pressing "d." Choose a very large, soft brush. You still have the Airbrush tool, so paint a soft drop shadow below the box with one smooth stroke. That's it!

Backlit Photo Backgrounds

This is an update of a technique from my previous book, and I think this version is much better, plus it has fewer steps and is easier to do. I got the idea after seeing Absolut Vodka's very slick print ad campaign, and I figured out how to create a similar background in Photoshop.

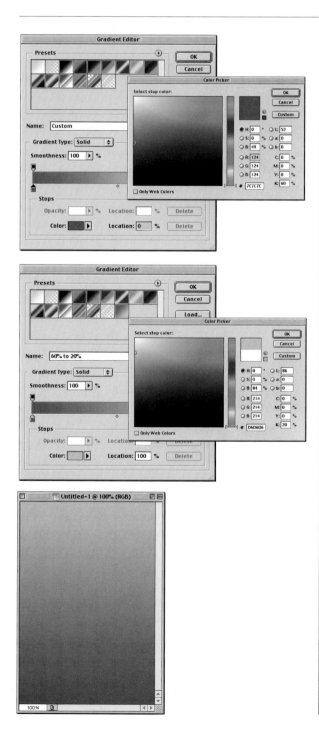

STEP ONE: Open a new document in RGB mode. Press "g" to get the Gradient tool. In the Options Bar click on the Gradient thumbnail to bring up the Gradient Editor. Click on the third gradient from the left in the top row (Black to White). Double-click on the black Color Stop (under the Editor Bar on the left) and in the CMYK fields enter C=0, M=0, Y=0, K=60. Click OK to set this Color Stop to a dark gray.

STEP TWO: Double-click on the white Color Stop (under the Editor Bar on the far right), and in the CMYK fields enter C=0, M=0, Y=0, K=20. Click OK to set this Color Stop to a light gray. Name this gradient 60% to 20% and click the New button to save it.

STEP THREE: Drag the Gradient tool from the bottom of your image window to the top so the lighter shade is on top (as shown).

continued

Quick Tip:
Nudging layers
You can nudge layers around pixel-by-pixel by switching to the Move tool (press the letter "v") then using the Arrow keys on your keyboard to nudge (slowly move) your layer either up, down, left or right.

STEP FOUR: Press Shift-M until the Elliptical Marquee tool appears in the Toolbox. Draw a selection in the center of your background. Press "q" to enter Quick Mask mode, and you'll see your selection represented by a clear circle, surrounded by a red tint.

STEP FIVE: Go under the Filter menu, under Blur, and choose Gaussian Blur. Enter 30 pixels (65 pixels for high-res, 300-ppi images) and click OK to blur the edges of your selection while in Quick Mask mode.

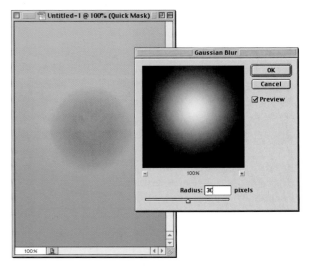

STEP SIX: Press "q" again to leave Quick Mask and return to Standard mode. Press Command-L (PC: Control-L) to bring up the Levels dialog. Drag the lower-left Output Levels slider to the right to around 200, and a soft spotlight effect will appear on your gradient background. Click OK. Press Command-D (PC: Control-D) to Deselect.

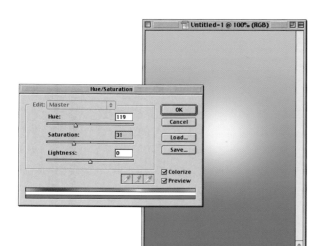

STEP SEVEN: Press Command-U (PC: Control-U) for Hue/Saturation. Check the Colorize box in the lower right-hand corner. Move the Hue slider to the right until the edges of your spotlight become green (around 117). You can also lower the Saturation slider if your glow color looks a bit too intense .

STEP EIGHT: Open your object image (in this case, a cellular phone), press the letter "v" to switch to the Move tool, then drag this object onto your spotlight document. Position it in the middle of your spotlight. Next, press Command-J (PC: Control-J) to duplicate your phone layer.

STEP NINE: Press Command-T (PC: Control-T) to bring up Free Transform. Hold the Control key (PC: Right-click), then click-and-hold inside the Free Transform bounding box to bring up a contextual menu. Choose Flip Vertical, then press Return (or Enter) to lock in your changes.

Quick Tip:
Escape that dialog box!
Almost anytime you're in a dialog box in Photoshop and want to get out of there fast, you can press the Escape key and the box will disappear with no changes made (the same as pressing the Cancel button in the dialog box).

continued

Quick Tip: Using the new Fill control

In Photoshop 7, there's a new field in the Layers palette called Fill. This has actually been in Photoshop since version 6.0, but previously it resided in the seldom-seen Blending Options dialog (which appears within the Layer Styles dialog box. Go figure!). What this puppy does is enable you to lower the Opacity (or fill) of a layer while leaving any Layer Styles applied to the layer at full intensity. Here's how to see it in action (and then it will make more sense): Create some type, add a Drop Shadow Layer Style, then lower the Fill (in the Layers palette) to 0% and all will become clear (young grasshopper).

STEP TEN: With the Move tool, drag this copy of your object down just below the original object to where their bottoms are just overlapping (as shown). Lower the Opacity of the copy to around 40%, then in the Layers palette, drag this copy layer down below Layer 1 (your original object layer). Go under the Filter menu, under Blur, and choose Motion Blur.

STEP ELEVEN: For Angle enter 0°, for Distance enter 13 (try 30 for high-res images), and click OK to blur the reflection a bit and put the focus back on the phone. Press "b" to get the Brush tool. In the Brushes palette, choose a soft-edged brush. In the Options Bar, change the Blend Mode to Behind, and lower the Opacity to 60%. Hold the Shift key and draw a straight line under the phone to add a soft shadow. Press Shift-M to get the Rectangular Marquee tool.

STEP TWELVE: In the Layers palette, click on the Background layer, then make a selection of the bottom half of the background. Press Command-J (PC: Control-J) to put this selected area on its own layer. Press "v" to switch to the Move tool, and drag this layer down until the edge of it appears just above the bottom edge of your object to complete the effect (as shown).

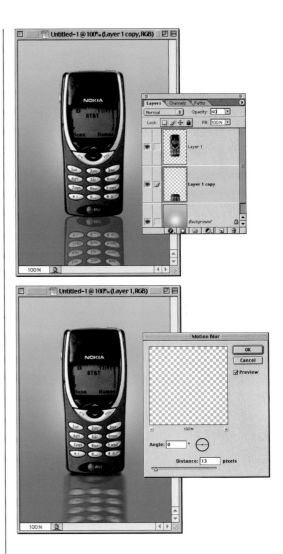

Illustrator Arc Trick

This is a trick I used to do from time to time using Adobe Illustrator, because even with Photoshop's Warp Text feature you couldn't really pull it off because this particular "arc" leaves the top of the letters straight and only arcs the bottom of the letter. This is a very popular technique in commercial logos and especially in logos for sports teams.

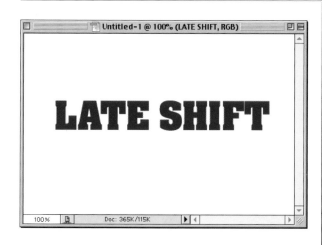

STEP ONE: Open a new document (RGB mode). Press "t" to get the Type tool and create your type.

STEP TWO: Go under the Layer menu, under Type, and choose Create Work Path. This will put a path around your type as if you drew it with the Pen tool. You'll be able to see the path around your letters.

STEP THREE: You no longer need your Type layer, so drag it to the Trash at the bottom of the Layers palette to delete it. Your path will still be visible (as shown). Press Shift-M to switch to the Elliptical Marquee tool. Draw a large ellipse and position it under your type (you can use the Spacebar to reposition your ellipse as you draw it). This will be used as a guide for the bottom of your arc letters.

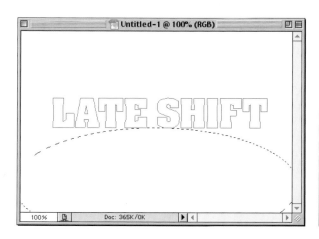

continued

Quick Tip:
Clearing out all those guides

If you use Photoshop's non-printing guides, they can really clutter up the screen sometimes, so if you want to get rid of them all quickly—don't drag them one-by-one back to the rulers (from whence they came). Instead, just go under the View menu and choose Clear Guides.

Quick Tip:
Aligning objects on different layers

You can align objects on different layers by linking them together (click once in the center column beside each layer you want to link), going under the Layer menu, under Align Linked, and choosing how you want your layers aligned from the menu.

STEP FOUR: While your selection is still in place, create a new blank layer by clicking on the New Layer icon at the bottom of the Layers palette. Go under the Edit menu and choose Stroke. For Width, choose 1 pixel, click on the Color Swatch and choose a color for your guide (I used PANTONE 2727, which is close to Photoshop's own guide color), and click OK. Deselect by pressing Command-D (PC: Control-D).

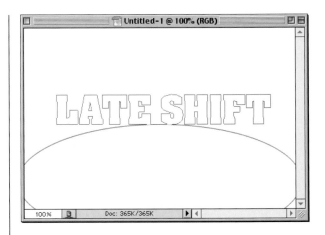

STEP FIVE: Press "z" to switch to the Zoom tool and use it to zoom in on the first letter in your word. Press Shift-A until you get the Direct Selection tool and click on the first letter to select the path.

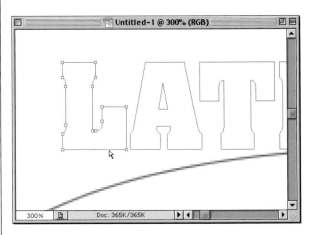

STEP SIX: Press Command-T (PC: Control-T) to bring up Free Transform. Click on the bottom-center point and drag straight down until the bottom of the letter touches the top of your "blue arc guide." Press Return (PC: Enter) to lock in your transformation.

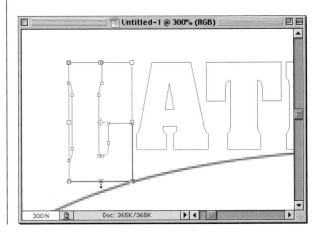

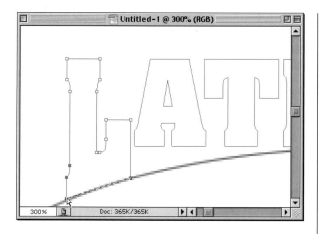

STEP SEVEN: Chances are, one part of the letter will still be a little ways above the arc. You should still have the Direct Selection tool, so use it to draw a selection around the bottom points of the letter that need to be pulled down to meet the arc. Then click on the path and drag it downward to meet the arc.

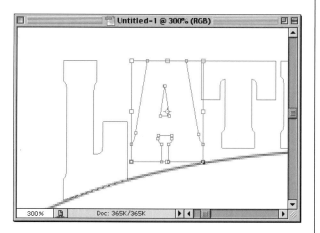

STEP EIGHT: Now, click the Direct Selection tool on the next letter. Press Command-T (PC: Control-T), and drag the bottom-center point down again to meet the top of the arc. Press Return (PC: Enter) to accept your transformation.

STEP NINE: Again, you'll have to select either one side of the letter, or one side of the descender, to drag down and make it fit to the arc. You may be able to select just one point, or you may have to select three or more and move them as a group to meet the arc. Repeat the process letter-by-letter (hey, I never said this was a fast technique).

Quick Tip:
Another Photoshop prank

Thanks to Photoshop 7, you can now pull one of my favorite Adobe Illustrator pranks in Photoshop on your Photoshop co-workers, friends, etc. that will drive them just this side of insane. That's thanks to the fact that in 7, Adobe put a pop-up list of language dictionaries in the Character palette for hyphenation and spelling. The simple trick is to change the dictionary from English USA to English UK. The next time they create some para-graph type, or run the spell checker…well, you get the picture. I've pulled this prank and in each instance, if they see the word English when the glance at the palette, they assume it's correct, and so far they've never noticed it was changed from English USA to English UK. Eventually, they just give up and do a full reinstall of Photoshop. It's a great way to turn some-body's day upside-down.

continued

Quick Tip:
Layer naming done right

After all these years, the naming of layers has been finally done right in Photoshop 7. Instead of Option-clicking (PC: Alt-clicking) to bring up a dialog box for naming your layers, just double-click on the layer's name, and the name becomes highlighted right there in the Layers palette. You can then type in a new name without any annoying dialog box at all...Ah, life is good.

STEP TEN: Once you've adjusted all the letters individually, press Command-0 (PC: Control-0) to view the overall arc (as shown). Now, go to the Layers palette and delete your blue oval guide layer by dragging it to the Trash icon at the bottom of the Layers palette.

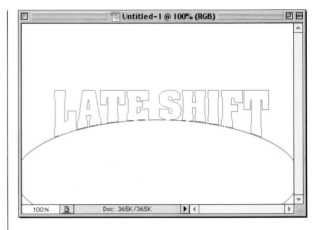

STEP ELEVEN: Go to the Paths palette and click on Work Path to choose your entire path. Then press Command-Return (PC: Control-Enter) to convert your path into a selection (as shown). In the Layers palette create a new layer by clicking on the New Layer icon.

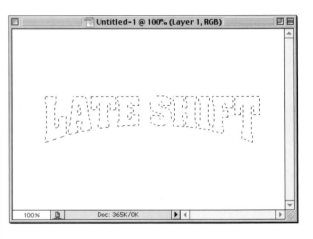

STEP TWELVE: Set your Foreground color to dark blue and press Option-Delete (PC: Alt-Backspace) to fill your type. Deselect by pressing Command-D (PC: Control-D). To stroke your type in yellow, choose Stroke from the Layer Styles pop-up menu, change the color to yellow, set the Width at 3 pixels, and click OK. Last, click on the background layer, press "d" to make your Foreground color, black then press Option-Delete (PC: Alt-Backspace) to fill your background with black.

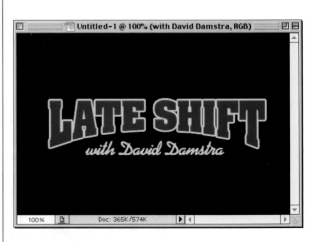

Spotlight Effect

I first saw a similar technique used in a print ad for a Ricoh digital camera, and what I particularly liked was the "noise" in the light beam that truly gave it a realistic look. You can tweak this technique a number of different ways, on different colored backgrounds, even on top of photographic images, once you've learned how to do it.

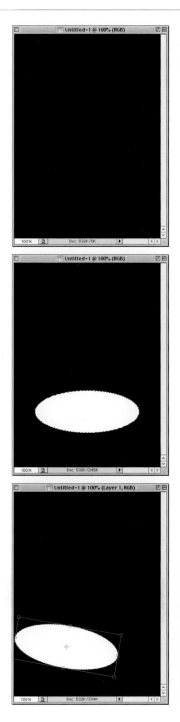

STEP ONE: Start with a 72-ppi document in RGB mode; in this case I created a 5.5x7" image. Press the letter "d" to reset your Foreground color to black, then press Option-Delete (PC: Alt-Backspace) to fill your background with black.

STEP TWO: Press Shift-M to switch to the Elliptical Marquee tool and draw a horizontal ellipse. Press the letter "x" to set your Foreground color to white. Press Option-Delete (PC: Alt-Backspace) to fill the ellipse with white.

STEP THREE: Press Command-T (PC: Control-T) to bring up the Free Transform function. Move your pointer outside the Free Transform bounding box, then click, hold, and drag downward to rotate the ellipse (as shown). Press Return (PC: Enter) to lock in the transformation. Press Command-D (PC: Control-D) to Deselect.

continued

Quick Tip:
Speeding up Photoshop by merging layers

Photoshop is a slave to file size: the larger the size of your file, generally speaking, the slower Photoshop goes (especially if you're short on RAM). Every time you add a layer, it significantly adds to the overall file size of your image. That's why it's sometimes a good idea to merge together layers that you don't think you'll need to adjust later on.

For example, if you have ten layers of type, you can save a lot of file size by rasterizing each of the Type layers and merging them into one layer by clicking on the top text layer and pressing Command-E (PC: Control-E) to Merge down. This takes the layer you're on and merges it with the layer directly beneath it. When you do this, your file size shrinks, and in many cases, Photoshop goes faster. Be careful when merging layers with Layer Effects applied, though, because they have Blend Modes assigned by default, and merging them can change or hide those effects.

When loading Action sets
in older versions of
Photoshop, you had to do
more digging than an
archaeologist to find
them (they were buried
deep within your drive,
nested inside folder after
folder). Not so in the
latest versions of
Photoshop; now they're
just one click away. Here's
how to load actions: From
the Window menu,
choose Show Actions to
bring up the Actions
palette. From the palette's
drop-down menu, choose
one of the Action sets at
the bottom. They'll
appear as a folder in your
Actions palette. Click the
right-facing triangle
beside the folder's name
to show the contents of
the folder. Scroll down
to the action you want
and click on it. Then click
the Play button (it's
the right-facing triangle
at the bottom of the
Actions palette) to run
it. Pretty sweet! Some
of the actions are pretty
decent. Others are... well,
let's just say they rhyme
with "fame."

STEP FOUR: To soften the
edges of the ellipse, go under
the Filter menu, under Blur, and
choose Gaussian Blur. Enter 6
pixels and click OK. In the
Layers palette, click on the
New Layer icon to create a new
layer, then press "g" to get the
Gradient tool. In the Options
Bar, click on the down-facing
arrow next to the Gradient
thumbnail to bring up the
Gradient Picker.

STEP FIVE: In the Gradient
Picker, choose the second
gradient from the left (the
Foreground to Transparent
gradient). Next, in the Options
Bar, click on the Reflected
Gradient (it's the fourth icon
from the left). Choose a warm
gray as your Foreground color
(I used PANTONE Warm Gray 6).
Click at the top center of your
white ellipse and drag to the
right about 1" past its edge to
apply the Reflected Gradient.

STEP SIX: Press the letter
"L" to switch to the Lasso
tool, and drag a selection
around the bottom of your
gradient that extends into the
bottom third of your white
ellipse (as shown). Go under
the Select menu and choose
Feather. For the Feather Radius,
enter 10 pixels (use 30 for
high-res, 300-ppi images), and
click OK. Then press Delete
(PC: Backspace) to remove
the gradient below the ellipse.

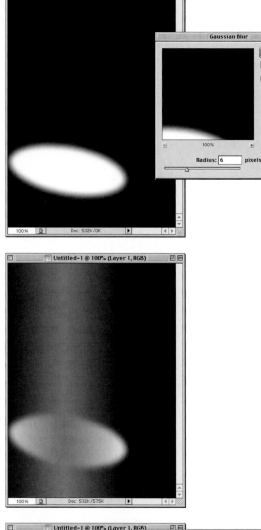

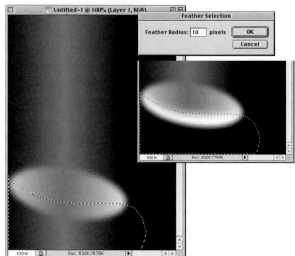

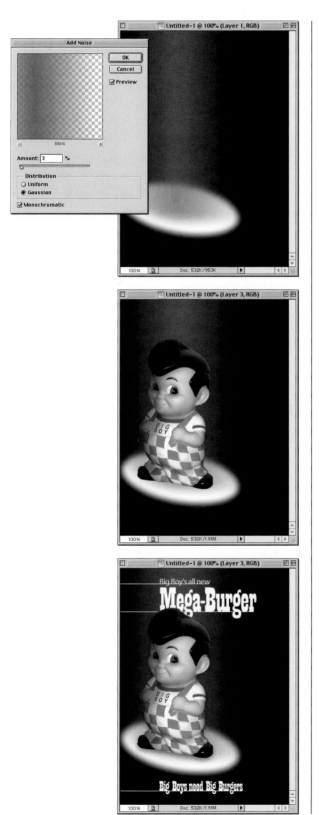

STEP SEVEN: Press Command-D (PC: Control-D) to Deselect. Go under the Filter menu, under Noise, and choose Add Noise. For Amount, choose 3, for Distribution choose Gaussian, turn on the Monochromatic checkbox, and then click OK. In the Layers palette, lower the Opacity of this layer to 75%.

STEP EIGHT: Open the object you want to place on your background image. Using the selection tool of your choice, select the object. Once it's selected, use the Move tool to drag the object onto your background image. Choose Drop Shadow from the Layer Style pop-up menu at the bottom of the Layers palette.

STEP NINE: For Opacity enter 85%, for Angle enter 90°, for Size enter 10, and click OK to apply a soft drop shadow. Go under the Layer menu, under Layer Style, and choose Create Layer to put the shadow on its own separate layer. Switch to the shadow layer in the Layers palette and use the Eraser tool to erase the parts of the shadow that appear above the bottom of the object to complete the effect.

Quick Tip:
What's in a name?
Adobe made a tiny change to a menu item that makes a whole lot of sense. To hide any of Photoshop's visual indicators (such as type highlighting, the Free Transform Bounding Box, non-printing guides, Slice borders, etc.) you would choose Show Extras. That's right, to hide the extras, you'd choose Show Extras. It was one of those menu commands that really made you scratch your head. Adobe changed that in Photoshop 7, and now it's just called "Extras." Either you want them or you don't, and as always, a checkmark next to the menu item lets you know if it's toggled on or off.

Quick Tip:
Name it the slow way?

Now that Photoshop has fixed the process of naming layers, do you miss the old Layer Properties dialog box? I know you don't, but just humor me. Hey, there actually is a reason you might want to access that annoying box—to color code your layer (ahhh, you forgot about that, didn't you?). Anyway, if you miss that annoying dialog, just Control-click (PC: Right-click) on the layer's thumbnail in the Layers palette and in the resulting pop-up menu, choose Layer Properties.

Comment Balloons

This technique caught my eye when I was watching TV one night and saw an ad for Cingular® Wireless. Later, I noticed that this same technique started popping up in their print ads. I wrote a tutorial on it in *Photoshop User* magazine, but thanks to Photoshop 7's additional built-in custom Shapes, the version shown here is much simpler and faster to do.

STEP ONE: Open a new document in RGB mode at 72 ppi. Click on the New Layer icon at the bottom of the Layers palette to create a new blank layer. Press Shift-U until the Custom Shape tool appears in the Toolbox (as shown).

STEP TWO: Once you have the Custom Shape tool, go up in the Options Bar and click on the down-facing triangle beside the current Shape thumbnail to bring up the Custom Shape Picker. When the Picker appears, click on the shape that looks like a cartoon "talk bubble" as shown (it's the one that follows the "No!" sign).

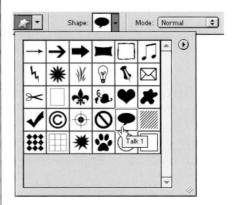

STEP THREE: Make sure that in the Options Bar you have the Fill Pixels icon (the third from the left) chosen so you create a filled shape and not a Shape layer or a Path. Then, use the Shape tool to draw a "talk bubble" on your layer.

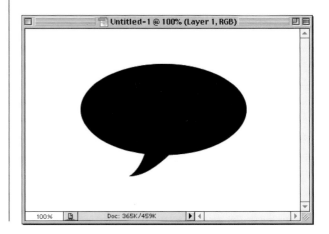

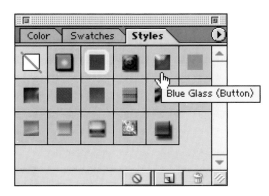

STEP FOUR: Go under the Window menu and choose Styles. In the Styles palette, click on the fifth default style from the left (it's called Blue Glass Button). This will apply the Blue Glass Button style to your balloon shape.

Quick Tip:
Slide it with your Arrow keys
In the Layers palette, you can move the Opacity and Fill sliders using your Left and Right Arrow keys. Each time you press the key, they decrease/increase 1%. To have them move in 10% increments, just hold the Shift key as you press the Arrow keys.

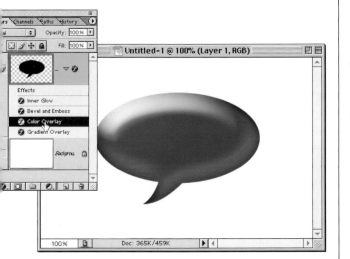

STEP FIVE: In the Layers palette, we need to remove the color from our shape, so go under Effects, click directly on the word "Color Overlay" and drag it to the Trash icon at the bottom of the Layers palette to delete the effect.

STEP SIX: In the Layer Style pop-up menu at the bottom of the Layers palette, choose Drop Shadow, and click OK to apply a drop shadow to your balloon. Last, to complete the effect, just add some type and you're done.

Quick Tip:
Brush changes update in two places at once

Now that Photoshop 7 has brushes available to you in two places (from the Options Bar and from the floating Brushes palette) you'd think that you'd have to go back and forth updating one or the other when you save or edit a brush. Luckily, Adobe designed it so changes you make in one palette are automatically carried through to the other palette, so that when you're editing and creating brushes, fear not—the other palette will know what you're doing and will be updated appropriately.

Transparent TV Type

I call this "TV Type" because you see a similar effect in the lower right-hand corner of your TV screen all the time. Although it's ubiquitous on television, I've seen this effect used in print and on the Web over and over again, and I like that it can be as subtle or powerful as you want just by using the Opacity slider.

STEP ONE: Open the image to which you want to add the effect.

STEP TWO: Press "d" to set your Foreground color to black. Press "t" to get the Type tool, then create your type.

STEP THREE: We now want to run a filter on the text, but we can't run a filter on a Type layer, so we'll first have to convert it to an image layer. Go to the Layers palette, Control-click (PC: Right-click) on your Type layer's name, and choose Rasterize Layer from the pop-up menu to convert it from a Type layer to an image layer.

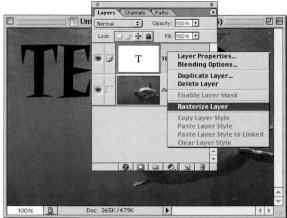

STEP FOUR: In the Layers palette, click on the Lock Transparent Pixels icon (it's the first icon from the left). Go under the Filter menu, under Stylize, and choose Emboss. When the Emboss dialog box appears, increase the Height to 5 (try 9 for high-res images) and click OK to apply a hard bevel to your type. Your type will turn gray, with highlights and shadows along the edges (as shown).

STEP FIVE: In the Layers palette, change the Blend Mode of this layer from Normal to Hard Light to make the gray fill disappear while leaving the highlights and shadows in place.

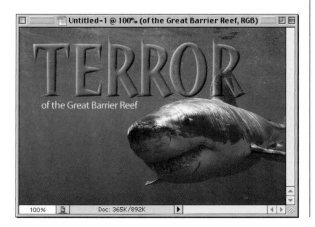

STEP SIX: Last, to round and smooth out the effect, with Lock Transparent Pixels still turned on, go under the Filter menu, under Blur, and choose Gaussian Blur. Enter 2 pixels (try 6 for high-res images), and click OK to apply soft shading inside the letter, completing the effect (as shown).

Quick Tip:
The secret to Batch Ranking

If you're using Photoshop 7's handy new File Browser, you probably already know that it allows you to rank images (Rank A, B, C, D, or E) to help you sort and organize them. However, what if you need to rank 50 or 60 images as Rank A? Do you have to go to 50 or 60 images individually and rank them one-by-one? It would seem so, because there's nothing in the drop-down palette about it, but here's the little secret tip that will make all your dreams come true (okay, it's something short of that, but it's a good tip). Don't use the File Browser's drop-down menu. Instead, first Shift-click on all the images you want to rank, and then Control-click (PC: Right-click) on one of them to bring up the contextual menu. Choose the rank you want from there, and it will automatically rank every file you chose. Thanks to Adobe's Graphics Evangelist Julieanne Kost for sharing this cool inside tip.

Quick Tip:
Paint tools have Blend Modes too

You're probably familiar with layer Blend Modes, where you change how a layer interacts with the layers beneath it. In Normal mode, it doesn't interact; it just covers whatever's beneath it. Well, Photoshop's paint tools have the same feature, and choosing any Blend Mode (other than Normal) allows your paint to interact with (be affected by) the colors in the image you paint on. These Blend Modes are accessed from the Options Bar when you have a paint tool selected.

Painting Away Color

You see this technique widely used in print ads and on TV. It's used very effectively in a print campaign for the Las Vegas nightclub Studio 54 (in the MGM Grand) where everyone in the image is black and white, but one person appears in full color, and it totally draws your eye. Here's how it's done.

STEP ONE: Open a color RGB image.

STEP TWO: Click on the Brush too, and up in the Options Bar, switch the Blend Mode from Normal to Color.

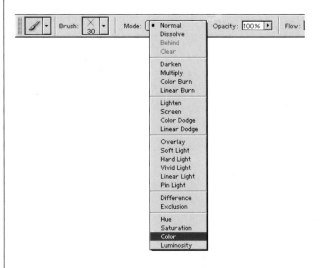

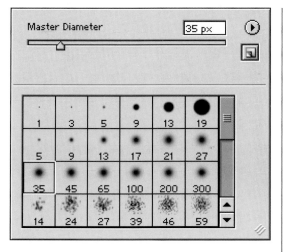

STEP THREE: From the Brushes palette, choose a soft-edged, medium-sized brush.

STEP FOUR: Start painting. As you paint, the color will disappear, leaving just grayscale in its wake.

Quick Tip:
How to delete extra brushes

If you've created a brush (or a number of brushes) that you don't want to appear in your Brushes palette, all you have to do is go to the Brushes Picker in the Options Bar and hold the Option key (PC: Alt key) and your cursor will change to an icon of a pair of scissors. Click once with the scissors on the brush that you want to delete and it's gone. If you decide that you want all of your new brushes deleted and that you want to return to the original factory default brushes, choose Reset Brushes from the Picker's pop-down menu.

Quick Tip:
Where the tablet controls are hidden

In Photoshop 7, Adobe moved the controls for pressure-sensitive tablet users (generally just called "Wacom Tablet users") into the expanded Brushes palette. On the left-hand side of the palette, you'll see a list of options. If you click on any of these options, their settings will appear in the palette. In many of the options' panels you'll find a pop-up menu for "Controls." That's where you'll find Pen Pressure, Pen Tilt, Thumbwheel control, and more.

Sparkle Trail

I saw a similar technique to this on a poster at Walt Disney World advertising their "Park Hopper" pass. The poster had a magic carpet with a trail of sparkles following it. I got up close and gave it a good look, and sure enough, it looked like a combination of Photoshop brushes. I thought it would be pretty cool to combine a number of brushes to create just one "sparkle trail" brush.

STEP ONE: Open a new document in RGB mode at 72 dpi. Press "d" to set your Foreground color to black, then create a new blank layer by clicking on the New Layer icon at the bottom of the Layers palette.

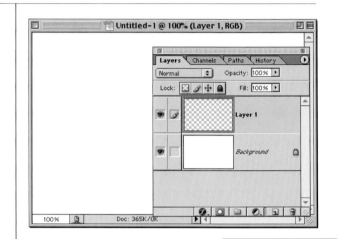

STEP TWO: Press "b" to get the Brush tool, then go under the Window menu and choose Brushes. Choose the 35-pixel, soft-edged, round brush from the default set of brushes. Click the brush in a few random spots within your image area. Don't paint a stroke; just click once for each spot.

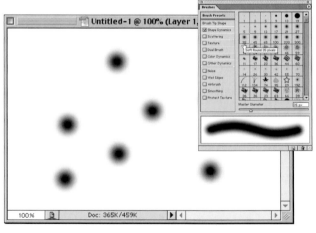

STEP THREE: Back in the Brushes palette, switch to the 21-pixel, soft-edged, round brush, and do the same thing—click once in a few random spots.

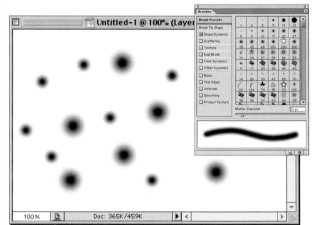

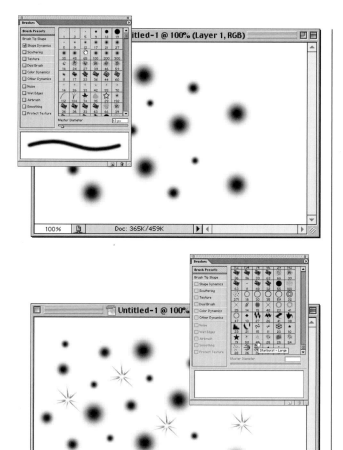

STEP FOUR: Now, switch to the 13-pixel, soft-edged, round brush and do the same thing again—clicking once in a few random spots.

STEP FIVE: In the Brushes palette's pop-down menu, choose Assorted Brushes, and when the dialog box appears, click OK to load these new brushes. Choose the 49-pixel brush named "Starburst - Large," and again click in a few random areas.

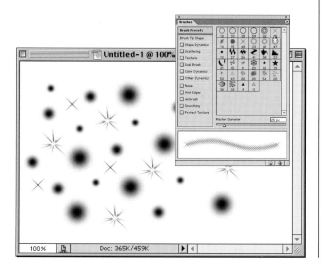

STEP SIX: Now, in the Assorted Brushes set in the Brushes palette, choose the 25-pixel brush named "Crosshatch 1," and again click a few times in random areas.

Quick Tip:
Renaming brushes
Don't like the name you gave your brush (which instead of "39-pixel soft-edge," you had named it "Frank," or "Cathy," or "Snoop Dogg")? Just Control-click (PC: Right-click) on the brush, choose Rename brush from the pop-up menu, and when the dialog box appears, type in a new name and click OK.

continued

Quick Tip:
F5 is back, baby!

Back in Photoshop 5 and 5.5, to bring up the floating Brushes palette, you'd press the F5 key on your extended keyboard. Well, when Photoshop 6.0 came out, the floating Brushes palette went away, and pressing F5 was just an exercise in futility. (When Photoshop 6.0 first came out, you could see Photoshop users pressing F5 over and over again, sobbing, "Why? Why!!!") Thankfully in Photoshop 7, the floating Brushes palette is back and along with it Adobe resurrected the classic F5 shortcut. Life is good again.

STEP SEVEN: Press "m" to switch to the Rectangular Marquee tool. Hold the Shift key and draw a square selection encompassing as many of the black paint daubs as possible (as shown). Now, go under the Edit menu and choose Define Brush. When the dialog box appears, name your brush Sparkles, and click OK to add your brush to the Brush presets.

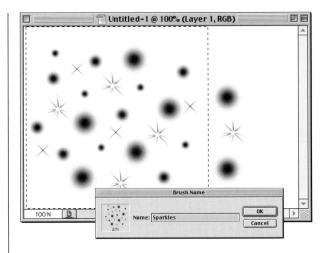

STEP EIGHT: Your new brush will be the last brush in the Brushes palette. Click on it to make it active (as shown).

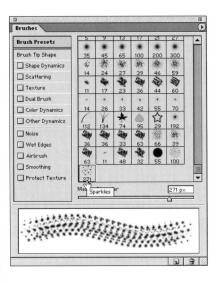

STEP NINE: In the list of options on the left side of the Brushes palette, click on the word "Brush Tip Shape" to make those options visible. Lower the Diameter of your brush to around 156 and increase the spacing to 50%. A preview of your changes appears at the bottom of the dialog box.

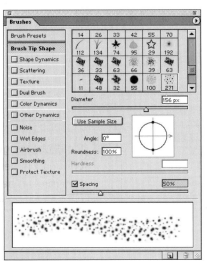

STEP TEN: Now, click on the word "Shape Dynamics" to make those options visible. Under Control, choose Fade, and enter 25 to have your brush strokes fade off (as shown in the preview at the bottom of the palette).

STEP ELEVEN: Then, click on the word "Scattering" to make its options visible. Increase the Scatter amount to 142%, the Count to 3, and the Count Jitter to 35%. (Note: these are not absolute values, so feel free to experiment. I was trying to create more of a flowing, random pattern, and used the preview at the bottom of the palette as a visual guide, and you should as well—let that be your guide, rather than the numbers.)

Quick Tip:
Starting from scratch with your brush

You want to edit a brush, or create a new one for that matter, and you want to start with a clean slate (i.e., you want all the option settings for the various brush controls set back to their defaults). Then, in the Brushes palette, click on the options you want to edit (e.g., Brush Dynamics, Scattering, Texture, etc.), and from the palette's drop-down menu choose "Clear Brush Controls." This will clear all the current settings and it also deselects the entire panel, so you may have to click on the option you want again, but when you do, all the default settings will be in place.

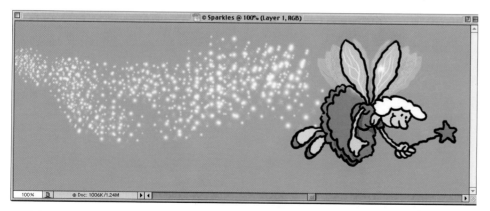

STEP TWELVE: Last, open the image where you want to add the sparkles. Add a new blank layer by clicking on the New Layer icon at the bottom of the Layers palette. Press "d" then "x" to set your Foreground color to white, then click-and-drag your new custom brush within your image, and you'll get the effect shown here.

Before you try the techniques in this chapter, it's important to understand what hi-tech interface design is.

Face Off
Hi-tech Interface Design

Many of you may already have a full understanding, but before you go any further into this chapter, I think it would be wise (for all parties involved) to test your understanding with a few simple questions. If you're able to answer these three simple queries without a single wrong answer, then this chapter is for you. However, if you miss one or more answers, you might want to skip ahead to the chapter on rainbows, puppies, and cuddly little teddy bears. Ready? Begin:
(1) Which of these is the name of a character in the new Star Trek Enterprise *series? (a) Lt. Shaq, (b) Ensign Puff Daddy, (c) First Officer Eminem, or (d) Subcommander T'Pol.*

(2) On Star Trek the Next Generation, *which of these is NOT a real location within the ship? (a) The Holo Deck, (b) The bridge, (c) Ten-Forward, or (d) Central Perk.*

(3) Which Star Trek TNG *character wound up on* Deep Space Nine *as well? (a) Commander Waffle, (b) First Officer Sausage, (c) Lt. Eggs'n'bacon, or (d) Lt. Worf.*

The answers are (and these are so obvious I hate to even write them): 1 b, 2 a, and 3 b. (They're actually all d of course, but you have to admit, it made you stop for just a second, didn't it?)

Quick Tip:
Want to increase your Canvas Size? Check Relative

Want to stop doing so much math when you go to the Canvas Size dialog box to add some extra space? Just check the Relative box (added in version 7) and type in how much space you want to add, rather than trying to determine how much to add to your current dimensions. Try it once and you'll see what I mean.

Designing the Core of Your Interface

This is the easiest technique we've found yet for creating the core of your interface (the core being the foundation upon which the rest of your interface is built). This version uses fewer steps than ever and lets the Layer Styles, rather than Channels, do most of the work.

STEP ONE: Open a new document in RGB mode. Press "p" to get the Pen tool. Create the outside shape of your interface using straight lines at different angles (no curves). When you get back to your starting point, click on it to complete your path. In this case, after creating the first path (top) I created a second below it, but it's not necessary.

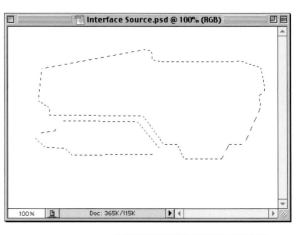

STEP TWO: Press Command-Return (PC: Control-Enter) to turn your path into a selection.

STEP THREE: Go under the Select menu and choose Save Selection to save your selection as a Channel. When the dialog appears, click OK. Then press Command-D (PC: Control-D) to Deselect.

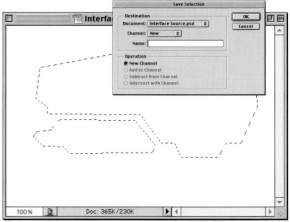

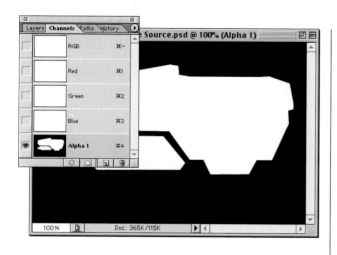

STEP FOUR: Go to the Channels palette and click on Alpha 1 (your saved interface channel). Your Alpha channel will be displayed onscreen (as shown).

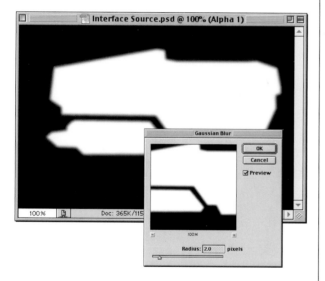

STEP FIVE: To round the corners of your interface, go under the Filter menu, under Blur, and choose Gaussian Blur. Apply a 2-pixel blur and click OK (the higher the blur, the rounder the corners will appear). Note: For high-res, 300-ppi images, apply a 5-pixel or more blur. To remove the blurriness and to make your round corners appear smooth, press Command-L (PC: Control-L) to bring up Levels.

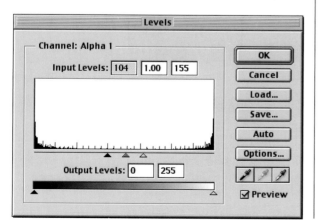

STEP SIX: When the dialog box appears, slide the far left and far right Input Levels sliders toward the middle (as shown). As you drag them, you'll notice the blurriness disappear and the corners start to smooth. Drag them until they are about $^1/_{16}$" from each other.

Quick Tip:
Why feathering is so important

Feathering affects the edge of your selection, and one of the main reasons to use it is to smooth the transition between your selection and the area surrounding it. Without the feathering there would be a harsh, obvious edge where your selection ends and the background begins.

This is a very popular technique in photo retouching, where it's used to smooth the transition in areas that have been copied and pasted to hide defects or unwanted elements in the image.

continued

Quick Tip:
Loading Selections

Numerous times in this book I ask you to put a selection around the contents of a layer by Command-clicking (PC: Control-clicking) on the layer's name in the Layers palette. You can use this same trick for loading Alpha Channels as a selection. Just go to the Channels palette and Command-click (PC: Control-click) on the channel to instantly load it as a selection. An even better trick is just to press Option-Command-4 (PC: Alt-Control-4) to load your first Alpha Channel. If you have other saved Alpha channels, you'd press 5, 6, etc.

STEP SEVEN: Click OK, and the outside of your interface becomes rounded (as shown).

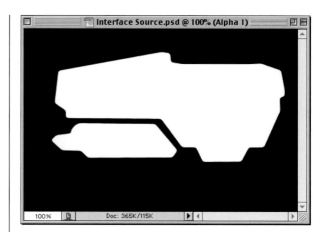

STEP EIGHT: Return to the Layers palette and click on the Background layer. Create a new blank layer by clicking on the New Layer icon at the bottom of the palette, then press Option-Command-4 (PC: Alt-Control-4) to load your Alpha Channel as a selection. Set a light gray as your Foreground color, and then fill the selection by pressing Option-Delete (PC: Alt-Backspace) as shown. Deselect by pressing Command-D (PC: Control-D).

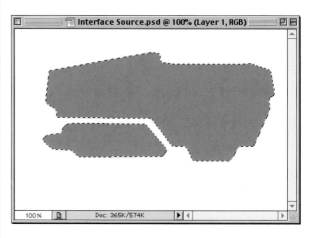

STEP NINE: Press "d" then "x" to switch your Foreground color to white. Press "m" to get the Rectangular Marquee tool and select inside areas of your interface. Press Delete (PC: Backspace) to knock these shapes out of your base interface (as shown). These are the areas you will fill with buttons, navigation, content, etc.

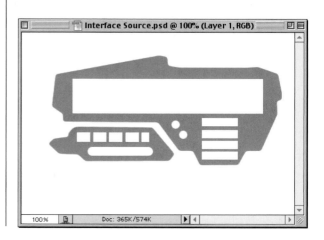

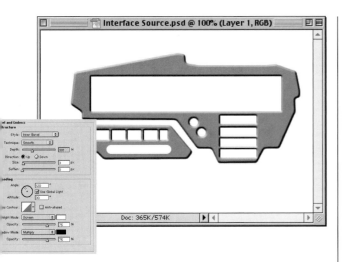

STEP TEN: Choose Bevel and Emboss from the Layer Style pop-up menu at the bottom of the Layers palette. When the dialog box appears, lower the Size to 2, increase the Depth to 300%, and click OK to add a bevel to your interface (as shown). At this point, the base of your interface is complete. The next two steps are totally optional for adding a metallic effect.

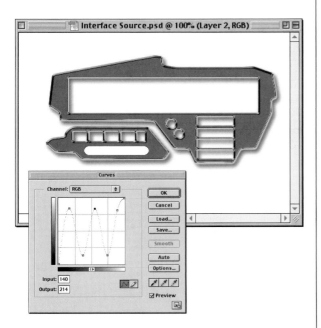

STEP ELEVEN: Add a new blank layer and drag it directly beneath your interface layer. Then, click back on your interface layer and press Command-E (PC: Control-E) to merge this interface layer with the layer beneath it. Press Command-M (PC: Control-M) to bring up the Curves dialog box. Create a curve similar to the one shown here, by clicking along the curve to add points. You'll add five points to create this curve. Click OK in the Curves dialog box to apply a metallic effect to your interface.

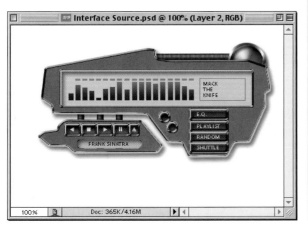

STEP TWELVE: Lastly, choose Drop Shadow from the Layer Styles pop-up menu to complete the base of your interface. Remember, this is just the base—what makes an interface cool is all the hi-tech goodies you add to it from later in this chapter. In the example shown here, I added buttons on layers beneath the interface, a Bevel and Emboss, and some text.

Quick Tip:
Why we run the Lighting Effects filter on the Background layer
You'll notice that in this book we often apply the Lighting Effects filter to the Background layer rather than a new blank layer. If you try to apply the Lighting Effects filter to a blank layer, you'll get an error message that reads "Could not complete the Lighting Effects command because the selected area is empty." It's right, ya know—a new layer is just an empty, transparent layer. However, the Background layer is actually filled with white, so you can apply the filter there. That's why we run it on the Background layer, load our original selection, and then put that up on its own layer.

Quick Tip:
Arrows, the easy way

You probably already know that if you're using the Line tool, you can add Arrow heads to your lines by going up to the Options Bar and clicking on the downward-facing triangle at the end of the Tool icons. A little dialog box will appear that lets you determine the Width, Length, and Concavity (whatever that is). That's math. Math is hard. Maybe that's why Adobe included a full set of very well-designed arrows in Photoshop 7 as custom shapes—all you have to do is switch to the Custom Shape tool, click on the Shape Picker (in the Options Bar) and from its drop-down menu choose Arrows. Ah, life is beautiful.

Creating Your Core Interface Using Shapes

This is another technique for creating your core interface, but rather than using the Pen tool, it uses Photoshop's Shape tools. The advantages—it's very fast and incredibly easy. The downside—you don't have quite as much control, and…well, that's all I could think of.

STEP ONE: Open a new document in RGB mode. Press "d" to make black your Foreground color. Then, create a new layer by clicking on the New Layer icon at the bottom of the Layers palette.

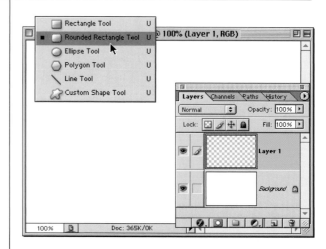

STEP TWO: Press Shift-U until the Rounded Rectangle Tool appears in the Toolbox. In the Options Bar, make sure the first icon (Shape Layers) is selected, then create the first piece of your base interface. This will add a special Shape layer to your Layers palette. Don't let that throw you, because it's only temporary.

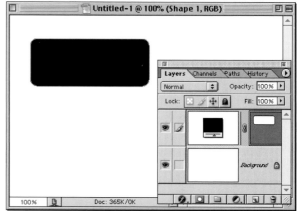

STEP THREE: Hold the Shift key, and you can continue adding more shapes over your original shape. Hold the Shift key, and the shapes will not create additional shape layers—they'll be added to your original shape, and you'll see the outlines (paths) of each shape as you work.

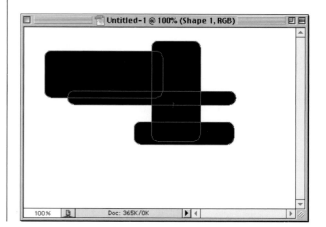

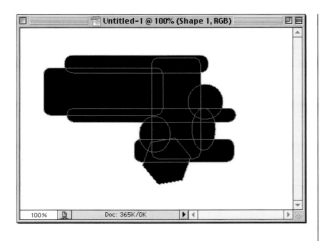

STEP FOUR: You can change to other Shape tools and add additional dimension to your interface base. Here I used the Ellipse tool and the Polygon tool (set to 6 sides) to expand upon my original shapes made with the Rounded Rectangle tool (as shown).

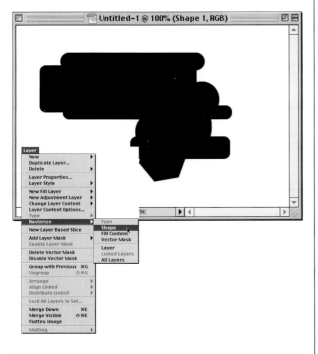

STEP FIVE: When the outside of your shape looks about right, go under the Layer menu, under Rasterize, and choose Shape. This converts your vector Shape layer into a regular image layer. That's the technique, but for the purposes of example, I took it a few steps farther. I started by filling the interface with a light gray and adding a Bevel and Emboss Layer Style.

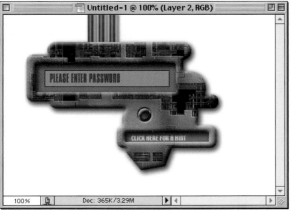

STEP SIX: Next I added a rectangular selection and pressed Delete (PC: Backspace) to knock a hole out of the interface. I created a smaller rectangle on the lower right and knocked that out as well. Then I created a new blank layer beneath the knockouts and filled them with a pale green. I added a texture to the interface, along with metal bars and a blue recessed button. (You can find all these techniques in this chapter; the only difference is that I didn't use the scan lines on the metal bars.) And, of course, I also added a drop shadow.

Quick Tip:
Creating your own textures

If you want to create your own textures in Photoshop, here are a couple of tips that might help:

• The Clouds filter is a great place to start building your textures because it already has a texture.

• Many textures are built using the Add Noise filter as a base. Generally, you'd start by filling the Background layer with a color and then running the Add Noise filter.

• Use Gradients as your base and build upon that. You can run filters, such as Polar Coordinates, Waves, Ripple, Glass, etc. on top of gradients to create your own custom textures.

• If you started with a noise background, try adding the Motion Blur filter to enhance your background.

• Use the Texturizer filter to add texture to flat colors or to enhance a noise background.

Adding Textures to Your Interface

Once you've created the core of your interface, you'll probably want to add a texture of some sort, either by choosing the Pattern Overlay Layer Style or using a photographic texture as shown in this simple technique.

STEP ONE: Open the document containing your core interface.

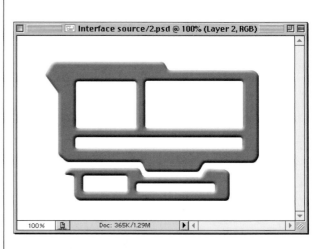

STEP TWO: Open the image texture that you'd like to use and drag it into your interface document so that it appears on its own layer. *(Note: This particular background image comes from a CD of hi-tech textures called "Amazing Sci-Fi Textures" from Marlin Studios.)*

STEP THREE: In the Layers palette, Command-click (PC: Control-click) on the interface layer to load it as a selection (as shown). Don't change layers; you should still be on the texture layer.

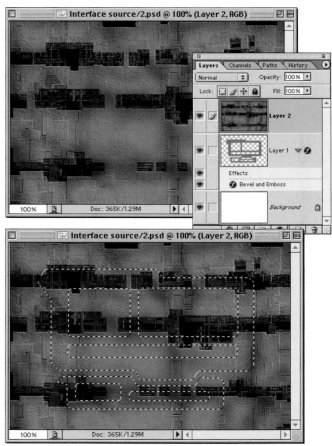

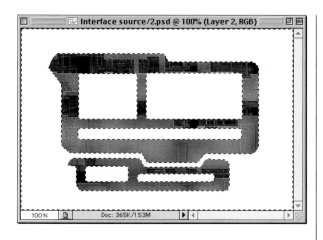

STEP FOUR: Press Shift-Command-I (PC: Shift-Control-I) to inverse the selection. Press Delete (PC: Backspace) to remove the excess texture from around your interface. Press Command-D (PC: Control-D) to Deselect.

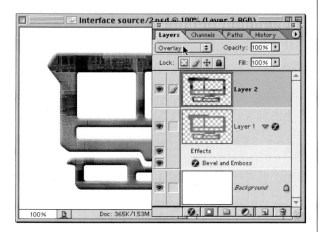

STEP FIVE: In the Layers palette, change the Layer Blend Mode of your texture layer to Overlay to let the texture blend in with the interface below it. Usually, Overlay mode looks best, but depending on the color of your texture, other blend modes, such as Hard Light, Soft Light, or Multiply, may look better.

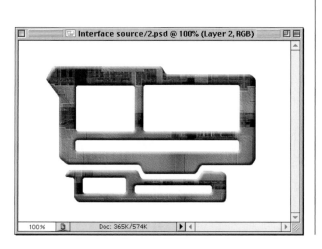

STEP SIX: When it looks good, hide the Background layer by clicking on the Eye icon beside the Background layer. Then, from the Layers palette's drop-down menu, choose Merge Visible to merge these two layers permanently together. You can make the Background visible again to complete the effect.

Quick Tip:
Selection super timesaver

If you've made a selection in Photoshop, there are a wide range of things you can do with that selection (besides dragging it around): you can feather it, save it, copy it to a layer, transform it, etc. Well, you can access a list of the things that you're most likely to do with your selection by holding the Control key and clicking-and-holding inside your selected area (PC: Right-click your mouse). A pop-up contextual menu will appear with a list of commands that you can apply to your selection. This is a huge timesaver and keeps you from digging through menus while you work.

Quick Tip:
Cool trick for eliminating backgrounds

In Step Four of the tutorial at right, we created a path and stroked it with the Brush tool to add a brush stroke along that path. You can use that same technique to help you remove an object from its background. Just draw a loose path (with the Pen tool) around the object you want to remove from its background (don't let it touch the edge of the object, just get close). Then follow Step Four in this tutorial but instead of choosing the Brush tool, choose the Background Eraser tool, then click OK. You'll be amazed because it traces around the edge of your image, erasing all the way around in about two seconds. Plus, it's fun to watch. Note: Make sure you choose a hard-edged brush for your Background Eraser tool before you try this trick.

Creating Wires

What would an interface be without some wires that house critical electrical components of the interface? (Okay, that's a stretch, but come on, you have to admit that, although they're not functional, they do look way cool!)

STEP ONE: Open a new document in RGB mode at 72 ppi. Create a new layer by clicking on the New Layer icon at the bottom of the Layers palette. Using the Pen tool, draw the path you'd like your wire to follow. Click, hold, and drag to create curves in your path.

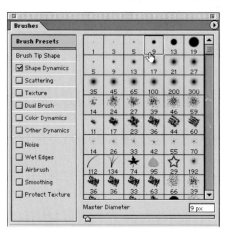

STEP TWO: Pick a new Foreground color (such as red or green). Press "b" to switch to the Brush tool. From the Brushes palette, choose a small, hard-edged brush.

STEP THREE: Go to the Paths palette, and in the drop-down menu, choose Stroke Path.

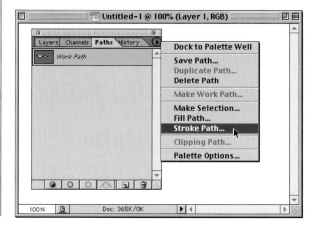

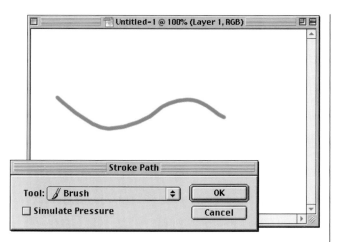

STEP FOUR: When the Stroke Path dialog appears, choose Brush from the Tool pop-up menu, and click OK to stroke your path with a hard-edged brush. You don't need the path you created anymore, so in the Paths palette, drag your Work Path into the Trash at the bottom of the palette to delete it.

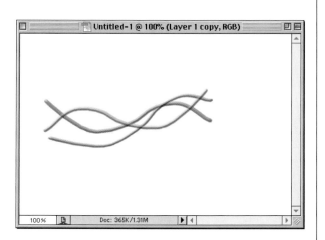

STEP FIVE: Choose Bevel and Emboss from the pop-up menu at the bottom of the Layers palette. Increase the Depth to 300% then click OK to complete your first wire. Drag this layer to the New Layer icon twice to make two duplicate layers. Press Command-T (PC: Control-T) to bring up Free Transform and slightly rotate each wire. Press Command-U (PC: Control-U) to bring up Hue/Saturation. Use the Hue slider to choose new colors for your two new wires and click OK.

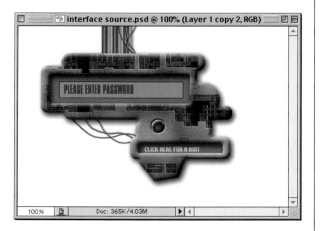

STEP SIX: Click on the Eye icon next to the Background layer to hide it, then choose Merge Visible from the Layers palette's pop-up menu to merge the three wire layers into one layer. Drag this layer into your interface and use Free Transform (Command-T [PC: Control-T]) to scale it to size to complete the effect. Here's an example of wires added in two places to an interface.

Quick Tip:
Bringing up the Info palette
Adobe assigned a few F-keys to bring up certain palettes and they're already preassigned when you install Photoshop. To bring up the Info palette, press F8, and it pops up. It also pops up automatically anytime you use the Color Sampler Eyedropper.

Quick Tip:
Creating one layer with the contents of all your layers

There's a little trick you can use that takes the layer you're on and converts it into a new layer that is a flattened version of all your layers. It doesn't actually flatten your layers; it gives you one single layer that looks the way your image would look if you flattened it at that point. To do this, start by creating a new blank layer, hold down the Option key (PC: Alt key), go under the Layers palette's drop-down menu, and choose Merge Visible. A new "merged contents" layer will now appear in your palette. Why would you need this? I have no earthly idea, but hey, you might need it one day, and now you know. However, you'll never remember which page this tip was on, and it'll take you hours to go through every tip in this book to find it, so maybe you're better off just forgetting this tip now, while you're still sane.

Embedding Objects into Your Interface

This is one of those instant effects where Photoshop does all the work, courtesy of a setting within the Layer Styles Bevel and Emboss dialog box.

STEP ONE: Open your interface file (you can download this file from the book's companion Web site).

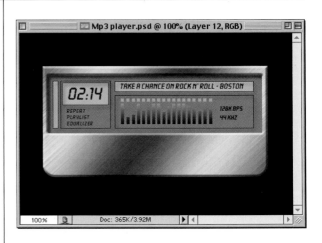

STEP TWO: Open the image that contains the interface elements you want to appear embedded into your interface. In this instance, it's a navigation bar and a Play button.

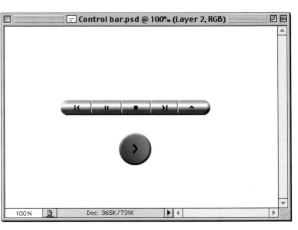

STEP THREE: Press "v" to get the Move tool. Click on the navigation bar layer, drag it into your interface document, and position it where you'd like it embedded (as shown).

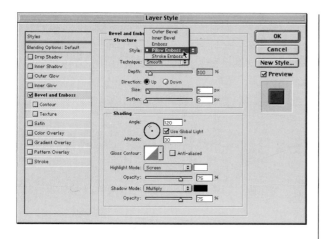

STEP FOUR: Choose Bevel and Emboss from the Layer Styles pop-up menu at the bottom of the Layers palette. When the dialog box appears, for Style choose Pillow Emboss.

STEP FIVE: When you click OK, the Pillow Emboss effect makes your navigation bar appear embedded into your interface. You can even move the bar around your image area and, because you applied a Layer Style, wherever it appears, the embedded effect goes with it. Return to the document with your interface elements.

STEP SIX: Click on the round Play button layer, drag it into your interface document, and position it where you want it. In the Layers palette, click on the words Bevel and Emboss on your navigation bar layer. Drag-and-drop the word onto your Play button layer, and the same effect will be applied to your button (as shown).

Quick Tip:
Shortcuts for aligning type

When you're working with type in Photoshop, you can change the alignment of your type (flush left, centered, flush right) by highlighting the type and using these simple keyboard shortcuts:

Align Left:
Shift-Command-L
PC: Shift-Control-L

Align Right:
Shift-Command-R
PC: Shift-Control-R

Align Center:
Shift-Command-C
PC: Shift-Control-C

Quick Tip:
**Layer Style
Angle tip**

In the Layer Styles dialog
box, a number of effects
have the Angle control,
which gives you control
over the angle of your
light source. But did
you know that if you
hold the Shift key while
adjusting the Angle, it will
snap to 15° increments?
You did? Rats!

Navigation Bar (from Previous Technique)

I was showing the previous pages to someone in my office, and they thought the embedding technique was cool, but sure enough, the first question they asked was, "Hey, how'd you create that navigation bar you used?" So…I thought I'd better include that too. Here it goes!

STEP ONE: Open a new blank document in RGB mode. Create a new blank layer by clicking on the New Layer icon. Press "d" to set your Foreground color to black. Then press Shift-U until the Rounded Rectangle tool appears in the Toolbox. In the Options Bar, for Radius choose 30, and click on the third icon from the left (Fill Pixels). Drag out your shape as shown.

STEP TWO: Hold the Command key (PC: Control key) and click once on the layer in the Layers palette to put a selection around your shape. Press "g" to get the Gradient tool, then press Return (PC: Enter) to bring up the Gradient Picker. From the Picker's drop-down menu, choose Metals. When the dialog appears, choose Append to add these gradients to your Gradient Picker.

STEP THREE: Choose the Silver gradient (shown in the inset in the previous step) and drag it from the top of your nav bar to about ¹/₂" past the bottom (shown in previous step). Press Shift-U until the Line tool appears in the Toolbox. Create a new layer, then hold the Shift key, and draw a straight line from just above your selected bar to just below (as shown) to add a divider to the bar.

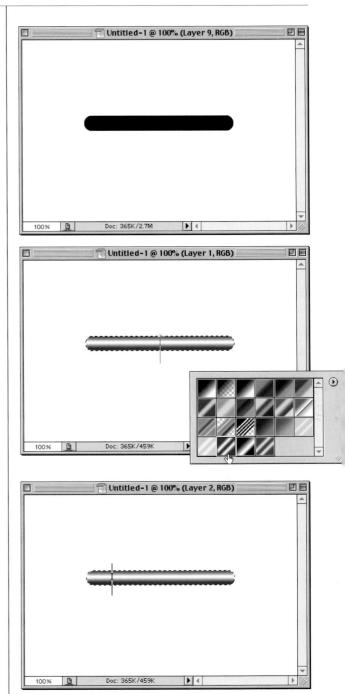

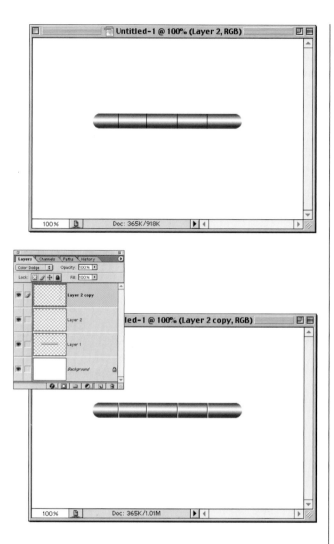

STEP FOUR: After you've drawn your first line, move over to the right and draw three more dividing lines in the same manner, until you have four lines (as shown). Press Command-D (PC: Control-D) to deselect.

STEP FIVE: Press Command-J (PC: Control-J) to make a duplicate of your lines layer. Press "x" to make white your Foreground color, then press Shift-Option-Delete (PC: Shift-Alt-Backspace) to fill your lines with white. Press "v" to get the Move tool, and press the Right Arrow key once to nudge these white lines over 1 pixel. In the Layers palette, change the Blend Mode of this white line layer to Color Dodge.

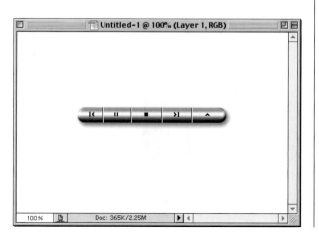

STEP SIX: Last, create a new layer, and then press Shift-L until the Polygonal Lasso tool appears in the Toolbox. Use it to draw the navigation symbols and fill each of them with black by pressing the letter "d", then Option-Delete (PC: Alt-Backspace). I also added a drop shadow, but with me, that pretty much goes without saying.

Quick Tip: Layer Set tip

If you have a bunch of layers to which you'd like to apply the same Blending Mode (or the same Opacity setting for that matter), link them all together, then choose "New Set from Linked" from the Layers palette's drop-down menu. All the linked layers will be put into a folder (Adobe calls it a set) within your Layers palette. That's no big deal, but the big deal is that whatever Blend Mode or Opacity setting you choose for your set is applied to all the layers automatically, as long as they remain in the set. Makes you stop and think, doesn't it?

Quick Tip:
Quick steel bars

The method on the right shows you how to create your own interface pipes using the Copper gradient preset that's already in Photoshop's Gradient Picker. But don't hesitate to try other gradients, including loading the Metals set of gradients (from the Picker's drop-down menu) to get your own custom look for your pipes.

Interface Pipes

This is one of my favorite interface techniques—creating tubes. I love 'em. They're great for connecting objects together or adding that hi-tech look to almost any existing object, and they look appropriate in almost any interface setting. Tubes rule. Try one and you'll fall in love.

STEP ONE: Create a new document in RGB at 72 ppi, then create a new blank layer by clicking on the New Layer icon at the bottom of the Layers palette. Press the letter "m" to switch to the Rectangular Marquee tool and drag a tall, thin rectangular selection in the size that you'd like your tube to be.

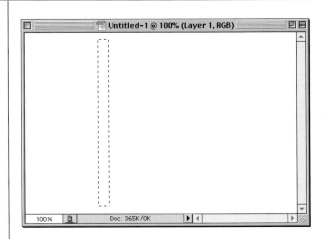

STEP TWO: Press the letter "g" to switch to the Gradient tool. In the Options Bar, click on the down-facing triangle next to the Gradient thumbnail to reveal the Gradient Picker. Choose the Copper gradient from the default set of gradients.

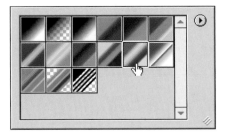

STEP THREE: With the Gradient tool, drag the gradient from the left side of your selection to the right to fill it with a gradient. Don't Deselect quite yet.

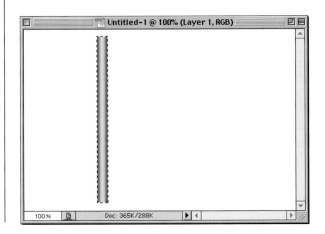

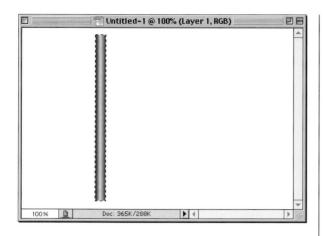

STEP FOUR: Next, press Shift-Command-U (PC: Shift-Control-U) to remove the copper color from your gradient, leaving you with a gray tube with white highlights. Next, go under the File menu and choose New.

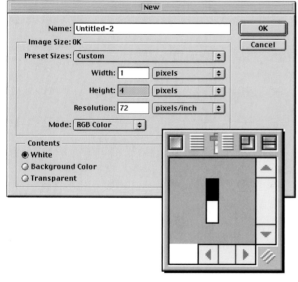

STEP FIVE: In the New dialog box, for Width enter 1 pixel, for Height 4 pixels, resolution 72, choose RGB mode, and click OK. Press Command-+ (PC: Control-+) a number of times to zoom in on your tiny document. Press Shift-B until the Pencil tool appears in the Toolbox. Use the Pencil tool to paint the top 2 pixels black in your 1x4-pixel document (as shown).

STEP SIX: Go under the Edit menu and choose Define Pattern. The Pattern Name dialog box will appear where you can name your pattern. Click OK. Now, return to your original Tube document (your selection should still be in place). Create a new blank layer by clicking on the New Layer icon at the bottom of the Layers palette.

Quick Tip:
Lighting Effects tips

We use the Lighting Effects filter quite a bit when we're creating interfaces and interface elements. Here are a few tips that will make using the Lighting Effects dialog even easier:

• Think of the Style pop-up menu at the top as a list of "presets," because that's exactly what they are.

• You can create your own styles (presets) by configuring the Lighting Effects the way you want and clicking on the Save button at the top of the dialog, just below the Style pop-up.

• To add another light, click-and-drag the Light icon into the preview, or hold the Option key (PC: Alt key) and click-and-drag a copy of your existing light.

• Press Option-Tab (PC: Alt-Tab) to jump from one light to the next.

• To delete any light, click on it and press Option-Delete (PC: Alt-Backspace).

continued

Quick Tip:
Changing the size of selections

Any time you have a selection in place, you can make that selection a few pixels larger or smaller by going under the Select menu, under Modify, and choosing Expand (to make your selection bigger) or Contract (to make your selection smaller). There's a weird thing about this function; when you make a large change either way, it doesn't keep the edges sharp and crisp—it tends to round (anti-alias) the edges a bit, so keep this in mind if you need to grow your selection by a large number of pixels. To see what I mean, draw a square selection, then go under the Select menu, under Modify, and choose Expand. Enter 15 (the maximum is 100) and click OK. Look at the edges of your selection—they're not square anymore, they're sort of rounded off at the corners. I haven't found a way around this; I try to keep my expansions to only 3 or 4 pixels and it works just fine.

STEP SEVEN: Go under the Edit menu and choose Fill. In the Fill dialog box, for Contents choose "Pattern" from the pop-up menu. Then, click on the down-facing triangle next to Custom Pattern to reveal your Pattern Picker. Choose the last pattern in the list (the tube lines you just created), then click OK to apply this pattern to your selection. Deselect by pressing Command-D (PC: Control-D).

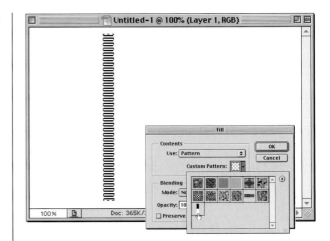

STEP EIGHT: In the Layers palette, change the Blend Mode to Multiply to add your lines to the gray tube on the layer below (as shown). Press Command-E (PC: Control-E) to merge the lines layer with the tube layer directly beneath it. Choose Drop Shadow from the Layer Styles pop-up menu at the bottom of the Layers palette. Lower the Opacity to 50% and click OK to apply a drop shadow.

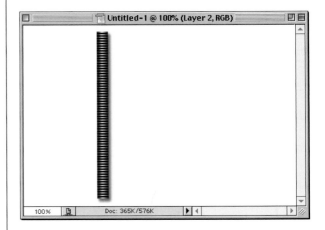

STEP NINE: As an optional step, you can bend the tube by going under the Filter menu, under Distort, and choosing Shear. When the dialog appears in the grid box, click on the line to add points and drag the points to bend the tube. The preview area in the dialog shows the amount of bend you're applying to the tube. When it looks the way you want (it's totally up to personal preference), click OK to apply the bend to the tube.

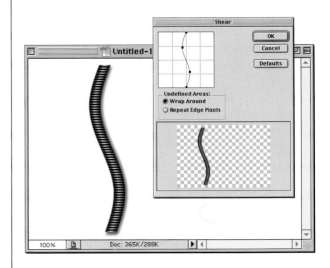

Screw Heads

Among the most popular interface add-ons are screw heads, which are very easy to create. The great thing about them is, once you've created some of these screw heads, you can save them in a separate document and anytime you need some, just open that document and drag them into your interface image. It's pretty handy. Kinda like having a Home Depot® on your hard drive.

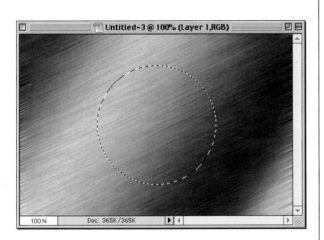

STEP ONE: Open a document in which you want to create this effect. (We used a brushed metal background with a technique shown in this chapter.) Create a new layer by clicking on the New Layer icon at the bottom of the Layers palette. Switch to the Elliptical Marquee tool, hold the Shift key, and draw a circle in the middle of your image area (We'll create a large screw head and shrink it down later to a usable size.)

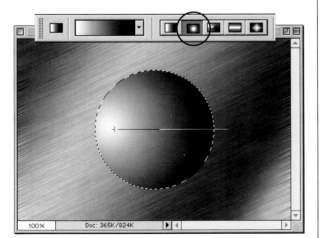

STEP TWO: Press "g" to switch to the Gradient tool. In the Gradient Picker in the Options Bar, select the Foreground to Background gradient (first one, top row). Press "d" then "x" to make your Foreground color white. Now, in the Options Bar, click on the Radial Gradient (it's the second icon from the left, circled). Click on the center left side of your circular selection and drag to the right.

Quick Tip:
Using the Clouds filter

The Clouds filter renders a random cloud pattern based on your current Foreground color. The clouds generated by the Clouds filter are usually pretty light in density, so if you want darker clouds, instead of choosing the Clouds filter, choose the Difference Clouds filter.

continued

STEP THREE: Deselect by pressing Command-D (PC: Control-D). Create a new blank layer by clicking on the New Layer icon at the bottom of the Layers palette. Switch to the Rectangular Marquee tool. Draw a tall thin rectangular selection (as shown). Don't worry about lining it up with the circle yet. Click on the Foreground Color Swatch, pick a medium-dark gray color, and fill your selection with gray by pressing Option-Delete (PC: Alt-Backspace).

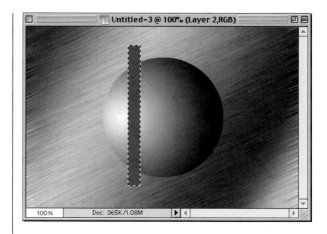

STEP FOUR: Deselect by pressing Command-D (PC: Control-D). Duplicate this layer by pressing Command-J (PC: Control-J). Press "d" to set your Foreground color to black and then press Shift-Option-Delete (PC: Shift-Alt-Backspace) to fill this rectangle with black. In the Layers palette, drag this black layer beneath your gray layer, then press "v" to get the Move tool. Press the Left Arrow key on your keyboard twice to nudge this layer left 2 pixels.

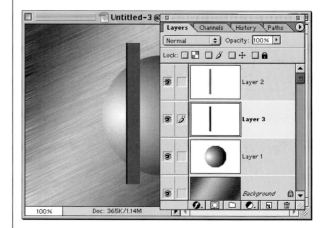

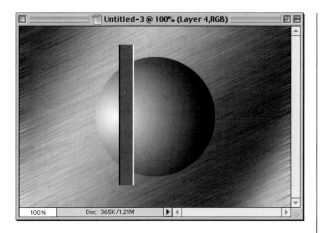

STEP FIVE: Press Command-J (PC: Control-J) to make a duplicate of your black rectangle layer. Press the letter "x" to make your Foreground color white, then press Shift-Option-Delete (PC: Shift-Alt-Backspace) to fill your rectangle with white. Press "v" to switch to the Move tool, then press the Right Arrow key four times to nudge this white layer two pixels to the right of the gray bar (as shown).

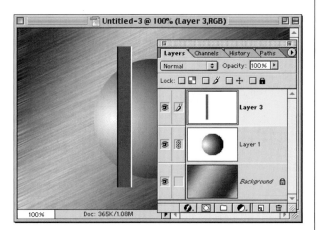

STEP SIX: Click on your top layer (the gray rectangle layer), then press Command-E (PC: Control-E) two times to merge these three layers into one layer. Then, click in the second column beside your sphere layer to link your top layer and the sphere layer together.

continued

Quick Tip:
Layer Styles and Global Light

When you use the Layer Style Drop Shadow to apply a shadow to a layer, Photoshop notes the angle of that shadow, and it makes every shadow on every layer go in that exact same angle. This feature is called Global Light, and by tying all your light sources together, you can adjust the position of this Global Light source on any layer, and all the other shadows will automatically follow suit.

This comes in handy if you've created a file with multiple Layer Styles and your client decides to change the angle of the sun (hey, it happens). Rather than going to every individual layer and changing the angle of every drop shadow, you can just go under the Layer menu, under Layer Style, and choose Global Light. When you change the angle here, all the other layers will change at the same time. You can also do the same thing by simply changing the angle of any shadow on any layer. If you want to have one layer with a shadow going a different direction, just uncheck the Use Global Light checkbox in the Drop Shadow dialog box.

Quick Tip:
Extract tool shortcut

If you have one of those incredibly hard-to-mask images, like someone with hair blowing in the wind or the delicate petals of a flower, there's a command in Photoshop that often works wonders. It's called the Extract command. In Photoshop 7, it now appears toward the top of the Filter menu and the keyboard shortcut is Option-Command-X (PC: Alt-Control-X). When you choose Extract, it opens your image in a whole new window with its own interface and tools. You use the Highlighter tool (like a Magic Marker) and draw a border around the object that you want to remove from its background. Click the Paint Bucket tool inside this border to tell Photoshop, "This is what I want to keep," and then click the Preview button to see what happens. One of the secrets to getting Extract to work its miracle is to use a very small brush for well-defined areas and a very large brush for less-defined areas (like windblown hair). Now here's the tip: Press-and-*hold* the Left or Right Bracket key to quickly change your brush size up or down 1 pixel at a time.

STEP SEVEN: Go under the Layer menu, under Align Linked, and choose Horizontal Centers. This will perfectly align your bar with the sphere. It's important (for an upcoming step) that you now unlink the two layers by clicking on the Link icon.

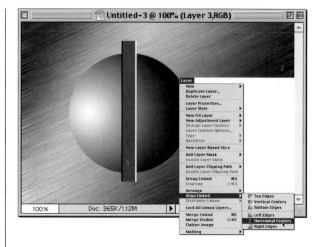

STEP EIGHT: By now I'm sure you've noticed that the rectangular bar extends beyond the top and bottom edge of the sphere. To remedy that, press Command-G (PC: Control-G), which groups the top image into the bottom image, and then press Command-E (PC: Control-E) to merge the two layers together.

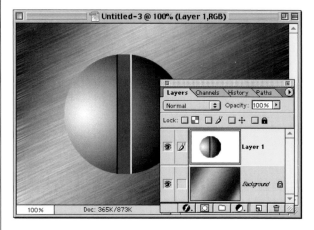

STEP NINE: Choose Bevel and Emboss from the Layer Styles pop-up menu at the bottom of the Layers palette. When the dialog box appears, simply change the Style to Pillow Emboss (which gives your screw head a sunken-in look) and click OK. Press Command-T (PC: Control-T) to bring up Free Transform. Hold the Shift key and scale your screw head down to size. Also, rotate the screw a bit as well.

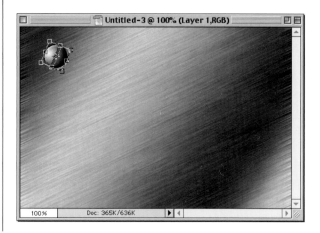

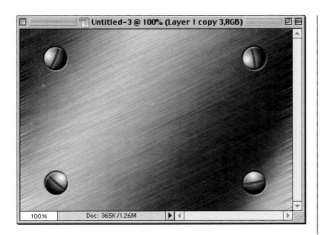

STEP TEN: Once you've got one finished screw, press Return (PC: Enter) to lock in your scale/rotation. To create more screws, hold Option-Command (PC: Alt-Control) and click-and-drag directly on the screw to make a duplicate. Move it into position where you'd like it, then bring up Free Transform again, and rotate it a little bit to give it a random look. Repeat this process for as many screws as you'd like.

Hi-tech Tubes

This is an updated version of creating tubes (at least from the way I did it in the previous versions of this book). It's based on a technique by Byron Rempel, with some tweaks and changes, including the use of Layer Styles. Again, we usually create these objects at a large size and then shrink them down considerably when it's time to apply them to our interface.

STEP ONE: Open a new document in RGB mode at 72 ppi. Create a new blank layer by clicking on the New Layer icon. Set your Foreground color to a medium gray. Press the letter "b" to switch to the Brush tool and choose a medium-sized, hard-edged brush. (I created a temporary, hard-edged brush, 35 pixels wide using the Master Diameter slider in the Brushes palette.) Paint a stroke to form the basic shape of your tube.

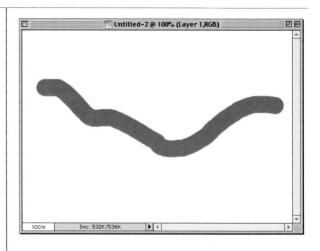

STEP TWO: Choose Bevel and Emboss from the bottom of the Layers palette. There are only three small changes here: (1) Increase the Size to 20; (2) increase the Highlight Opacity to 100%; and (3) increase the Shadow Opacity to 100%. Click OK to apply this soft bevel effect to your tube shape.

STEP THREE: Hold the Command key (PC: Control key) and click once on your layer's name in the Layers palette to put a selection around your tube. Then, go under the Select menu, under Modify, and choose Expand. Enter 3 pixels and click OK to expand your selection by three pixels (as shown).

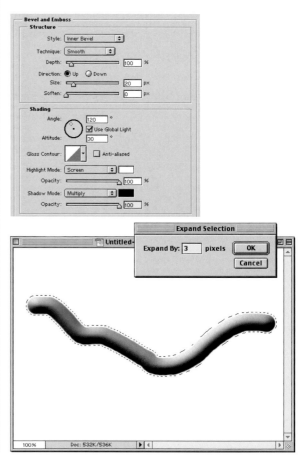

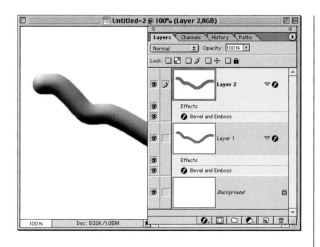

STEP FOUR: While your selection is still active, create another new blank layer. Press Option-Delete (PC: Alt-Backspace) to fill this layer with your gray Foreground color. In the Layers palette, click directly on the word Bevel and Emboss (on Layer 1) and drag-and-drop it on Layer 2 (the layer you just created) to add the same soft-beveled effect to your larger, 3-pixel gray tube layer.

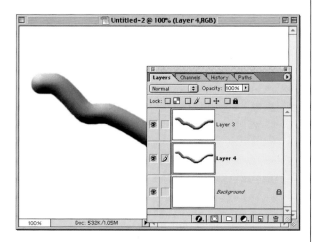

STEP FIVE: Deselect by pressing Command-D (PC: Control-D). Create a new blank layer by clicking on the New Layer icon at the bottom of the Layers palette. Drag this blank layer directly beneath Layer 2 (your second gray beveled layer). Then, click on the top tube layer and press Command-E (PC: Control-E) to merge it with the blank layer beneath it. Repeat this with the other tube layer as well until you have just two layers with no Layer Styles (as shown).

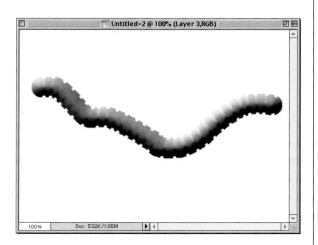

STEP SIX: Press "e" to switch to the Eraser tool. Choose either a 3- or 5-pixel, hard-edged brush tip (depending on how big your tube is) and start at one end erasing straight lines from the top layer. What I do is click once on one side of the tube, hold the Shift key, and click again on the other side of the tube, and Photoshop erases along a straight line. Follow the contours of your tube from left to right, erasing little lines out of the top tube layer.

Quick Tip:
Adjust those Options on the Fly

Want to quickly change the tolerance setting for a tool (say the Magic Wand tool for example)? You don't have to go up into the Options Bar, just press "w" to get the Magic Wand tool, then press the Enter key and the first field in the Options Bar will automatically become highlighted. All you have to do is type in your setting and you're set.

continued

Quick Tip:
Why choose Monochromatic Noise?

Every time we use the Noise filter (which is quite often in this book, particularly in this chapter), we also check the Monochromatic box at the bottom of the Add Noise dialog. The reason is that if Monochromatic is not turned on, you get noise that is composed of little red, green, and blue dots, and that can get in the way of colorization that will often take place later on in the tutorial.

STEP SEVEN: Once you've erased lines all along the top layer, choose Drop Shadow from the Layer Styles pop-up menu at the bottom of the Layers palette. Only one change here—just lower the Distance setting to 1, then click OK to apply this drop shadow to your top layer. Press Command-E (PC: Control-E) to merge your top tube layer with the bottom tube layer.

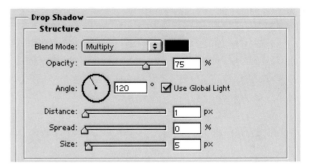

STEP EIGHT: Now we'll add a little "grit" to our tube by going under the Filter menu, under Noise, and choosing Add Noise. When the dialog box appears, enter 2% for Amount, change Distribution to Gaussian, check the Monochromatic box, and then click OK. The tube is now complete and ready to be sized down and added to or combined with other interface elements.

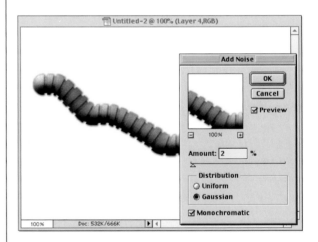

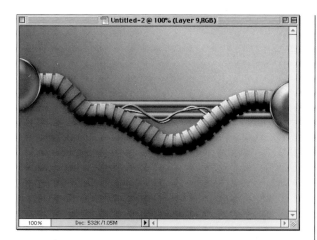

STEP NINE: I added two steel bars below (from the Steel Bar tutorial, but I left off the scan lines in this instance), then I added two wires (from the Wires tutorial). At each end I made a circle, filled it with Photoshop's Silver Metals gradient, contracted 3 pixels, added a new layer and a black fill. Then I went to the Styles palette and clicked on the fifth default style (Blue Glass) in the palette. To remove the color, I merged this layer down with a blank layer and pressed Shift-Command-U (PC: Shift-Control-U). Lastly, I added a light-gray to dark-gray gradient as a background and for good measure, I put a drop shadow on everything!

Quick Tip:
Adding file name extensions
This tip is for Mac OS 9.x and earlier users of Photoshop, many of whom do not add the three-letter file name extension to the end of their saved files, because the Mac platform doesn't require it. However, if you're sharing files with Photoshop users with PCs, you'll need to add the appropriate extensions so that they can open the files on their PCs. There's a Preference setting for adding these automatically, but if you only need the extension added once in a while, all Mac users have to do is hold the Option key when choosing the File Format in the Save As dialog, and Photoshop automatically adds the three-letter extension for you.

Quick Tip:
Transparent Gradients

In most cases, we're either using a Foreground to Background gradient, using one of the preset color gradients, or creating our own custom gradient; but one of the most useful (and coolest) gradients is the Foreground to Transparent gradient. When you set the Gradient tool to this gradient style and drag the gradient in your document, it goes from your Foreground color to transparent (just what it sounds like it would do).

Steel Rivets

This is a new twist on the rivet tutorial I included in the 6.0 version of the book. This one takes advantage of the Bevel and Emboss Chisel Hard feature and its Gloss Contours to create a shiny metallic texture on the metal.

STEP ONE: Open your interface (or the object to which you want to add steel rivets). Switch to the Elliptical Marquee tool and draw a small circular selection at the size you want your rivets to appear.

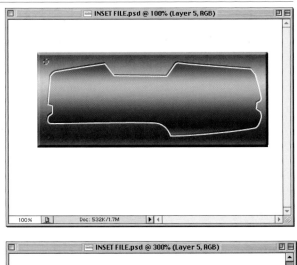

STEP TWO: Press Command-+ (PC: Control-+) a couple of times to zoom in on the area where you made the selection. Press "g" to switch to the Gradient tool. Click on the Gradient Picker (the down-facing arrow up in the Options Bar) and choose the Black to White gradient (it's the third one on the top row), and then drag the Gradient tool from the top of the selection to the bottom (as shown).

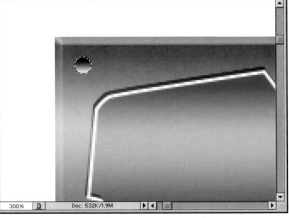

STEP THREE: Choose Bevel and Emboss from the Layer Styles pop-up menu at the bottom of the Layers palette. For Technique, choose Chisel Hard. Increase the Depth to 200% and the Size to 10. Increase the Highlight Opacity to 100%, and lower the Shadow Opacity to 50%. Turn on Anti-aliasing and from the Gloss Contour Picker (the down-facing arrow next to the Contour thumbnail), choose Ring (as shown).

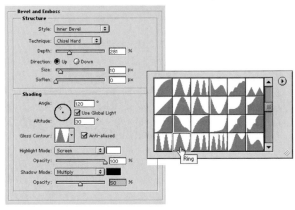

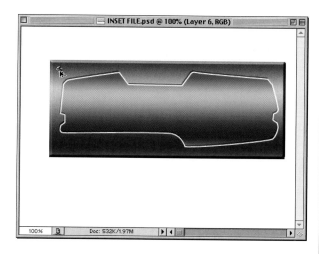

STEP FOUR: Hold the Option and Command keys (PC: Alt-Control) and drag a copy of the rivet.

STEP FIVE: Continue dragging rivets until they're all in place. Deselect by pressing Command-D (PC: Control-D).

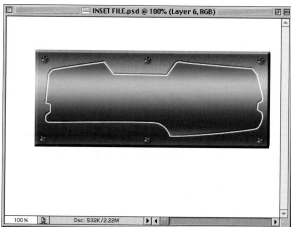

STEP SIX: This last step is optional, but since it's adding a drop shadow, don't you think it should be mandatory? Just choose Drop Shadow from the Layer Style pop-up menu at the bottom of the Layers palette. When the dialog box appears, lower the Distance amount to 1, and click OK to complete the effect.

Quick Tip:
Finding the right Gradient

When you have the Gradient tool, you can access the built-in preset gradients (and your own custom gradients) from the Gradient Picker. This is found in the Options Bar by clicking on the down-facing triangle just to the right of the Gradient thumbnail (which shows your currently selected gradient). When you click on this triangle, it reveals the Gradient Picker. By default, the Foreground to Background gradient is the first swatch on the top row in the Gradient Picker. It's a smart thumbnail, because it changes to display your currently selected Foreground and Background colors.

Quick Tip:
Gradient Picker shortcut

Want to save yourself a trip to the Options Bar every time you need to pick a different gradient? Try this super shortcut. While you have the Gradient tool, just press Return (PC: Enter) and the Gradient Picker will pop up within your image area, right where your pointer currently is.

Brushed Metal

If you're creating interfaces, it's just a matter of time before you say, "Ya know, I could really use some brushed metal." I know, it sounds unlikely, but it happens (more often than I'd care to admit). Here's how to whip up some brushed metal from scratch (just like grandma used to make).

STEP ONE: Open a new document in RGB mode. Press "g" to switch to the Gradient tool. Up in the Options Bar, click on the down-facing arrow next to the Gradient thumbnail to bring up the Gradient Picker. From the default set of gradients, choose the Copper gradient (as shown).

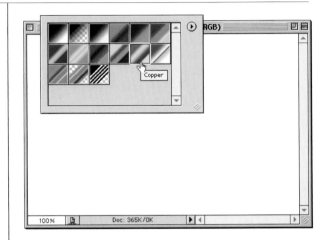

STEP TWO: Take the Gradient tool and drag it from the top of the image window to the bottom, but you need to do these two things: (1) drag at a slight angle (as shown); and (2) start at the top but drag about an inch past the bottom of the image window (its easier than it sounds). Then release to create the gradient shown.

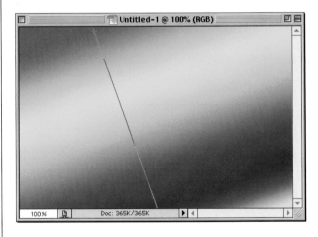

STEP THREE: Press Shift-Command-U (PC: Shift-Control-U) to remove the copper color from your gradient.

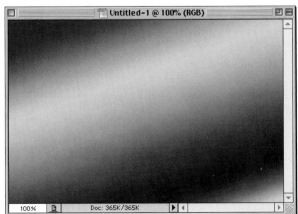

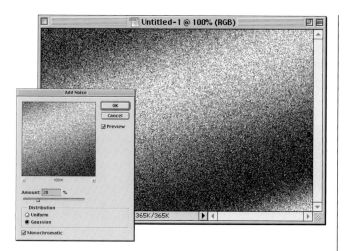

STEP FOUR: Go under the Filter menu, under Noise, and choose Add Noise. When the Add Noise dialog box appears, enter 20 for Amount, and click OK.

Quick Tip:
A sharper brushed metal?

If you try the brushed metal effect shown here and it doesn't look sharp enough to you, it's not unusual for designers to add an Unsharp Mask filter to the brushed metal to help accentuate the edges created by the Motion Blur. Give it a try and see which version you like best—sharpened or not.

STEP FIVE: Go under the Filter menu, under Blur, and choose Motion Blur. When the Motion Blur dialog box appears, enter 33° for Angle , and 75 for Amount.

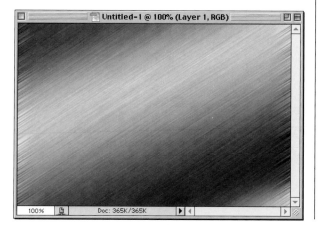

STEP SIX: When you click OK, Photoshop applies the Motion Blur to your image, completing the effect. Note: Take a look at the left and right edges and you can see that these areas don't look as good as the rest of the image., To get around that, we often make our new document about 1/2" wider than we really need so we can crop it down later to remove those harsh edges.

Quick Tip:
What about that collage in Step Six?

I created that collage from scratch, in the style of what I refer to as "Euro collages" (since they seem to have started and proliferated there). I started with a black background. To create the big green blob, I created a layer and used the Polygonal Lasso tool to draw a random shape that I filled with green. Next, I painted some random strokes on the edges with a darker green stroke. Then I just kept duplicating this layer, rotating or flipping it horizontally, and changing the Blend Mode of each copy (usually to Screen). After I had four or five layers, I would merge them together, duplicate that layer, rotate, change the Blend Mode, and nudge it over an inch or so. I did this over and over again for about 10 minutes. Then I finally ran the Wave filter on it, duplicated this layer, changed the Blend to Screen, and did it all again. I ran Wave yet again, and then created a new layer on top and filled it with "hi-tech nonsense," such as grids, a pattern of "+" signs, 1-pixel lines, 1-pixel circles, and

continued

Hi-tech Grids

This is an even faster way to create cool hi-tech grids than we showed in the previous versions of the book. This one saves the grid as a pattern so you can access it anytime you want. In the last step, we add the grid to a "Euro collage." Read the sidebars here for more on how I created the collage.

STEP ONE: Open a new document in RGB mode in pretty much any size you'd like. Create a new blank layer by clicking on the New Layer icon at the bottom of the Layers palette. Next, press "d" to make black your Foreground color.

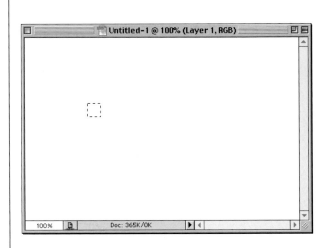

STEP TWO: Press "m" to get the Rectangular Marquee tool, hold the Shift key, and draw a selection at the size you want your grid squares to be. Go under the Edit menu and choose Stroke. When the dialog box appears, enter 1 pixel for Width, and choose Outside for Location.

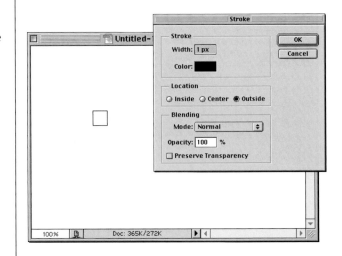

STEP THREE: Go under the Image menu and choose Trim. When the Trim dialog box appears, just click OK and your canvas will be trimmed (cropped) down to an exact fit about your grid square.

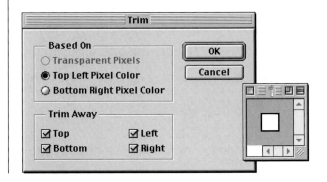

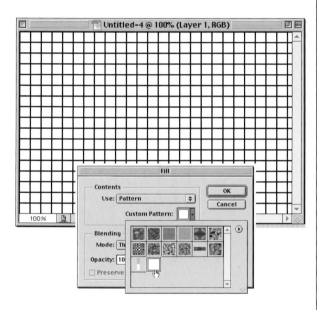

STEP FOUR: In the Layers palette, click on the Eye icon in the first column beside the Background layer to hide it from view (this will give your grid a transparent background). Go under the Edit menu and choose Define Pattern. When the dialog box appears, give your grid a name and click OK.

STEP FIVE: Now switch to the document where you want to apply your grid. Create a new layer by clicking on the New Layer icon at the bottom of the Layers palette. Go under the Edit menu and choose Fill. For Contents, use Pattern. Click on the down-facing triangle next to the Pattern thumbnail to bring up the Pattern Picker. Your pattern will be the last one in the Picker. Click on the pattern you created, click OK, and your layer will be filled with the grid.

STEP SIX: You can now drop this grid onto other backgrounds, you can recolor it, etc. Here, I dragged and dropped the grid into a collage in the right lower corner and the left upper corner. I changed my Foreground color to white, and pressed Shift-Option-Delete (PC: Shift-Alt-Backspace) to fill the grid lines with white. Lastly, I used Free Transform to scale each down to size.

continued from facing page

boxes—all in white, and I lowered the Opacity of this layer to about 12%. The tentacles? It's the Steel Bar with one end pinched (using Free Transform), then I used the Wave filter on it and ran the same Curve setting as I did for the "Designing the Core of Your Interface" tutorial at the beginning of this chapter. There's also some tiny type at 3 points. It's just gibberish (since it's three points, who would know?), but I can tell you what it is—it's the dialog from a rerun of *Frasier* that was on while I was creating the collage on my laptop. Oh, I almost forgot—I added a white Outer Glow behind the green glob, and to create those stretched lines, I made a 2-pixel wide selection as deep as my whole green glob—then I pressed Command-J (PC: Control-J) to put it up on its own layer. I went to Free Transform and simply grabbed the center right point and dragged all the way across the image. Then I changed the Blend Mode until it looked cool and also added the numbers 01, 02, 03, etc. in Helvetica Black, in white. Then I lowered the Opacity to around 12%. That's it (in a nutshell).

Yummy Metal Web Buttons

In this day and age, if you have to make a Web button, it better be pretty slick. Here's a technique for making a yummy-looking, metallic-like, plastic, reflecto-looking thingy that is . . . well, pretty slick.

STEP ONE: Create a new document (RGB, 72 ppi). Create a new blank layer by clicking on the New Layer icon at the bottom of the Layers palette. Draw a circular selection using the Elliptical Marquee tool. Press "d" then "x" to set your Foreground color to white. Press "g" to switch to the Gradient tool.

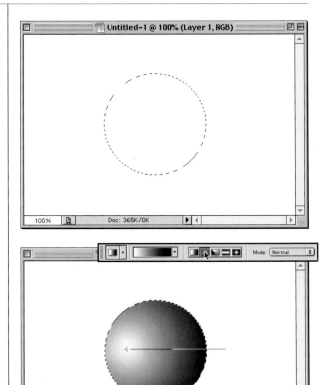

STEP TWO: In the Options Bar, click on the down-facing arrow next to the Gradient thumbnail to bring up the Gradient Picker. Choose the Foreground to Background gradients (it's the first one). Then close the Picker, and in the Options Bar, click on the Radial Gradient icon. (It's the second one from the left.) Drag a White to Black gradient from the left center of the selection to about $1/4$" past the edge (as shown).

STEP THREE: Press "d" to make black your Foreground color. Create a new layer by clicking on the New Layer icon in the Layers palette, then in the Gradient Picker choose the Foreground to Transparent gradient (it's the second one from the left, top row). In the Options Bar, choose the Linear Gradient (it's the first one). Drag the Gradient tool from the top of your selection to the middle to fill the top with black (as shown).

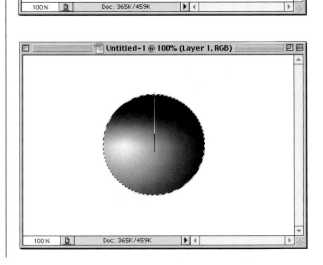

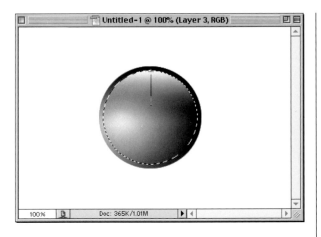

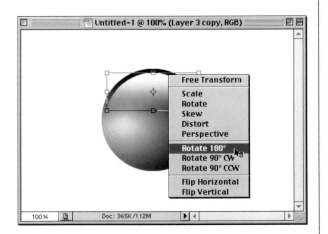

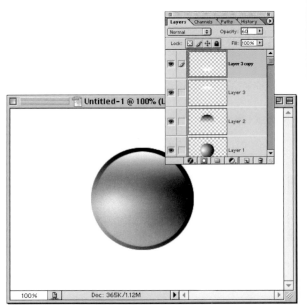

STEP FOUR: In the Layers palette, lower the Opacity to 75%. With your selection still in place, create a new layer. Go under the Select menu, under Modify, and choose Contract. Enter 6 pixels and click OK. Press "x" to set your Foreground color to white, then drag from the top of your selection through about one-third of your selected area. Press Command-D (PC: Control-D) to Deselect.

STEP FIVE: Go under the Filter menu, under Blur, and choose Gaussian Blur. Enter 3 pixels and click OK. Duplicate your top layer by dragging it to the New Layer icon. Press Command-T (PC: Control-T) to bring up Free Transform. Control-click (PC: Right-click) inside the bounding box, then choose Rotate 180° from the pop-up menu, and press Return (PC: Enter).

STEP SIX: Press "v" to switch to the Move tool. Drag this layer straight down almost to the edge. In the Layers palette, lower the Opacity of this layer to 60% (as shown).

Quick Tip:
Make 'em big

Many designers prefer to create their Web graphics at a much larger physical size (like two- or three-times bigger) than the final size that the graphic will be on the Web page. This is especially helpful when the final size is very small, like Web buttons—which would be hard to create from scratch at their actual size. If you decide to go this route, you can scale your object down to its final size by using Free Transform and sizing down before you save the file for the Web.

continued

Quick Tip:
Loading selections

Most of the time in this book we ask you to go under the Select menu and choose Load Selection to load a selection saved as an Alpha Channel. However, you can also load a selection by going to the Channels palette, clicking on the Alpha Channel you want to load as a selection, and dragging it to the Selection icon at the bottom of the Channels palette. (It's the first one from the left.) Click back on the RGB channel to view the entire RGB image again with the loaded selection.

STEP SEVEN: Go back to Layer 3 (the layer below your current layer) and press Command-T (PC: Control-T) to bring up Free Transform. Hold the Shift key, grab the bottom right handle, and shrink this white gradient by around 15%. Press Return (PC: Enter) to lock in the transformation. Hide the Background layer and choose Merge Visible from the Layers palette's pop-up menu.

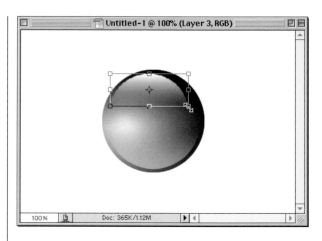

STEP EIGHT: Choose Drop Shadow from the Layer Style pop-up menu at the bottom of the Layers palette and click OK. Then, press Command-U (PC: Control-U) to bring up Hue/ Saturation. Click the Colorize button and move the Hue slider to choose a color for your button.

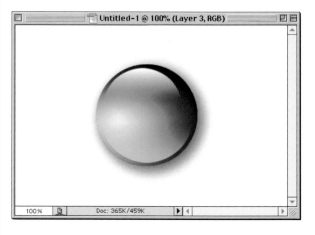

STEP NINE: Here's the final effect. I scaled the button down in size, then I duplicated the button layer twice, and used Hue/Saturation to change the color of one to red, and one to yellow. I also added a scan line effect to the Background layer using the technique shown in the "Down and Dirty Tricks" chapter, but instead of using black for my scan lines, I used 20% gray.

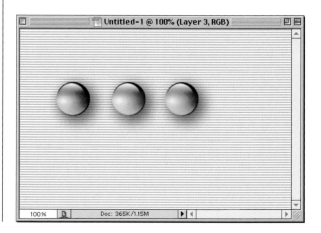

8

Here we are, sadly, at the last chapter of the book (I cried when I wrote it. Well, at least parts of it). But I don't

Saturday Night Special
Special Effects

want you to think, just because it's the last chapter, that I've run out of cool things to share. Au contraire (gratuitous use of French in everyday conversation, inspired by Frasier). I specifically saved this chapter for last, and I named this chapter "Special Effects" because that's just what these effects are—special. Oh sure, I toyed with other names, like "Zowie-wowie effects," "Turbo-mondo spasmatic effects," and even "Intergalactic alien death-ray effects," but those names just weren't special enough for the effects I had planned for this chapter. But before you launch into the chapter and begin creating effects with an unbridled zeal heretofore hidden beneath layers of conformity and years of ingrained neo-conservatism (I'm not sure what any of that means, but my publisher told me to use a lot of big words), I just want to thank you for spending these special moments with me. See, how could I name this chapter anything but "special effects?"

Stretched-pixel Backgrounds

This technique is very popular in those trendy Euro-collages that are showing up everywhere. They're great as backgrounds for collages and as collage elements where the tops and bottoms are cropped off, and then the Blend Mode is changed to blend in with other elements in the collage.

STEP ONE: First a little set-up. Go under the Window menu and choose Info to bring up the Info palette. Click-and-hold on the + icon at the bottom left-hand corner of the dialog, and a pop-up menu of measurement units will appear. Choose Pixels to have the Info palette display measurements in pixels (as shown).

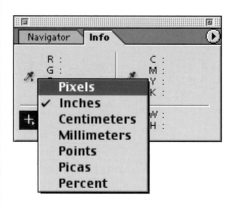

STEP TWO: Open an image you want to use for the effect. Images with lots of variation in color seem to create the most interesting stretched pixel effects. Press "m" to switch to the Rectangular Marquee tool. Draw a tall thin selection that's only 2 pixels wide (the "W" setting in the bottom right of the Info palette shows you how many pixels wide your selection is as your drag it).

STEP THREE: Press Command-J (PC: Control-J) to put your selected area on its own separate layer. Then press Command-T (PC: Control-T) to bring up Free Transform. Grab the right center point (as shown) and drag to your right.

STEP FOUR: Continue dragging until your pointer extends beyond the edge of your document window. You'll see what appear to be seams in your stretched pixels, but they'll go away once you lock in your transformation.

STEP FIVE: Press Return (PC: Enter) to lock in your transformation. Your stretched pixel effect is on its own layer above your image, so you no longer need the Background layer. Now you can delete it by dragging the background into the Trash icon at the bottom of the Layers palette.

STEP SIX: You can then use your stretched-pixel image by dragging it out farther (I did the same thing again in the example shown here—I just stretched it some more using Free Transform). To see a stretched-pixel effect in use, turn to the Interface chapter, go to the tutorial for creating hi-tech grids, and look at the illustration in Step 6. There, you'll see a stretch pixel effect clearly used in the background.

Quick Tip:
Running filters on CMYK images

The next time you convert a file to CMYK format, take a trip under the Filter menu and you'll find something that may surprise you. Many of the filters are grayed out (unavailable). Once you've converted to CMYK, you don't want to convert back to RGB to use these filters, because when you convert back to CMYK again, it's going to re-separate your image and cause untold horrors to your separation (okay, it's not that bad, but it's not a good thing to do).

Instead, here's a trick that lets you apply any filter to CMYK images. Go to the Channels palette and click on a color channel (for example, Cyan). Now, look under the Filter menu—the filters are back, baby! You can now apply the filter to each individual CMYK channel. It takes a little longer, but it'll get the job done. Here's a tip to speed up the process: Run the filter on the Cyan channel, press Command-2 (PC: Control-2) to switch to the Magenta Channel, and then press Command-F (PC: Control-F) to run the filter again. Repeat this for the Yellow and Black channels.

Quick Tip:
Change your view anytime

When you open a filter dialog, or any dialog such as Levels or Curves, most of your menus are grayed out while you're in that dialog. However, one menu that's almost always available is your View menu. Your keyboard shortcuts for accessing View menu items also still work, even though you're in a dialog box.

Try it for yourself: Open an image, bring up the Gaussian Blur filter dialog, then look at the menu bar up top. View is still available, you can just reach out and choose a new view or use the keyboard shortcut of your choice.

Electric Type

This is a take-off on the old lightning effect, but in this method you have some control over how and where the lightning will be applied, and although we're using type in this example, this will also work with an object. If applied correctly, this technique can be very shocking (sorry about that).

STEP ONE: Open a new document in RGB mode at 72 dpi. Press "d" to make black your Foreground color. Press "t" to get the Type tool and create your type (I used the Helvetica Ultra Compressed font).

STEP TWO: In the Layers palette, Command-click (PC: Control-click) on your Type layer's name to put a selection around the letters. When the selection is in place, you can hide the Type layer by clicking on the Eye icon in the first column beside it. Now click on the Background layer.

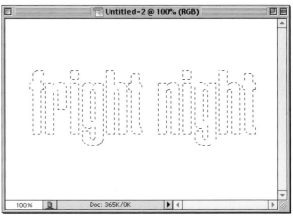

STEP THREE: Your selection should still be in place, so go under the Edit menu and choose Stroke. For Width enter 8 pixels, for Location choose Outside, and click OK to put an eight-pixel stroke around your selection. Now you can Deselect by pressing Command-D (PC: Control-D).

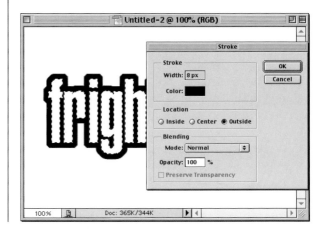

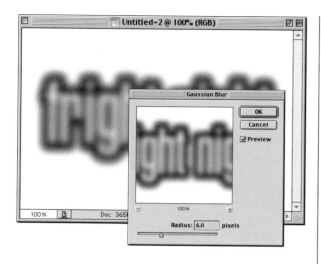

STEP FOUR: Go under the Filter menu, under Blur, and choose Gaussian Blur. When the dialog appears enter 6 pixels and click OK to blur your stroked type.

Quick Tip:
Don't like the lightning pattern? Request a new one

One of the great things about the Clouds filter is that the pattern it generates is totally random, so if you do the effect at left and don't like the way your lightning spikes look, just start from scratch and redo the Clouds filter. Each time you do it, you'll get a different cloud effect and a different set of spikes in your lightning.

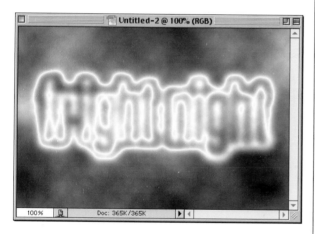

STEP FIVE: Go under the Filter menu, under Render, and choose Difference Clouds. This will generate the electric stroke around your type, but to enhance the effect, press Command-I (PC: Control-I) to Invert the clouds and make the electric stroke stand out more.

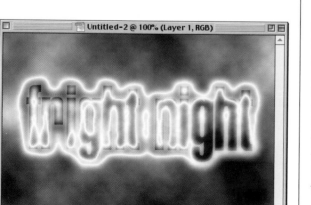

STEP SIX: Press Command-U (PC: Control-U) to open the Hue/Saturation dialog box. Check the Colorize box in the lower right-hand corner, then move the Hue slider up to 215 for a blue tint. Last, click on your Type layer to make it visible and change its Blend Mode to Overlay, to give you the effect shown here.

Quick Tip:
Apply changes to multiple layers

There are a number of changes and transformations you can apply to multiple layers at once. The first step is to go to the Layers palette and link together the layers that you want to affect. This is done by clicking in the second column beside each layer you want to link. A tiny link icon will appear indicating that the layer is now linked to your currently active layer. Once that's done, whatever transformation (such as scaling, rotating, etc.) you do to your active layer will also affect all your linked layers.

Ripped Edge Technique

While working on this book, I showed some color proofs of a page to a friend and he asked how we created the ripped edge effect we sometimes use when showing menus or the Options Bar (we "rip" the menu or Options Bar because sometimes they're too long and we'd have to make them very small to fit.) He thought I should include the technique in the book, so here it is.

STEP ONE: Open the image you want to rip (in this case, I'm going to use a screen capture of Photoshop's Layer menu—the longest of Photoshop's menus) but this technique will work just as well on any image. As you can see, to display the entire menu here, the menu items are very small. You have to get this menu up on its own layer with none of the white background, so press "w" to switch to the Magic Wand tool.

STEP TWO: Click once in the white area to the right of the word Layer to select that area (shown in fig. 1). Then press Shift-Command-I (PC: Shift-Control-I) to inverse your selection (which selects everything *but* that white area (shown in fig. 2). Now press Shift-Command-J (PC: Shift-Control-J) to cut just the menu out of the background and put it up on its own separate layer (shown in fig. 3).

fig. 1   fig. 2

fig. 3

STEP THREE: Press "L" to switch to the Lasso tool, and draw a jaggy selection through the part of the menu that you want to tear away (as shown). I started drawing the jaggy part first, then I went outside the image window and went around to the point where I started making this selection.

STEP FOUR: Press Shift-Command-I (PC: Shift-Control-I) to inverse your selection, selecting the part of your image you no longer want visible. Press Delete (PC: Backspace) to delete this area (as shown). Then, press the Up Arrow key four times to nudge your selection up about 4 pixels into your menu (as shown).

STEP FIVE: Press Command-L (PC: Control-L) to bring up the Levels dialog. Drag the lower-left Output Levels slider to the right until it reads 220 (as shown). Then click OK. This lightens the 4-pixel-high selected area to almost white. Now press Command-D (PC: Control-D) to Deselect.

STEP SIX: Choose Drop Shadow from the Layer Style pop-up menu at the bottom of the Layers palette. Increase the Size to 8 and click OK to complete the effect. With the drop shadow applied, the area you lightened in the previous step is now visible, and that area helps give a more realistic rip effect. When cropped to size, you can see how much bigger we can now display the menu (as shown here).

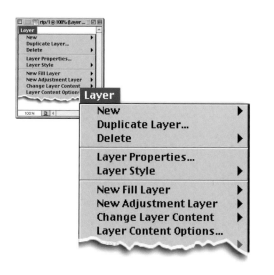

Quick Tip:
Detaching a Layer Effect from its layer

When you apply a Layer Effect, the effect is attached directly to your layer. So if you apply a Layer Effects Drop Shadow to a Type layer, that shadow is attached to your Type layer. If you'd like to separate that drop shadow onto its own layer, you can go under the Layer menu, under Layer Style, and choose Create Layer. When you do this, a new layer is created that contains just the effect (in this case it would contain the drop shadow). If you try this when you've applied a Bevel and Emboss Layer effect, it separates the highlights to one layer and the shadows to another. However, in the case of Bevel and Emboss, they're still grouped with the original layer as a clipping group. To remove the clipping group, press Shift-Command-G (PC: Shift-Control-G). You'll see that you now have three separate layers.

Quick Tip:
Viewing only your active layer and hiding the rest

If you have a multilayered document, you can look at just the layer you're working on (or any one layer for that matter) by holding the Option key (PC: Alt key) and clicking on the Eye icon in the first column next to it in the Layers palette. This immediately hides all other layers from view, leaving only your chosen layer visible (and any Layer Styles you have applied to other layers). To show all the layers again, hold the Option key (PC: Alt key) and click on the Eye icon again for your layer, and the rest will instantly reappear.

Multicolor Glow

Although we're doing this effect on type, it really isn't a type trick, because you can apply this multi-color glow to any object on a layer. This is an easy technique, thanks to Photoshop's Layer Styles and a few little tweaks by you.

STEP ONE: Open a new document in RGB mode at 72 dpi. Press the letter "d" to set your Foreground color to black, and fill your Background with black by pressing Option-Delete (PC: Alt-Backspace).

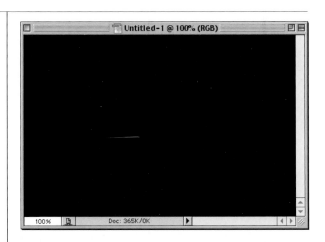

STEP TWO: Using the Type tool, create your type. It will appear on a layer above the Background, but because they're both black, you'll have to hide the Background layer to see your type. So click on the Eye icon next to your Background layer to hide it from view. Position your type as you'd like (as shown) and then click in the column where the Eye icon used to be to make your black background visible again.

STEP THREE: Go under the Layer menu, under Layer Style, and choose Outer Glow. When the dialog box appears, click on the light yellow Color Swatch (okay, I admit it—it's beige. Yecch!), and when the Color Picker appears, choose white as your color and click OK. In the Outer Glow dialog box, change the Blend Mode to Normal and click OK to apply a white glow to your letters.

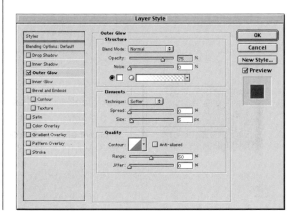

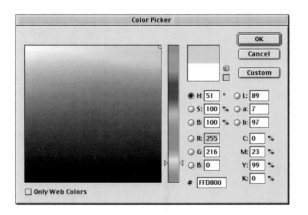

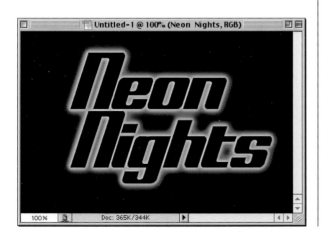

STEP FOUR: In the Layers palette, make a copy of your Type layer by dragging it to the New Layer icon at the bottom of the Layers palette. Drag this copy layer below your original Type layer. Then double-click directly on the little *f* that appears right before the words Outer Glow (in your copy) to bring up the dialog box's current settings. Click on the white Color Swatch and change the color to yellow.

STEP FIVE: Increase the Size amount to 8, Spread to 25, and click OK to apply a yellow glow that extends beyond your original white glow.

STEP SIX: Make a copy of this yellow glow Type layer by dragging it to the New Layer icon at the bottom of the Layers palette, and drag this new copy layer below your yellow Type layer. Double-click directly on the words "Outer Glow" in the Layers palette to bring up its dialog box with its current settings. Click on the yellow Color Swatch and change the color to purple. Increase the Size to 12 and click OK to apply the final glow. Now it appears that your glow starts with white and then radiates out to yellow, then to purple, creating a multicolored glow.

Quick Tip:
Copying Layer Styles to other layers

Once you've applied a Layer Style to a layer, you can apply that same effect (with the exact same settings) to any other layer. The slow sloth-like way is to go under the Layer menu, under Layer Style, and choose Copy Layer Style. Then go back to the Layers palette, click on the layer where you want the effects, then sloth your way back under the Layer menu, under Layer Style, and choose Paste Layer Style.

A much faster (and more fun) way is to hold the Control key (PC: Right-click) and click-and-hold on your layer in the Layers palette. A pop-up menu will appear and you can choose Copy Layer Style. Hold the Control key (PC: Right-click) and click-and-hold on the layer in the Layers palette where you want to copy the effect. Choose Paste Layer Style from the pop-up menu that appears. Try it once, and you'll never go digging under the Layer Style menu again.

Quick Tip:
How to move a layer to another document and have it appear in the exact same spot

There's a quick trick for duplicating a layer and having it appear in another document in the exact same position as in the original. In the Layers palette, click on the layer you want to duplicate, then in the Layers palette's drop-down menu, choose Duplicate Layer. When the dialog box appears, under Destination, choose your other document from the pop-up menu (or new if you want it to appear in a brand-new document), and click OK. Your layer will be duplicated to its new document in the exact same spot as in the original.

Metallic Glass Effect

Although I'm doing this technique on type, it works pretty well on just about any shape or a logo, so don't think of it necessarily as a type effect (that's why I put it here in this special effects chapter). What I like about this technique is the transparency created by feathering and knocking out the inside of the letters that's only evident when you place the effect over a background.

STEP ONE: Open a new document in RGB mode at 72 ppi. Click on the Foreground Color Swatch and pick a color to use for your type (I chose PANTONE 646). Press "t" to get the Type tool and create some very large type (as shown). Next, convert this Type layer into an image layer by going under the Layer menu, under Rasterize, and choosing Type.

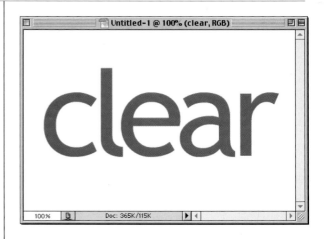

STEP TWO: Create a new layer by clicking on the New Layer icon at the bottom of the Layers palette. In the Layers palette, Command-click (PC: Control-click) on your text layer to put a selection around your text. Go under the Select menu, under Modify, and choose Contract. When the dialog box appears, enter 2 pixels, and click OK.

STEP THREE: Set your Foreground color to white by pressing the letter "d" then the letter "x." Fill your selection with white by pressing Option-Delete (PC: Alt-Backspace). Deselect your type by pressing Command-D (PC: Control-D).

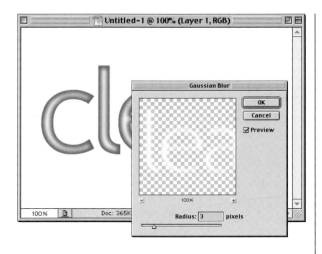

STEP FOUR: Go under the Filter menu, under Blur, and choose Gaussian Blur. Enter 3 pixels and click OK to blur your white type. Change this layer's Blend Mode from Normal to Overlay. Press Command-E (PC: Control-E) to merge your white blurry layer with your original type layer directly below it.

STEP FIVE: Go under the Layer menu, under Layer Style, and choose Bevel and Emboss. Increase the Size to 10, the Highlight Mode Opacity to 100%, and click OK.

STEP SIX: Go under the Filter menu, under Artistic, and choose Plastic Wrap. For Highlight Strength enter 15, for Detail enter 9, for Smoothness enter 7, and then click OK.

continued

Quick Tip: The limits of Bevel and Emboss

Photoshop's Bevel and Emboss Layer Style works really well on low-res, 72-ppi images, but unfortunately when you're using high-res, 300-ppi images, the effect of the Bevel and Emboss filter is much less. For example, a Depth of 20 gives a very thick, sharp inner bevel on a 72-ppi image, but the same setting of 20 on a 300-ppi image gives a softer, smaller bevel that seems to have about 30% to 40% of the intensity of the low-res version.

There's really no practical way around this in Photoshop, but if you want this type of bevel effect for high-res images, Alien Skin's Eye Candy collection of Photoshop plug-ins has an Inner Bevel filter that's first-rate, and it works well on high-res images. Find out more at their Web site at www.alienskin.com.

Quick Tip:
Moving selections from one document to another

If you have an active selection in a document, and you want the exact same selection in another open document, you can drag-and-drop just the selection (and not its contents) from one open document to another. To make this work, all you have to do is make sure you have a selection tool active (e.g., Lasso, Rectangular Marquee, Magic Wand, etc.), and with that tool, click in the center of your selection and drag it over to the other open document.

STEP SEVEN: Go to the Layers palette, hold the Command key (PC: Control key), and click on your text layer to put a selection around your text. Create a new layer by clicking on the New Layer icon at the bottom of the Layers palette. Fill your selection with white by pressing Option-Delete (PC: Alt-Backspace). Deselect by pressing Command-D (PC: Control-D).

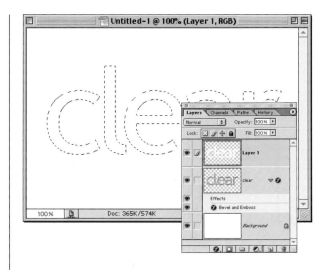

STEP EIGHT: Go under the Filter menu, under Sketch, and choose Chrome. When the Chrome dialog box appears, enter 10 for Detail, 10 for Smoothness, and click OK.

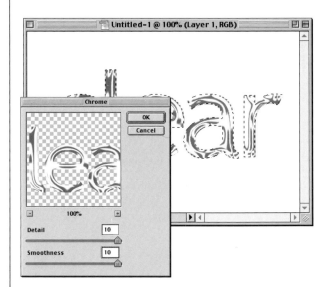

STEP NINE: Change the layer Blend Mode for this layer from Normal to Multiply, and lower the Opacity to 75%. Hide your Background Layer (click on the Eye icon), then choose Merge Visible from the Layers palette's pop-down menu.

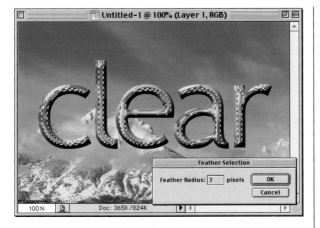

STEP TEN: Open a background image, drag it into your type document, and in the Layers palette, drag this image below your text layer. While in the Layers palette, hold the Command key (PC: Control key), and click on your text layer to put a selection around your text. Go under the Select menu, under Modify, and choose Contract. When the dialog box appears, enter 5 pixels and click OK. Go under the Select menu and choose Feather. Enter 3 pixels, and click OK (this will soften the edges of your selection).

Quick Tip:
Toggling through open documents
If you have more than one document open at the same time in Photoshop, you can toggle through your open documents by pressing Control-Tab (PC: Right-click-Tab).

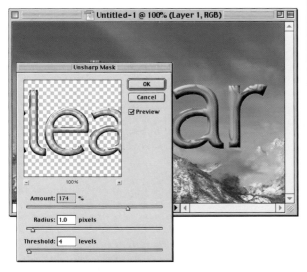

STEP ELEVEN: Now, press Delete (PC: Backspace) to create transparency within the type, while keeping the edges intact. Deselect by pressing Command-D (PC: Control-D). Last, go under the Filter menu, under Sharpen, and choose Unsharp Mask. Increase the Amount to 174, set the Radius to 1, and the Threshold to 4.

STEP TWELVE: When you click OK, the sharpening adds a glassy, metallic-like shine to your type, and completes the effect.

Credit Card from a Photo

In the old days, unless you worked for Visa, MasterCard, or American Express, your chance of designing a credit card was fairly slim, but now there are phone cards, frequent flyer cards, frequent shopper cards, slot club cards, convention badges, and about a hundred other reasons why you may need this effect, primarily as a mockup to show clients.

STEP ONE: Open a new document in RGB mode at 72 dpi. Press "d" to set your Foreground color to black, then create a new layer by clicking on the New Layer icon at the bottom of the Layers palette. Press Shift-U until the Rounded Rectangle tool appears in the Toolbox. In the Options Bar, set the Radius to 10, then draw your rounded corner box at the size of a credit card (approximately $3\frac{1}{2}$" by $2\frac{1}{4}$").

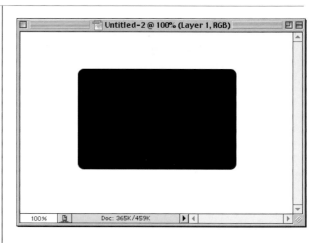

STEP TWO: Open the image you want to use in your credit card. Press "v" to get the Move tool and drag it into your credit card document. In the Layers palette, lower its Opacity to 50% to help you see when resizing the image. Press Command-T (PC: Control-T) to bring up Free Transform. Hold the Shift key, grab a corner point, and drag inward to size down your image (as shown).

STEP THREE: Press Return (PC: Enter) to lock in your changes and in the Layers palette, raise the Opacity of this layer back up to 100%. Now press Command-G (PC: Control-G) to place your photo inside the black credit card shape on the layer below it.

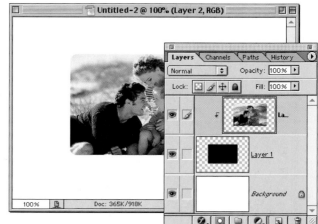

STEP FOUR: The grouping you just did is temporary, so press Command-E (PC: Control-E) to permanently merge your photo layer with the credit card shape layer, leaving you with just a Background layer and your rounded corner photo layer. Choose Drop Shadow from the Layer Style pop-up menu at the bottom of the Layers palette. When the dialog appears, just click OK.

STEP FIVE: Create a new layer by clicking on the New Layer icon at the bottom of the Layers palette. Press "m" to get the Rectangular Marquee tool, and draw a rectangle at the bottom of your credit card that's just a bit wider and covers about one-sixth of your image (as shown). Press "x" to set your Foreground color to white, then press Option-Delete (PC: Alt-Backspace) to fill your selection with white.

STEP SIX: Press Command-D (PC: Control-D) to Deselect. Then press Command-G (PC: Control-G) to Group the two images (put the white into the credit-card shape), and then press Command-E (PC: Control-E) to merge the two layers together once again (as shown).

Quick Tip:
How to navigate your image when you're zoomed in close
When you've zoomed in on an image, trying to navigate using the scroll bars is frustrating at best, because when you're zoomed in really close, even a small move with the scroll bar can move the area you're working on totally out of the image window. Instead, when you've zoomed in, hold the Spacebar and your pointer will temporarily change to the Hand tool, and you can click-and-drag around your image. This is an ideal way to move quickly around your zoomed image, without the frustration of the scroll bars. When you release the Spacebar, you immediately switch back to the tool you were using.

continued

STEP SEVEN: Press "t" to get the Type tool and enter the type that will appear at the bottom of the card (I used the Trajan font, with the Anti-aliasing set to Sharp in the Options Bar).

STEP EIGHT: Create a new layer by clicking once on the New Layer icon at the bottom of the Layers palette. Press "m" to get the Rectangular Marquee tool and draw a rectangle in the upper left-hand side of the card, starting at the top edge (as shown). Press "d" to set your Foreground color to black, and then press Option-Delete (PC: Alt-Backspace) to fill with black. Again, press "t" to get the Type tool and enter the appropriate type.

STEP NINE: Next, while we have the Type tool, we'll add some "credit card type" to our image. Press the letter "x" to change your Foreground color to white and then add your text. I used the OCRA font from Adobe—but just adding the font isn't enough. Choose Bevel and Emboss from the Layer Style pop-up menu at the bottom of the Layers palette.

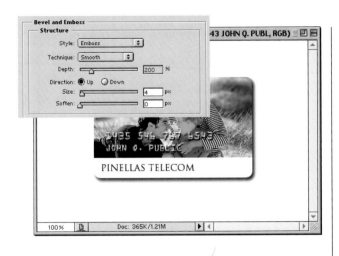

STEP TEN: When the dialog appears, for Style choose Emboss. Increase the Depth to 200%, decrease the Size to 4, and click OK to give your type the stamped on look (as shown). In the Layers palette, hide the Background layer by clicking on the Eye icon in the first column to the left of the layer. Choose Merge Visible from the palette's drop-down menu.

STEP ELEVEN: Press Command-T (PC: Control-T) to bring up Free Transform. Move your pointer outside the bounding box and click-and-drag up to your left to rotate the card counterclockwise a little. Then, hold Shift-Option-Delete (PC: Shift-Alt-Back-space), grab one of the top corner points, and drag inward to create a bit of a perspective effect.

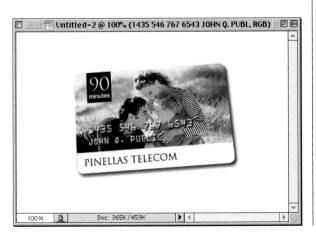

STEP TWELVE: Press Return (PC: Enter) to lock in your rotation and perspective, which completes the effect.

Quick Tip:
File Browser tips

When you're working in Photoshop 7.0's File Browser you can use the Arrow keys to move from image to image in the preview window. But if you hold the Shift key while you use the Arrow keys, it will keep your original image selected, then select the image in the direction you moved with the Arrow key. For example, if you click an image, hold the Shift key, and click the Right Arrow, it adds the image to the right of your current image to your selection of images. Every time you Shift-Right Arrow over, it adds another image. If you then Shift-Up Arrow, that image is added, and so on.

Quick Tip:
Changing the mode of line art
If you open a line art scan (in Bitmap mode) in Photoshop, you'll have to convert it to a color mode before you can add color (that makes sense, right?). But Photoshop doesn't let you convert from Bitmap mode straight to RGB; you have to make an intermediate stop in Grayscale mode along the way. When you're in Bitmap mode, RGB mode is grayed out as a choice until you're in Grayscale mode. When you choose Grayscale (from the Mode menu) you'll be greeted with a dialog asking for Size Ratio. Leave the Size Ratio at 1 and click OK to convert your line art into Grayscale mode. Then, when you go under the Mode menu, RGB will be available as a mode choice.

Colorizing Line Art

Colorizing line art is really very simple: Start out by switching to RGB color mode, create selections inside your line art, and then colorize the selections on layers.

STEP ONE: Scan your line art image in RGB mode if possible, because your image has to be in a color mode if you're going to add color to it. If your line art image is already in Grayscale mode, you can simply go under the Image menu, under Mode, and choose RGB Color.

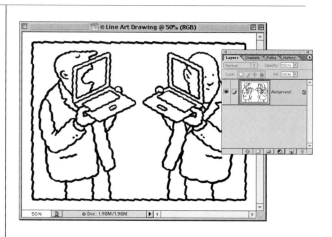

STEP TWO: Your scanned image will appear on the Background layer, but we need to convert it to a regular layer. In the Layers palette, double-click directly on the name "Background" and a dialog will appear where you can name your new layer. Name it "Lines" and click OK to convert your Background layer in a regular layer.

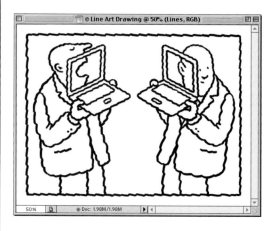

STEP THREE: Create a new blank layer by clicking on the New Layer icon at the bottom of the Layers palette. Then, go under the Layer menu, under New, and choose Background from Layer. This converts your just-created blank layer into a Background layer (we want one again, because it provides a white backdrop to work upon).

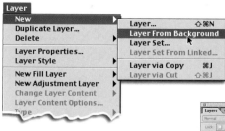

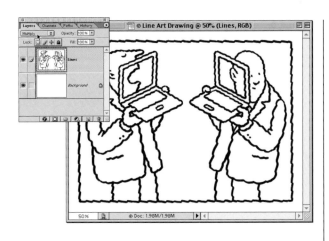

STEP FOUR: In the Layers palette, click on your Lines layer. Change its Blend Mode from Normal to Multiply. This makes the white areas of your lines layer transparent, leaving only the black lines visible (you can't see this onscreen yet, but you will soon). Press "w" to switch to the Magic Wand tool. Click once inside an area you want to colorize and the Magic Wand tool will select that area.

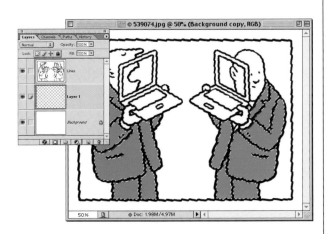

STEP FIVE: In our example, we clicked on the suits. (Note: You can use any selection tool you'd like: Lasso, Pen Tool, etc.) Next, hold the Command key (PC: Control key) and click on the New Layer icon. This creates a new layer directly beneath your lines layer and this is where you'll add your color. Choose a Foreground color, then press Option-Delete (PC: Alt-Backspace) to fill your selected area with color.

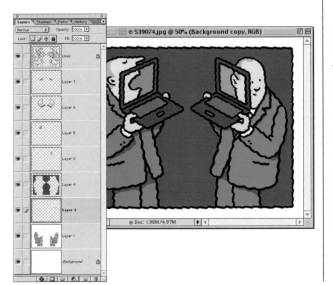

STEP SIX: Press Command-D (PC: Control-D) to deselect. You'll continue this same process to colorize the rest of the image: click on the Lines layer, select an area with the Magic Wand tool, Command-click (PC: Control-click) on the New Layer icon to create a new layer under the Lines layer, pick another Foreground color, and then fill on that layer.

Quick Tip:
Design tip
Filling your selections with a flat color can make your colorization look, well…flat. Instead, try filling your line art with a gradient that goes from a lighter color to a much darker shade of that same color. For example, set your Foreground color to light pink and your Background color to a very dark pink. Make your selection on the Line layer, create your new layer below it, switch to the Gradient tool by pressing the letter "g" (make sure your chosen gradient is Foreground to Background), then drag this gradient from left to right through your selection. This gives the illusion of a light source and adds interest to your image. Note: Remember to drag your gradient in the same direction consistently so that your "shadows" will fall on the same side throughout your image (i.e., always drag from left to right, top to bottom, etc.).

Painting Using a Photo as Your Guide

Photoshop 7's new Brush engine includes a great collection of brushes and brush controls to give you more traditional paint effects. Felix uses this particular technique to create a paint effect by using a photograph as a template and painting on top of it using specialized brushes.

STEP ONE: Open the photo you want to use as the basis of your painting.

STEP TWO: Go under the Window menu and choose Brushes. In the list of Options on the left side of the dialog, click on the words "Brush Presets" to make those options visible. In the Brushes drop-down menu, choose Wet Media Brushes. When the dialog box appears, click OK to load this set of brushes.

STEP THREE: Create a new Layer by clicking on the New Layer icon at the bottom of the Layers palette. Then press "b" to get the Brush tool, and in the Brushes palette, choose the brush named "Dry Brush on Towel." Hold the Option key (PC: Alt key) to temporarily toggle to the Eyedropper tool, then click the Eyedropper on the color under the area where you want to start painting.

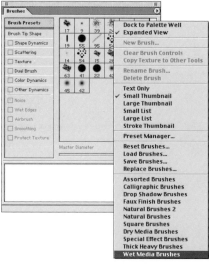

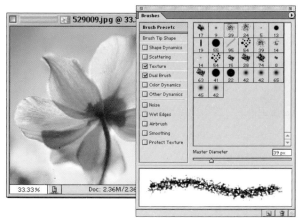

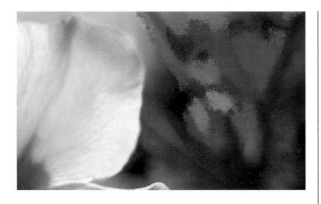

STEP FOUR: Although you'll be painting on your new layer, you're going to use the Background layer image as a tracing template. Begin painting and try to mimic the shapes and colors from the background onto Layer 1 using the Brush tool.

STEP FIVE: You'll need to vary the size of your brushes as you paint and use smaller brushes to paint more detailed areas. Letting some of your brush strokes overlap will give your image a more painted look.

STEP SIX: Once you've painted over the entire image area, we can help the overall effect look more painted by adding texture. To do this, go under the Filter menu, under Texture, and choose Texturizer. When the dialog box appears, for Texture choose Canvas, lower the Scaling to 80%, and click OK to put a light texture over your image. If the texture seems too intense, go under the Edit menu and choose Fade Texturizer. When the dialog appears, lower the Opacity slider to lessen the effect of the filter.

Quick Tip:
Another way to delete brushes
Another way to delete a brush is to Control-click (PC: Right-click) on it in the Brushes flyout menu and a contextual menu will pop up where you can choose Delete Brush from the menu.

Quick Tip:
Too much Liquid? Undo it!

If you're used to the
Photoshop 6 version of
Liquify, you're used to the
"one undo" limitation that
makes you really stay on
your toes when working
in Liquify. Well, you'll be
happy to know that in
Photoshop 7 you can
now "mess up" all you
want, because Adobe
added multiple undos.

Giant Plasma Screen

Just because only multi-millionaires can afford huge flat-panel plasma screens, doesn't mean you can't use digital versions of them at will in your own advertising and self-promotion projects by slapping a giant plasma screen on any flat surface that you see fit. Feel the power!

STEP ONE: Open the image where you want to add a giant plasma screen. (In this case, we're going to add it to the side of a building. This is what I mean by "giant" plasma screen.) Press Shift-L to get the Polygonal Lasso tool and select the area where you want your giant plasma screen to appear (as shown). Press "d" to make your Foreground color black .

STEP TWO: Create a new blank layer, then press Option-Delete (PC: Alt-Control) to fill your [handwritten: *Shift-Alt-Backspace*] selection with black. Go under the Select menu and choose Contract. Enter 8 and click OK to shrink your selection by 8 pixels. Now, hold the Option key (PC: Alt key), switch to the Polygonal Lasso tool, and trim off another $1/4$" off the bottom of your selection (as shown).

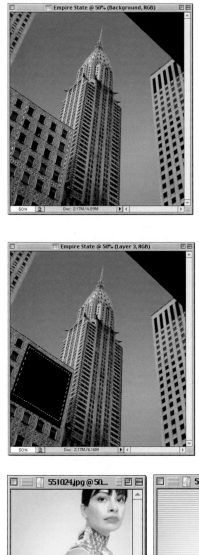

STEP THREE: Open the image you want in your plasma screen. To add scan lines, create a new layer, press "x" to set your Foreground color to white, and fill by pressing Option-Delete (PC: Alt-Backspace). Go under the Filter menu, under Sketch, and choose Halftone Pattern. Set the Size to 1, Contrast to 5, Pattern Type to Line, and click OK to add black/white lines.

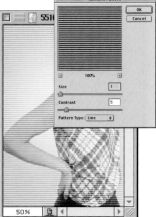

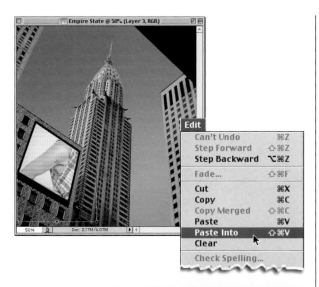

STEP FOUR: Change the Layer Blend mode to Overlay, then press Command-E (PC: Control-E) to merge the two layers into one. Press Command-A (PC: Control-A) to Select All, then press Command-C (PC: Control-C) to copy the image. Switch back to your building image. Go under the Edit menu and choose Paste Into. Your image will appear on its own layer.

STEP FIVE: It's important that your image have the same perspective as your building, so press Command-T (PC: Control-T) to bring up the Free Transform function. Hold the Command key (PC: Control key), grab one of the corner points, and drag it to fit the side of the building. You'll have to adjust all four sides, lining up each side with the angle of the building. When the image's angle looks right, press Return (PC: Enter).

STEP SIX: Last, add a made-up plasma manufacturer's name below the image in white. (Note: It's very important to match the overall contrast of the pasted image with the contrast of the building photo you're pasting into. If the image looks too dark or too light, press Command-L [PC: Control-L] to bring up Levels, and use the Left and Right bottom Output Levels sliders to lighten or darken as needed.)

Quick Tip:
Spell Checking très magnifique
You probably know by now that there's a spell checker in Photoshop 7 (Thank God!), but what you may not realize is how powerful that spell checker really is. It not only checks English, but comes with spell-checking dictionaries for French, Italian, German, Spanish, Dutch, Swedish, Canadian French, and a bunch more. The trick is to find where you choose which language you want. You do it from a pop-up menu that's been added to the bottom of the Character palette. Ah, très magnifique.

Quick Tip:
Bringing back color to your line art

In the tutorial shown at right, we take a photograph and convert it to a black-and-white line drawing, and then morph the two together at the end. But another technique you may want to consider is not morphing, but instead, after you've created the line art drawing in Step 5, just switch to the History Brush tool. Lower the Opacity to about 20%, and lightly paint back in the original image. When you paint with the Opacity set that low, it's the color that appears first, and you can create an effect of almost a watercolor wash under your line drawing that really looks slick. Give it a try after you finish the full tutorial at right and see what you think.

Photo to Line Art Morph

This is a great little trick that morphs line art with a photograph of the same subject. I've seen this used numerous times, most recently in a backlit ad on the terminal wall at LAX. Anyone who remembers the award-winning video for the song "Take On Me" by the group "a-ha" will experience a momentary '80s flashback when they try this technique.

STEP ONE: Open the image you want to morph into a line drawing of itself.

STEP TWO: Press Command-J (PC: Control-J) to create a duplicate of your Background layer. While on this duplicate layer, go under the Filter menu, under Stylize, and choose Find Edges (as shown).

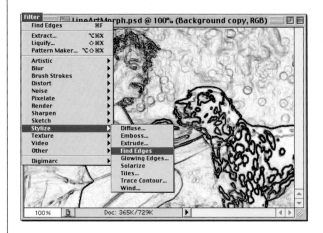

STEP THREE: Press Shift-Command-U (PC: Shift-Control-U) to remove all the color from the image (running the Find Edge filter introduces lots of highly saturated patches of color, so removing the color is a must).

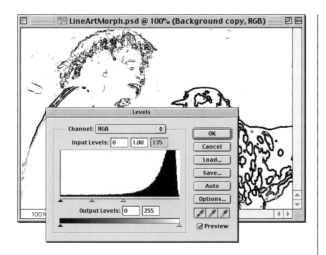

STEP FOUR: Now that the color is gone, we need to remove some of the leftover "noise" and unnecessary detail created by the Find Edge filter. Press Command-L (PC: Control-L) to bring up the Levels dialog. Drag the top-right Input Levels slider to the right to "blow out" the extra detail, leaving just the most substantial lines (as shown).

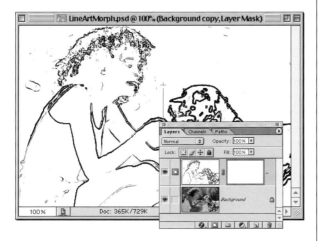

STEP FIVE: Next, in the Layers palette, click on the Layer Mask icon (as shown in the inset at left). Make sure your Foreground color is set to black. Press "g" to get the Gradient tool. Press Return (PC: Enter) to bring up the Gradient Picker, and make sure the first gradient (the Foreground to Background gradient) is selected. Drag the Gradient tool from the center of your image downward.

STEP SIX: As you drag downward, the top of the image will become transparent, revealing the original photo on the layer behind, and it will smoothly blend into the line art version of your image (as shown). If you want to add a little color to your line art, change the Blend Mode to either Lighten, Vivid Light, or for a lot of color, try Overlay.

Quick Tip:
If the Blend isn't right, drag again
In the tutorial at left, I ask you to drag a gradient on a Layer Mask to reveal the photo on the layer below it. The nice thing about this technique is that if it's not right the first time you try it, just keep dragging until it does look right. Every time you drag again, it creates an entirely new mask. Also, try painting on the mask (actually, it looks like you're painting on the layer, but it's really painting on the mask, so don't let that throw you) using solid black to reveal the layer below, or solid white to cover it back up.

Quick Tip:
Creating new brushes

You can create a new brush by choosing New Brush from the Brushes flyout menu's pop-down menu, but there's a quicker way—just click your pointer once in any open space within the Brushes palette and the New Brush dialog box will appear.

Wire Frame Effect

This trick isn't an entire effect by itself—it's more of a collaging element that you'd add to an existing collage, but that hasn't hurt its popularity. These instant wire-frame techniques are popping up in lots of the latest cutting-edge collage work.

STEP ONE: Open a new document in RGB mode at 72 dpi. Press Shift-L until the Polygonal Lasso tool appears in the Toolbox (or just click-and-hold on the Lasso tool for a moment and a flyout menu will appear where you can choose the Polygonal Lasso, as shown).

STEP TWO: Use the Polygonal Lasso tool to draw a polygonal shape. Start by clicking once, then move the pointer to a new position, click again, and a straight line will connect the two points. Continue clicking in different areas to create your polygonal shape, and when you're done, click back on the first point where you started, and your lines will become a selection (as shown).

STEP THREE: Go under the Edit menu and choose Stroke. For Width enter 1 pixel, for Color make sure it's black, and for Location choose Center. Click OK to put a black stroke around your selection. Now press Command-D (PC: Control-D) to Deselect.

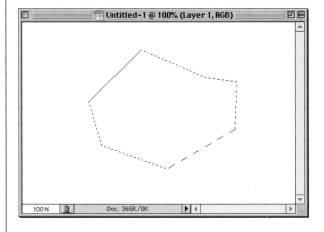

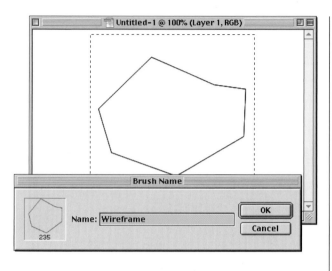

STEP FOUR: Press "m" to get the Rectangular Marquee tool, hold the Shift key, and draw a square selection entirely around your polygonal shape (as shown). Then go under the Edit menu and choose Define Brush. A dialog box will appear where you can name your brush (as shown). Enter a name and click OK to save this brush to your Brushes palette.

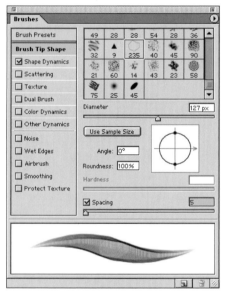

STEP FIVE: Choose Brushes from the Window menu, and in the list of options on the left side of the dialog box, click on the words "Brush Tip Shape" to bring those options forward. Adjust the Diameter of your brush to your desired size (I lowered my size down to 127 pixels) and then lower the Spacing slider to 5 (as shown). A preview of your edited brush stroke will appear at the bottom of the palette. Your wire frame brush is now complete.

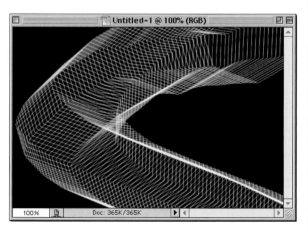

STEP SIX: Now you can add this wireframe effect to any collage. If you want to replicate the example shown here, open a new document in RGB mode. Press "d" to set your Foreground color to black and press Option-Delete to fill the background with black. Press "x" to set the Foreground color to white. Create a new layer, then paint a long curved stroke with your brush to create the effect shown here.

Quick Tip: Saving your brushes

Do you need to save any custom brushes you create? Any brush you create is automatically saved. The next time you launch Photoshop, that brush will automatically appear in the same position in your Brushes menu. However, if you reset your brushes to their factory defaults (by choosing Reset Brushes from the Brushes drop-down menu), that brush will be gone forever. If that's a concern to you, make sure you save your new set of brushes by going under the Brushes flyout menu's drop-down menu and choosing Save Brushes. What I do is delete all the other brushes by holding the Command key (PC: Control key) and clicking once on them. Then, when I'm down to just the one brush I created, I choose Save Brushes from the Brushes Options Bar flyout menu, name that brush with a name I'll remember (such as Acme Co. logo), and save it in the Brushes folder, inside the Preset folder, inside my Photoshop folder. Whew!

Since the beginning of Photoshop history (back when dinosaurs roamed the earth) when you had one image open onscreen and you opened a second image, the way the images were displayed within your monitor was called "cascading." What that meant was, when you opened an image, it would open in front of the existing image (as you've already experienced countless times). However, in Photoshop 7, Adobe added a new document view that has been in page layout programs for years, and my guess is you're going to love it. It's called "Tile" and what it does is tile all your open documents one beside the other filling your monitor. Photographers should love this, because they can open up to 10 or 12 proofs and display them side-by-side on their monitor. Tile is found under the Window menu under Documents. Open up three or four images then choose Tile and you'll see what all the fuss is about.

3D Cubes

Another of those collaging elements that are very trendy right now and that are showing up in some of the latest cutting-edge collages are 3D cubes. They've caught on in such a big way, and what's nice is that they make use of Photoshop's almost useless 3D Transform filter. And, anything that brings that old dog to some sort of useful life is worth of a look, don'tcha think?

STEP ONE: Open a new document in RGB mode and make it 8"x8". (This technique works best with a large square image.) Create a new layer by clicking on the New Layer icon at the bottom of the Layers palette.

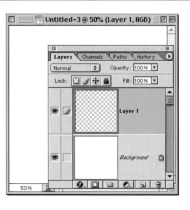

STEP TWO: Go under the Filter menu, under Render, and choose 3D Transform. When the dialog box appears, click on the Options button, and in the resulting dialog box, turn OFF Display Background (it's on by default, so you'll have to turn it off, as shown).

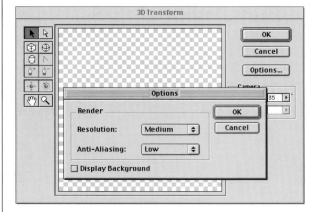

STEP THREE: Click on the Cube tool and drag out a tall rectangular shape. Then press "a" to get the Direct Selection tool, click on the only point showing at the top of your cube, and drag to the left or right to lean your cube (as shown). Then, draw another rectangular cube, and lean it too.

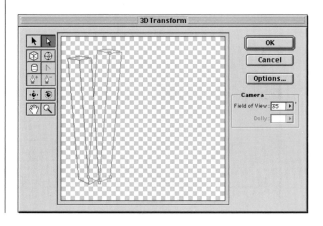

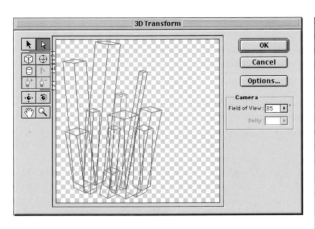

STEP FOUR: Continue this process of adding rectangular cubes and tilting them to the left or right until you have a number of cubes in place. If you have the patience, the more cubes, the merrier (so to speak).

STEP FIVE: After you've completed drawing your cubes, press "R" to switch to the Trackball tool. The background will turn black and your cubes will turn solid white. Click the Trackball tool in the center of your cubes and drag your pointer to the right. As you do, your cubes will rotate in the preview window, and if you drag far enough, the "backside" of your cube shapes will appear, complete with shading on all sides (as shown).

STEP SIX: Click OK and your shapes will be rendered onto your layer. Choose Drop Shadow from the Layer Style pop-up menu at the bottom of the Layers palette, and click OK to add a drop shadow. Also, press Command-U (PC: Control-U) to bring up Hue/Saturation. Click the Colorize button, choose a color with the Hue slider, and click OK to colorize your cubes and complete the effect.

Here's an example (left) of the 3D cube effect used in Digital Vision's Infinity collection.

Quick Tip: Brush size changes in Photoshop 7

Here's a tip about a feature in Photoshop 7 that didn't make big headlines, but when you realize what it means, it's absolutely mondo-crazy big! The feature is the Master Diameter slider in the Brushes palette (found under the Window menu, choose Brushes). This enables you to change the size of a selected brush. I know that sounds like no big deal because you could always change the size of a brush, right? Well, not always. You see, previous versions of Photoshop let you change the size of round soft-edged and hard-edged brushes, but NOT the custom brushes. This meant that if Adobe created a cool custom brush at 25 pixels, that's the size it was stuck at. So, for high-res images, many of those smaller custom brushes were totally unusable because they were too small. Now, just pick ANY custom brush and make it the size you want it. Even if you create your own custom brush, it's totally scalable with the Master Diameter slider. Way, mondo-crazy cool!

Quick Tip:
**Load those
sets, baby!**

Back in Photoshop 6,
Adobe introduced
loadable Presets (collec-
tions) of Brushes, Patterns,
Shapes, etc. What was
nice, rather than digging
through dialog boxes to
dig up sets buried in
folders on your computer,
now you could load these
presets right from the
palette's drop-down
menus. What was bad
was the quality of those
presets. They were, (and
I'm being as kind as
possible here) incredibly
lame. Adobe fixed that in
Photoshop 7 and now
includes lots of usable
shapes, patterns, brushes,
and other presets.
Not only that, there are
many more sets than in
Photoshop 6. So if you
haven't loaded some
sets in a while, it's time
to take another look.

Blending a Logo into a Photo

Adding a logo to an existing image is an extremely popular technique (recently I've seen logos added to the bottom of swimming pools, tennis courts, race tracks, and buildings), but often it's obvious that the logo was added digitally, usually because the designer didn't work to blend it in—they just stuck it there and that's how it looks—stuck there. Here's how to hide your tracks.

STEP ONE: Open the photo to which you want to add a logo.

STEP TWO: Open the logo you want to add to the image and drag it into your image (as shown). If the client has provided you with an EPS of their logo, go under the File menu and choose Place to add the logo. The logo will then appear with a bounding box around it, so you can size it appropriately while it's still a vector logo. Press Return (PC: Enter) to rasterize the logo onto a layer.

STEP THREE: Press Command-T (PC: Control-T) to bring up Free Transform. Rotate the logo to match the angle of the pool. Next, hold the Command key (PC: Control key) and click-and-drag the top center point to the right to skew the logo a bit to the right (as shown). When it looks about right, press Return (PC: Enter) to lock in your transformation.

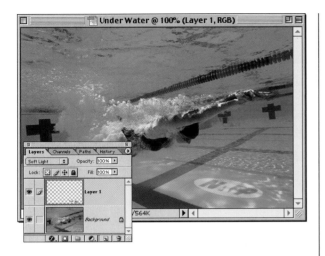

STEP FOUR: In the Layers palette, change the Blend Mode for this layer to Soft Light to help it blend into the water. When you're doing this technique, using a logo of your own, Soft Light might not be the right mode, so press "v" to switch to the Move tool, then press Shift-+ (the plus sign) to rotate through the different modes until you see one that looks right for your logo.

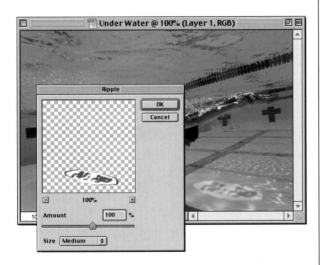

STEP FIVE: To help make the logo look a bit more "underwater," go under the Filter menu, under Distort, and choose Ripple. We'll use the default settings of 100% Amount and Medium Size. Click OK to apply a ripple effect to your logo.

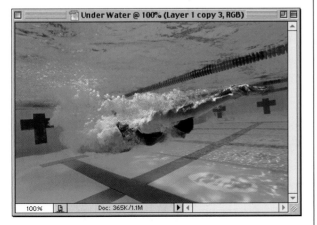

STEP SIX: Last (and this is a surprisingly critical step, even though it's so simple), lower the Opacity of your logo layer by quite a bit (I lowered mine to 50%) to complete the effect. Most designers trip up by leaving the logo at 100% Opacity. This is what makes the logo look "slapped on" and is a dead giveaway that it was added after the fact, so don't get caught—lower that Opacity.

Quick Tip:
Save that mesh!
If you're a Liquify user (and I know that you are), Photoshop 7 lets you do something previous versions did not—you can now save the mesh that you create and apply it to another image. So what's the big deal about that? Well, you could apply your Liquify adjustments on a low-res version of your image, save the mesh, then apply that same mesh to a high-res version of the same image. This has some very interesting implications (none of which I can think of at this time, but I've always wanted to use that sentence).

Quick Tip:
Hyperspace is just one filter way

I have to tell you that this is the one tip in the book that will probably only be used by guys, because even I have to admit that it's so geeky, I almost didn't include it. You noticed I said "almost." In the tutorial on the right, if you feel at some point (like just after Step Four, perhaps) that you need to go into hyperspace (and I know you will), here's how: Go under the Filter menu, under Blur, and choose Radial Blur. For Blur Method choose Zoom, and for Amount choose something around 50, and click OK. Now it won't look quite right yet because the zoom will cause things to be too dark, so press Command-L (PC: Control-L) to bring up Levels. Then drag the top right Input Levels slider to the left until the stars come again, hurling you helplessly into the deep unknown (blah, blah, blah, etc.) You might want to leave off the Lens Flare at this point, ya know, in the interest of good taste. ;-)

Instant Star Field

This is one of those "create something from nothing" techniques and within just a few seconds, you've got an instant star field. This makes a great background for collage projects or you can add it to existing images. Warning: While replicating this technique, you may feel an uncontrollable urge to say things like "Make it so!" and "To the Transporter room." This will pass.

STEP ONE: Open a new document in RGB mode at 72 dpi. Press "d" to make black your Foreground color, then press Option-Delete (PC: Alt-Backspace) to fill your background with black.

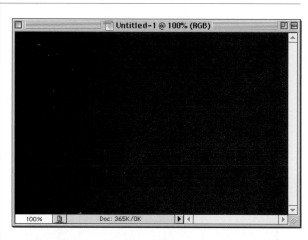

STEP TWO: Go under the Filter menu, under Noise, and choose Add Noise. For Amount enter approximately 40%, for Distribution choose Gaussian, check Monochromatic, and click OK.

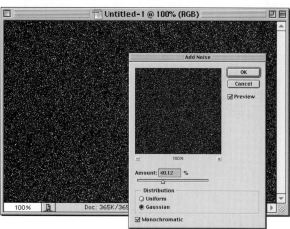

STEP THREE: Go under the Filter menu, under Blur, and choose Gaussian Blur. For Radius enter 0.5 (half a pixel) and click OK to apply just a slight blur to your noise.

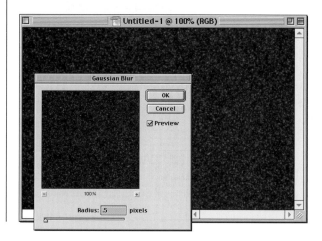

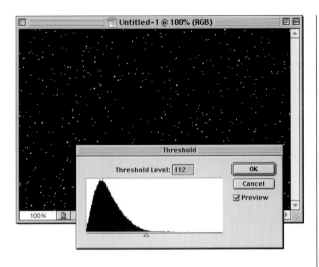

STEP FOUR: To bring out the starfield in your noise, go under the Image menu, under Adjustment, and choose Threshold. When the Threshold dialog box appears, drag the slider to the left until the "stars come out," then click OK. Press Command-F (PC: Control-F) to apply another 0.5-pixel Gaussian Blur to soften the stars.

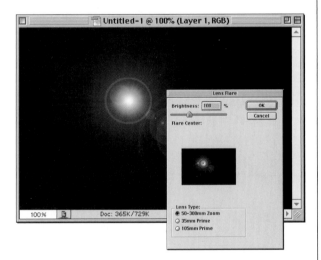

STEP FIVE: To enhance the "out in space" look, I generally add a Lens Flare effect to the starfield. Add a new layer by clicking on the New layer icon at the bottom of the Layers palette. Fill it with black by pressing Option-Delete (PC: Alt-Delete). Next, go under the Filter menu, under Render, and choose Lens Flare. Use any brightness setting or Lens Type you like. (I used the defaults settings shown here.) Click OK.

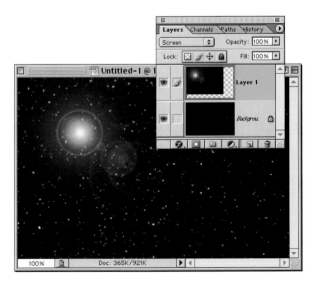

STEP SIX: Last, to bring the Lens Flare into your starfield, just change the Blend Mode of this layer to Screen (as shown) which completes the effect.

Quick Tip:
How to copy a flattened version in a multilayered document

When you make a selection on a layer and press Command-C (PC: Control-C), Photoshop copies the selected area from that layer into memory. But did you know that you can copy from all your visible layers (as if from a flattened image), by adding Shift to that keyboard shortcut? That's right. To do that press Shift-Command-C (PC: Shift-Control-C), and it captures everything inside your selected area as if it was a flattened background image.

Water Drops

This was one of the most popular techniques from the previous version of this book, so I wanted to include it in this update. We've come up with a faster, easier way to create the drop since then, however, so the new updated version is shown here.

STEP ONE: Open a new document in RGB mode and create a new layer by clicking on the New Layer icon at the bottom of the Layers palette. Press the letter "d" then the letter "x" to set your Foreground color to white, then fill this new layer with white by pressing Option-Delete (PC: Alt-Backspace).

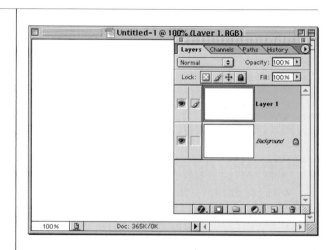

STEP TWO: Go under the Filter menu, under Noise, and choose Add Noise. For Amount enter 400%, for Distribution choose Gaussian, check Monochromatic, and click OK.

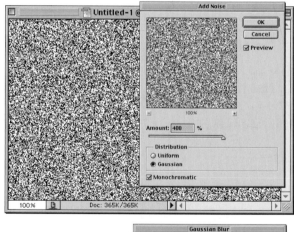

STEP THREE: Go under the Filter menu, under Blur, and choose Gaussian Blur. Add a 5-pixel blur, and click OK.

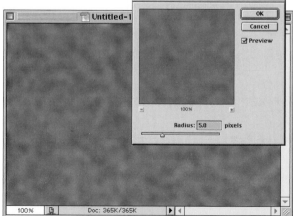

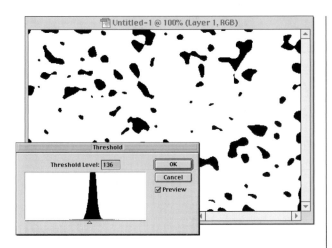

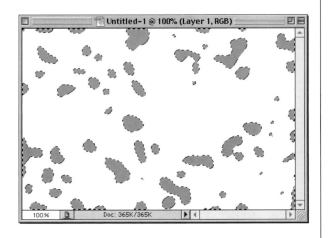

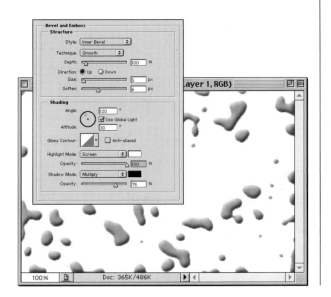

STEP FOUR: Go under the Image menu, under Adjustment, and choose Threshold. When the dialog box appears, drag the slider slightly to the right until the rounded spots start to appear fairly large, and click OK. Press Command-F (PC: Control-F) to add another 5-pixel Gaussian Blur. Go to Threshold again and move the slider toward the right until you have even bigger raindrop-looking spots.

STEP FIVE: Switch to the Magic Wand tool, click it once on any white area surrounding your drops to select all the white, and then press Delete (PC: Backspace). Press Shift-Command-I to inverse your selection (which selects all the spots). Click on the Foreground Color Swatch to bring up the Color Picker. In the RGB fields enter R=181, G=181, B=181, and click OK to choose light gray. Press Option-Delete (PC: Alt-Backspace) to fill your water drops with gray.

STEP SIX: Deselect by pressing Command-D (PC: Control-D). Choose Bevel and Emboss from the Layer Style pop-up menu at the bottom of the Layers palette. When the dialog box appears, increase the Soften amount to 6. In the Shading section increase the Highlight Opacity to 100% and click OK to add highlights and shadows to your water drops (as shown).

Quick Tip:
Selecting just one letter, rather than the whole word

We've been using the Command-click (PC: Control-click) on the layer's name trick to put a selection around your type throughout this book. But that puts a selection around all your text. What if you want to select just one or two letters? You can do it, but first you have to rasterize your Type layer by going under the Layer menu, under Rasterize, and choosing Type. You might be tempted to try selecting the letter with the Magic Wand tool, but don't—it'll leave behind little edge pixels if you move the type. Instead, try this: Draw a very loose selection around the letter or letters that you want to select (don't touch the edges of the letters, just make a loose selection). Hold the Command key and press one of the Arrow keys on your keyboard. Your letter will be immediately selected with no messy edge pixels, so now you can colorize it, move it, or do whatever.

continued

Quick Tip:
Setting shades of gray

Photoshop is such an incredibly powerful program that surely there would be a little slider or pop-up menu for creating shades of gray, right? Well, there is one, it's just a bit hidden. Go under the Window menu and choose Show Color to bring up the Color palette. In the drop-down menu, choose Grayscale Slider. A slider will appear that goes from 0% to 100% and you can slide it to the percentage of gray that you want.

Another popular way, though a bit more cumbersome, is to click on the Foreground Color Swatch and in the CMYK fields of the Color Picker, enter 0 for Cyan, Magenta, and Yellow. Under Black, enter 40, and click OK. This gives you a shade of gray without any CMY in it, whereas the Color palette gives you a gray color build, with percentages of Cyan, Magenta, and Yellow.

STEP SEVEN: Choose Stroke from the Layer Style pop-up menu at the bottom of the Layers palette. When the dialog box appears, lower the Size to 1, set the Position to Center, and lower the Opacity to 50%. Click on the Color Swatch and choose a dark gray, and then click OK to put a dark gray stroke around your water drops (as shown). Hold the Command key (PC: Control key) and click on the New Layer icon to create a new blank layer beneath your current layer.

STEP EIGHT: In the Layers palette, click on the water drops layer, then press Command-E (PC: Control-E) to merge your water drops layer with your blank layer. Next, Command-click (PC: Control-click) on your water spots layer to put a selection around the spots. Press Option-Command-F (PC: Alt-Control-F) to bring up the Gaussian Blur dialog again, but this time lower the Radius to 1, then click OK to slightly blur the inside of your water drops. Deselect by pressing Command-D (PC: Control-D).

STEP NINE: Last, open the image where you want to apply the water spots, and change the Blend Mode of the water drops layer to Hard Light to make the gray center of the drops transparent, leaving just the highlights and shadows visible (as shown).

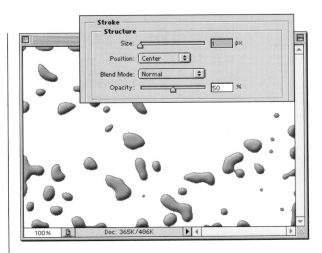

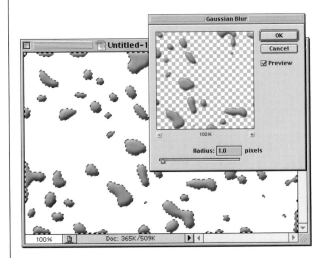

INDEX

INDEX

FONT LISTING

PHOTO AND ILLUSTRATION CREDITS

All Stock Images
Courtesy of Digital Vision
(www.digitalvisiononline.com)

Bill Lindsay
Page 54

Felix Nelson: Illustration of computer on
page 134 book cover, guitar illustration 155,
soda can 272. Photos: 160, 179, 187

Scott Kelby
Pages 89, 91, 94, 231

Marlin Studios
Sci-fi texture on page 206

COLOPHON

The book was produced by KW Media
Group using all Macintosh computers,
including a Power Mac G4 450-MHz, Power
Mac G4 500-MHz, a Power Mac G4 Dual
Processor 500-MHz, and an iMac. We use
LaCie, Sony, and Apple Studio Display
monitors.

Page layout was done using Adobe
PageMaker 6.5 and QuarkXPress 4.1. Our
graphics server is a Power Mac G4, with a

60-GB LaCie external drive, and we burn
our CDs to a Sony Spressa 12X CD-RW.

The opening paragraph of each
technique is set in Adobe Minion at 9.5
points on 13 leading, with the Horizontal
Scaling set to 95%. The headers for each
technique are set in Helvetica Black at 14
points on 17 leading, with the Horizontal
Scaling set to 95%. Body copy is set using
Adobe MyriadMM_400 RG 600 NO at 9.5

points on 13 leading, with the Horizontal
Scaling set to 95%.

Screen captures were made with Snapz
Pro and were placed and sized within the
layout program. The book was output at 150
line screen, and all in-house printing was
done using a Xerox Phaser 850 DX.

ADDITIONAL PHOTOSHOP RESOURCES

**National Association of Photoshop
Professionals (NAPP)**
The industry trade association for Adobe®
Photoshop® users, and the world's leading
resource for Photoshop training, education,
and news.

http://www.photoshopuser.com

KW Computer Training Videos
Scott Kelby is featured in a series of 18
Photoshop training videos, each on a
particular Photoshop topic, available from
KW Computer Training. Visit the Web site
or call 727-733-6225 for orders or more
information.

http://www.photoshopvideos.com

PlanetPhotoshop.com
"The Ultimate Photoshop Site" features
Photoshop news, tutorials, reviews, and
articles posted daily. The site also contains
the Web's most up-to-date resource on
other Photoshop-related Web sites and
information.

http://www.planetphotoshop.com

Photoshop Killer Tips
Scott is also co-author, with Felix Nelson, of
the best-selling book *Photoshop 6 Killer Tips*,
and the book's companion Web site has all
the info on the book, which is also available
at bookstores around the country.

http://www.photoshopkillertips.com

Adobe Photoshop Seminar Tour
See Scott live at the Adobe Photoshop
Seminar Tour, the nation's most popular
Photoshop seminars. For upcoming tour
dates and class schedules, visit the tour
Web site.

http://www.photoshopseminars.com

Mac Design Magazine
"The Graphics Magazine for Macintosh
Users" is a tutorial-based print magazine
with how-to columns on Photoshop,
Illustrator, QuarkXPress, Dreamweaver,
GoLive, Flash, and more. It's also packed
with Photoshop tips, tricks, and shortcuts
for your favorite graphics applications.

http://www.macdesignonline.com

PhotoshopWorld
The annual convention for Adobe
Photoshop users, it has now become the
largest Photoshop-only event in the world.
Scott Kelby is technical chair and education
director for the event, as well as one of the
instructors.

http://www.PhotoshopWorld.com

Photoshop Photo-Retouching Secrets
Scott is also author of the book *Photoshop
Photo-Retouching Secrets,* which details the
inside secrets of photo restoration and
retouching techniques in Photoshop.

http://www.photoretouchingsecrets.com

Photoshop Hall of Fame
Created to honor and recognize those
individuals whose contribution to the art
and business of Adobe Photoshop has had
a major impact on the application or the
Photoshop community itself.

http://www.photoshophalloffame.com

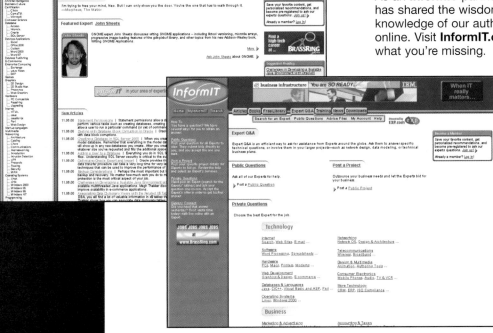

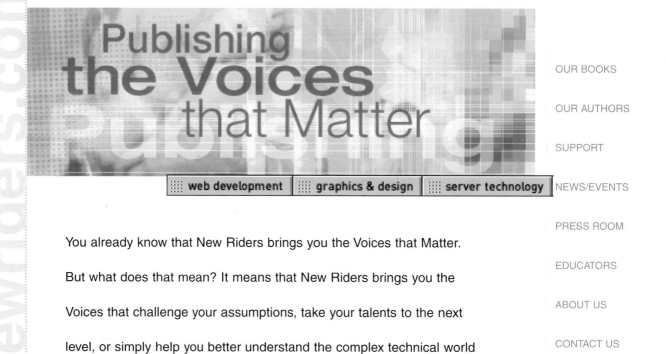

Photoshop 7 Killer Tips
Scott Kelby
0735713006
$39.99

**Photoshop 7
Down & Dirty Tricks**
Scott Kelby
0735712379
$39.99

Photoshop 7 Magic
Sherry London,
Rhoda Grossman
0735712646
$45.00

Photoshop 7 Artistry
Barry Haynes,
Wendy Crumpler
0735712409
$55.00

Inside Photoshop 7
Gary Bouton, Andy Anderson,
Robert Stanley, J. Scott Hamlin,
Daniel Will-Harris,
Mara Nathanson
0735712417
$45.00

**Photoshop Studio with
Bert Monroy**
Bert Monroy
0735712468
$50.00

**The Photoshop 7
Answer Book**
Dave Cross
0735712387
$25.00

**Photoshop Restoration
and Retouching**
Katrin Eisemann
0789723182
$49.99

**Photoshop Type Effects
Visual Encyclopedia**
Roger Pring
0735711909
$45.00

**Creative Thinking in
Photoshop**
Sharon Steuer
0735711224
$45.00

VOICES THAT MATTER

VISIT OUR WEB SITE

WWW.NEWRIDERS.COM

On our Web site you'll find information about our other books, authors, tables of contents, indexes, and book errata. You will also find information about book registration and how to purchase our books.

EMAIL US

Contact us at this address: **nrfeedback@newriders.com**

- If you have comments or questions about this book
- To report errors that you have found in this book
- If you have a book proposal to submit or are interested in writing for New Riders
- If you would like to have an author kit sent to you
- If you are an expert in a computer topic or technology and are interested in being a technical editor who reviews manuscripts for technical accuracy

- To find a distributor in your area, please contact our international department at this address. **nrmedia@newriders.com**

- For instructors from educational institutions who want to preview New Riders books for classroom use. Email should include your name, title, school, department, address, phone number, office days/hours, text in use, and enrollment, along with your request for desk/examination copies and/or additional information.
- For members of the media who are interested in reviewing copies of New Riders books. Send your name, mailing address, and email address, along with the name of the publication or Web site you work for.

BULK PURCHASES/CORPORATE SALES

If you are interested in buying 10 or more copies of a title or want to set up an account for your company to purchase directly from the publisher at a substantial discount, contact us at 800-382-3419 or email your contact information to corpsales@pearsontechgroup.com. A sales representative will contact you with more information.

WRITE TO US

New Riders Publishing
201 W. 103rd St.
Indianapolis, IN 46290-1097

CALL US

Toll-free (800) 571-5840 + 9 + 7477
If outside U.S. (317) 581-3500. Ask for New Riders.

FAX US

(317) 581-4663

New Riders

WWW.NEWRIDERS.COM

Using a Wacom® Tablet with Adobe® Photoshop® 7.0

Photoshop's behind-the-scenes photo-editing power...

1. Dynamically change tool size

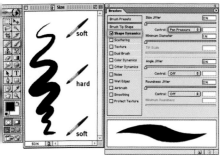

A Wacom graphics tablet gives you the power to change the size of any of Photoshop's 20 pressure-sensitive tools with pen pressure. Press softly to get a thin stroke – press harder to get a thicker stroke. And by the way, the Wacom-enabled tools in Photoshop 7.0 are the Paintbrush, Pencil, Airbrush, Rubber Stamp, Pattern Stamp, History Brush, Art History Brush, Eraser, Background Eraser, Smudge, Blur, Burn, Healing Brush, Sharpen, Dodge, Sponge, Magnetic Lasso, Magnetic Pen, Liquify Warp, and Liquify Twirl (whew)!

2. Change tool opacity on the fly

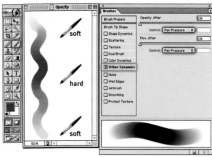

You're probably familiar with using the Paintbrush's opacity to add a gentle wash of color. You can also vary the opacity of some of the other tools such as the Rubber Stamp tool to gently blend while cloning an old photo. Or give the Art History brush a try – press lightly with your pen for transparent strokes, press harder for more opaque strokes. And when you have the hang of using opacity, move on to using opacity and size at the same time!

3. Blend colors while you paint

Being able to change color during a paint stroke can give you some great effects. Set the Photoshop 7.0 Paintbrush to be color-sensitive in the Color Dynamics sub-palette and try it out. Set the Paintbrush to be both color-sensitive and size-sensitive, and you can paint blades of grass that vary from dark to light green, or add a warm glint of light to a photograph of a chrome fender. *(And for the adventurous, add "Texture" as well – be sure to select "Texture Each Tip" to make your brush pressure-sensitive as well.)*

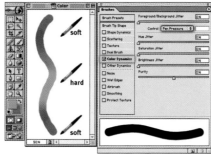

4. Try a little tilt

Photoshop has always had a special place in a tablet user's heart as the first major pressure-sensitive application. Photoshop 7.0 steps into another league, offering Photoshop fans tilt sensitivity for the first time. Select the Shape Dynamics sub-palette, and you can set the Angle to be affected by Pen Tilt. Modify a round brush to be an angular calligraphy brush, tilt the pen to the left or right, and you'll get beautiful calligraphic brushstrokes. *(By the way, almost all of the pressure-sensitive tools are tilt-sensitive too!)*

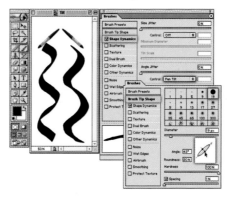

5. A finger on the Wacom Airbrush

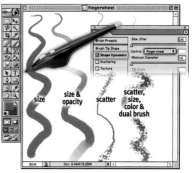

Wacom's Airbrush Pen now offers Photoshop 7.0 users a new method of control – the Fingerwheel. Grab the Wacom Airbrush, select the Photoshop Paintbrush, and you can set size, opacity, scatter, color, and more to respond to the roll of the fingerwheel. Check out the examples above – try some different variations with pressure, fingerwheel, and tilt to get an amazing amount of creative control.

6. Put it all together

Now imagine editing photographs with some of your favorite Photoshop techniques and the Wacom tablet. Control size and opacity with pressure to create accurate layer masks, burn and dodge quickly, and make subtle color corrections exactly where you want them.

7. The comfort you need

With all the great new features Photoshop 7.0 has, you may find yourself spending a little more time in front of the computer than you normally do. But don't worry – the Intuos2 Grip Pen is the perfect Photoshop 7.0 tool for more than just its good looks. The Grip Pen features an enlarged cushioned "grip" that reduces grip effort by up to 40%. It also makes the hours you spend exploring Photoshop 7.0 comfortable, as well as fun.

Visit **www.wacompowertips.com** today for more great tips and a chance to pick out the Intuos2 tablet that's right for you.

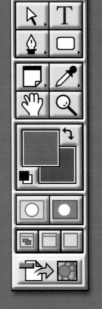